CW00953978

Profit Power Economics

MIA DE KUIJPER

Profit Power Economics

A New Competitive Strategy for Creating Sustainable Wealth

2 May 2013

OXFORD
UNIVERSITY PRESS

2009

OXFORD
UNIVERSITY PRESS

Oxford University Press, Inc., publishes works that further
Oxford University's objective of excellence
in research, scholarship, and education.

Oxford New York
Auckland Cape Town Dar es Salaam Hong Kong Karachi
Kuala Lumpur Madrid Melbourne Mexico City Nairobi
New Delhi Shanghai Taipei Toronto

With offices in
Argentina Austria Brazil Chile Czech Republic France Greece
Guatemala Hungary Italy Japan Poland Portugal Singapore
South Korea Switzerland Thailand Turkey Ukraine Vietnam

Copyright © 2009 by Mia de Kuijper

Published by Oxford University Press, Inc.
198 Madison Avenue, New York, NY 10016

www.oup.com

Oxford is a registered trademark of Oxford University Press

All rights reserved. No part of this publication may be reproduced,
stored in a retrieval system, or transmitted, in any form or by any means,
electronic, mechanical, photocopying, recording, or otherwise,
without the prior permission of Oxford University Press.

Library of Congress Cataloging-in-Publication Data
Kuijper, Mia de.
Profit power economics : a new competitive strategy
for creating sustainable wealth / Mia de Kuijper.
p. cm.
Includes bibliographical references.
ISBN 978-0-19-517163-1
1. Strategic planning. 2. Profit. 3. Information technology—Management.
I. Title.
HD30.28.K85 2009
658.4'012—dc22   2008048624

9 8 7 6 5 4 3 2 1

Printed in the United States of America
on acid-free paper

For Napier Collyns

CONTENTS

Introduction

On a crisp April morning in 2004, I embarked upon an encounter with economic heresy.

The Charles River was sparkling in the bright sunlight. The sky was a brilliant blue, the color that we associate with clear vision. I was wearing a white cotton shirt and a dark suit: fine quality, strong fabric. As I walked through the Yard to the Harvard Faculty Club on Quincy Street, I noticed that the grass was about to come out.

I had returned to Cambridge for a reunion of Harvard economics PhDs. The high point of the gathering was an address by one of our famous alumni. There were two types of economists in the audience: those who, like me, had ventured into the "real world" and those who had remained in academia.

Our famous speaker made what passes for a joke among economists: "We economists, we work to make markets perfect. But all you guys"—referring to those of us not in academia—"all you do is look for places where markets are not perfect so that you can earn profits."

To an economist, a perfect market is one that works so efficiently that any profit beyond the bare minimum is competed away. In general, perfect markets have been thought to exist only in theory, because for a market to function perfectly, several conditions must be met, including what economists call perfect information, an ideal state in which all existing information regarding anything and anybody is immediately available to all market participants at very low cost.

I laughed politely at the joke but wondered if those of us in the commercial world deserved to be viewed as profit-seeking heretics. Then a more interesting thought crossed my mind: Economic reality is rapidly approaching the theoretically ideal state of perfect information. I knew this because I had been immersed in the advances of computing and communications recently, while working at AT&T. Thanks to progress in a wide array of technologies coupled with investments to put these advances to use around the globe, what was once just a theoretical condition for perfect markets is well on its way to becoming an actuality. Where they aren't here already, ubiquitous connectivity and cheap, easily available information—perfect information, in other words—are just around the corner. Everywhere. Globally.

What does the near achievement of perfect information mean for markets? Will more perfect information (and everything else being equal) unequivocally contribute to making markets more perfect, as the theory predicts? Will profits, therefore, be competed away? How can companies maximize value in an era of perfect information? How can investors identify the companies with the greatest value potential?

As I was thinking about this, a more heretical question, as far as classical economics was concerned, arose: Was the theory right or could perfect information cause market failures? Could more information, therefore, increase opportunities for profits (again, everything else being equal)? Was it possible that parts of the *classical economic theory itself* and *the familiar strategies that were based on it needed to be rethought?*

The idea that we should need fresh economics and new strategies is not that far-fetched. The bulk of our mainstream economic theories were developed well before anyone envisioned what perfect information, should it come to pass, would do to our economic foundations. Some components of mainstream economics predate not only the 21st century but the 20th as well. While a number of forward-thinking economists are addressing these disconnects, many of the mainstream theories that are still espoused in textbooks were developed in the days before there was a direct phone line between the White House and the Kremlin. But now we live in the era of *Slumdog Millionaire,* a movie whose game-show-contestant hero finds both his girlfriend and his fortune because of instant information and ubiquitous connectivity. These days, mobile phones and televisions are commonplace even in the slums of Mumbai.

From Brazil to China to India, it looks as if the vanishing cost of information is enabling markets and global competition. The abundant information flow seems to be helping to create new companies, new industries, and new markets.

Yet some companies, clearly, still generate extraordinary profits. Coca-Cola, the Industrial and Commercial Bank of China, Microsoft, and Wal-Mart appear to maintain profit power in spite of the advance of cheap information. Is this sustainable?

And the corollary of cheap information, our increasing interconnectedness, is causing unpredicted waves of global popularity and baffling spirals of global distress. How do these dynamics work? How did Google become a powerhouse? Why did consumers snap up Apple's iPod in such overwhelming numbers, when rival products were as good or better, and often cheaper? Furthermore, we find ourselves surrounded by large-scale failures of financial markets. Why did so many investments across the global financial system turn sour simultaneously? Activities like these operate in markets that are especially rich in information—and yet these are the markets, oddly, that display a tendency to work in unfamiliar ways and that seem the least likely to obey the laws of supply and demand.

To investigate the effect of perfect information on the global economy and the implications for business and investing strategies, I drew on my work with numerous high-profile firms. I reexamined profit strategies that have been field-tested over years of experience. I also studied countless examples of business success and failure from enterprises around the globe. I revisited economic theories old and new; I delved into cutting-edge work in related fields, such as network mathematics. I examined the impact of abundant information and connectivity on the prospects for long-term value creation, on the sources of profits, the behavior of groups, the efficiency of markets, corporate business models, and on the nature of competition.

My conclusion: perfect information is rewriting the rules of the global economy. I have written this book to help leaders of companies, not-for-profits, and governmental organizations, as well as investors and entrepreneurs, formulate strategies that will put them ahead of the curve of economic change. Below, I highlight the key insights of the book. I enumerate the 12 essential facts about the evolving business environment, define the best way to measure business success, summarize the new strategy playbook in terms of one commandment and four rules, describe the tools and templates found in this book, and give an overview of the major trends driving global economic change. Finally, I will explain how this book is organized.

12 Essential Facts about the Transparent Economy

A new economy, which I call the transparent economy, is evolving before our eyes. Every business, every nonprofit, and every government organization will have to change profoundly if it is to succeed in the rapidly evolving business environment. Here are the 12 most important facts I learned about the transparent economy:

1. The movement toward transparency is unstoppable.
2. Transparency is challenging not just one, but most—or even all—industries in fundamental ways.
3. The seven benefits of transparency—reduced search costs, global wage and price competition, cheap and easy coordination of activities over distance, cheap and easy monitoring of people and processes over distance, the end of information asymmetries, falling transaction costs, and the feasibility of intricate contracts and conditional deals—give organizations a great deal more freedom in how they conduct their affairs, who they do business with, and how large they can become.
4. Access to cheap, plentiful information and levels of connectivity unlike anything we have ever experienced before are changing how people make economic decisions. This radically changes the behavior of participants in markets.
5. Many of the concepts and assumptions that we currently use to understand markets no longer work, including the concept of market equilibrium and the simplifying assumption of normal distributions.
6. There are new concepts and tools that we can use to understand the new market dynamics. These are based on network dynamics and power laws.
7. In transparency, profits are not necessarily competed away. Instead there are more opportunities for companies to create extraordinary profits.
8. For companies, the key to achieving these extraordinary profits is profit power. Likewise, for investors, profit power is the key to identifying companies with extraordinary profits.
9. There are 12 sources of profit power, which I call power nodes. A power node is a thing, position, skill, dynamic, or process that a company can reliably use to influence financial outcomes for itself and for other commercial enterprises in either a positive or negative way.
10. Vertically integrated companies and traditional industry boundaries are breaking apart.
11. Focused companies, working with other focused companies in distributed business arrangements, are becoming the new dominant business "structure."

12. The rules for competition and competitive strategy are being rewritten completely. Competition is becoming more intense. Competitive battles are being fought in three dimensions: vertical (up and down the value chain), horizontal (in established markets), and horizontal (across traditional industry boundaries).

Given these facts and the magnitude of the economic transformation now underway, how do companies and investors identify and evaluate the most promising new opportunities? Ultimately, they must create (and then implement) corporate and investment strategies that allow them to move *with* instead of *against* the powerful current of economic transformation. This means throwing out the tattered old strategy playbook and learning some new plays.

Keeping Score

The guiding principle of this book is that *the objective of corporate strategy is to create value.* When I recommend or evaluate corporate strategies in the later chapters of this book, the key test of merit will be whether a strategy builds long-term value. Profit is the means to an end, which is for an enterprise to create and build long-term value for its employees, its shareholders, and potentially other stakeholders. "Value" does not mean the drive at all cost for short-term profits such as quarterly earnings per share. Such nearsighted goals have often turned out to be detrimental to the pursuit of long-term value. In this book, "value" is equivalent to "wealth"; "profits" is shorthand for "economic profits," which is equivalent to "risk-adjusted long-term returns"; and "maximizing profits" means maximizing long-term value and sustainable wealth.

The New Strategy Playbook

The 12 insights about transparency lead us to transparency-age-appropriate answers to the four core strategic decisions all businesses face: what to own, how to structure the organization, how to conquer competitive threats, and how to read the marketplace and win. Below, I summarize the strategy playbook for the transparent economy in terms of one commandment and four rules. The specific applications of these guidelines will vary from company to company, from investor to investor, and from marketplace to marketplace, but the basic instructions remain the same.

▨ The Commandment for Maximizing Profits

Know Your Power Nodes

Power nodes are the sources of profit power, which is the single most effective tool for maximizing value in the transparent economy. Profit power is economic clout—the ability of a company to hold on to the value it itself has created, as well as to extract a share of profits from its competitors, to create incremental value for itself and for its partners in business relationships, and to shape the risks it and others will take on. It is the profit power of its brand, for example, that lets Coca-Cola run its global beverages business with a maximum of return and a minimum of investment and risk. Nothing is more important to a company's ability to build and sustain value than its ability to wield profit power. Being "the best" does not guarantee that your company can hold on to its hard-earned gains. Only profit power does that. In transparency, the presence or absence of power nodes is the key determinant of the prospects for profits. This book identifies the 12 power nodes that are effective in the transparent economy and explains what they are, how to create them, and how to use them in order to elevate long-term values. Some power nodes, like brands, have been around for a long time. Others, like hubs, are relatively new and relate to a dynamic rather than to a position.

▨ The Four Rules for Maximizing Profits

Once you are aware of power nodes, use these four rules to evaluate your business and investment prospects and to create a strategy for maximizing long-term value.

I. Focus, Focus, Focus

To maximize profits, be focused: own only businesses with power nodes. Transparency is enabling a vast expansion in the numbers and types of companies, many of them in markets for intermediate goods and operating across traditional industry boundaries. Business leaders and investors now have unprecedented choice about what businesses to own. "Focused" companies—those concentrated on providing a single element of the value chain—can operate efficiently and attract capital. In transparency, thanks to new technologies, it is no longer necessary for firms to own companies at every vertical step of the value chain in order to function efficiently or to compete. New technologies are also enabling focused companies to expand globally, transcending previous limitations of scale. Microsoft is an example of a company that has been focused yet has crossed industry boundaries time and again and has become large and global.

The most valuable focused companies are the ones that own power nodes and know how to use them. A focused company with a strong power node in the middle of a value chain, like Intel, may enjoy leverage over profits, while a company with a famous line of consumer products and a large market share in final packaged consumer goods, like Nestlé, may turn out to have little profit power relative to big chains of shops or providers of their ingredients. Whether you are a corporate executive or an investor, this book will show you how awareness of power nodes and focus can improve your strategic choices, your investment decisions, and your value analyses.

2. Adopt New Business Models and Mind Your Power Relationships

In transparency, a nexus of relationships replaces vertical integration as the prevailing archetype for "the firm" and every other organization. While companies can perform well as focused entities, long-term relationships (rather than arms-length transactions) can be beneficial in dealing with vagaries of markets, motley crews, etc. Perfect information allows wide latitude for establishing, monitoring, and coordinating ongoing relationships. Therefore, focused companies have an unparalleled degree of freedom in deciding how to organize. We can expect many innovative arrangements that won't involve full ownership. This book includes an exhaustive three-part checklist (that builds on the research in industrial organization of the past few decades) that you can use to decide on the optimal structure of your organization. Corporate leaders must use every single technological tool available to implement the structural arrangement that will maximize profits.

In particular, companies with profit power can use structure to further increase returns. Focused companies with a power node can be at the center of long-term distributed business arrangements, orchestrating the relationships to provide positive sum benefits to all, while seizing the bulk of the returns and allocating risk in the most advantageous manner. This can allow emerging global companies, for instance, to grow rapidly without destroying their returns. Profit power is the glue that holds the arrangements in a distributed business model together. The cultivation of power relationships is likely to become an essential management skill.

3. Fight Fiercely in Three Dimensions

We need a radically new approach to competitive strategy. In transparency, companies can expect to compete in multiple dimensions, namely: vertically (in the same value chain), horizontally in the same sector or market, and horizontally across traditional industry boundaries. Competition is no longer one-dimensional, i.e., uniformly horizontal. New competition is no longer over horizontal market share either; it is over risk-adjusted returns. In many cases, *the key determinant of long-term value is now the ability to defend or extract returns from vertical competitors in the same value chain.* The fierce 3-D rivalries that we are seeing increasingly will essentially be power node battles. The relative strength of one company's power node vis-à-vis the power nodes of its competitors in multiple dimensions will determine the level of returns that the company can expect. This book gives many examples of companies that have won 3-D competitive battles by skillful use of their power node.

4. Get Ready for Powerlaw Marketplaces

Perfect information and high levels of connectivity cause new dynamics in groups and in marketplaces because they fundamentally change the way people make economic decisions. I call this new style of decision making "interdependent decision making." The dynamics of interdependence (coupled with a number of conditions that we will find in transparency) can create success on a phenomenal scale—the kind of scale we have observed in YouTube, Facebook, *Harry Potter*, Oprah Winfrey, and iPods—because it makes large groups (of buyers, or of voters, for instance) behave like a special kind of network, one that is characterized by powerlaw distributions. "Power law" is a mathematician's term for a type of distribution that, in everyday parlance, is often called the 80–20 principle. The 80–20 principle is operating when, for example, 20 percent of a company's products are responsible for 80 percent of its sales. Over the course of this book, readers will become very familiar with power laws, powerlaw networks, and the interesting way that powerlaw markets stay in a state of continuous yet well-defined flux.

Most of us are accustomed to patterns that follow another set of rules entirely. In the past, the distributions of purchases, votes, guesses, and other choices were often assumed to be random. A random (also called "normal") distribution has a mean. When distributions are normal, we can reasonably expect the average of many choices to regress to the mean and therefore crowds can be "wise." This does not happen in transparency in the case of powerlaw distributions. They do not have means; instead we see multiple hubs. Hubs are the points with the predominant number of links in a power-law network. Think *Harry Potter* or Google. "Tipping," which is equivalent to one point getting all the links and the other points getting none, is less common in transparency because of the prevalence of powerlaw distributions and major and minor hubs. In the transparent economy, we have the technology to infinitely customize products for individual consumers, but we find that the powerlaw dynamics of mass consumer marketplaces cause actual consumer choices to be concentrated according to the 80–20 principle.

In order to master the art of winning the hearts and minds of consumers in powerlaw marketplaces, we must "flip" our perspective 180 degrees. No longer can we "push" a message into a marketplace. To succeed, we must learn to use the energies of the marketplace to draw consumers to our products and services.

This discussion is of equal importance to for-profit as to not-for-profit and governmental organizations.

Tools and Templates

This book is a strategic tool; it is not an economics text. My intention is to help corporate leaders, investors, individual entrepreneurs, and leaders of not-for-profit organizations to anticipate the effects of transparency, and to provide readers with tangible, practical strategies to prosper in the years ahead. This book offers step-by-step instructions to implement these strategies by means of user-friendly templates for each of the four rules for maximizing profits. You will also find dozens of real-life illustrations. I have repeatedly applied this sort of methodology to lay the groundwork for concrete results, and I believe readers can do the same.

The Forces Driving the Transparent Economy

How is perfect information transforming our economic fundamentals?

In transparency, perfect information and the potential for extraordinary profits coexist, practically as well as theoretically. By better understanding the underlying forces that are creating transparency, we can successfully benefit from the momentum that these forces create.

As the cost of information plummets, it drives two inevitable trends, one arising from the other. The first is the trend toward perfect information. Perfect information itself drives a second inevitable trend—the rise of interdependent decision making.

The first trend toward perfect information is already erasing many marketplace imbalances and other economic inefficiencies. For executives, entrepreneurs, investors, and individual employees this means new degrees of freedom but also fierce global competition from an unprecedented number of fronts.

Contrary to expectations, due to the second trend, of increasing inter-dependence of decision making, *perfect information also creates a new set of market failures.* Therefore, the potential for *extraordinary profit and for long-term value creation is an economic reality, even in the light of perfect information* and absence of other market failures. This is the key insight that will help us formulate a new economic paradigm based on the dynamics of networks in conditions where information is perfect.

Admittedly, I am hardly the first to observe that markets don't always work the way the classical theories say they should. As the legendary investor Warren Buffett is said to have remarked, "I'd be a bum on the street with a tin cup if the markets were always efficient." The contribution of this book to economic theory is to demonstrate why markets do not work perfectly even when, or rather, especially when, information becomes perfect, and to show how we can make practical use of this insight. The challenge to the premise that perfect information leads to perfect markets is important well beyond academic debate, because many policymakers in both business and government base their strategies—knowingly or not—on this assumption.

How This Book Is Organized

This book is divided into parts that follow the same logic as the path of discovery.

Part I discusses profit power and power nodes, giving readers concrete examples of how power node strategies produce extraordinary valuations (chapter 1).

Part II focuses on how our economic reality is reshaped by the underlying driver of change, the vanishing cost of information (chapters 2–5).

Part III is an in-depth look at how transparency will affect the four core decisions that all businesses face: what to own (company focus), how to structure their organization, how to conquer competitive threats, and how to read their marketplace and define a winning strategy (chapters 6–10).

Part IV discusses the new strategy playbook, including the power node Commandment and the Four Rules for Maximizing Profits in Transparency (chapter 11).

Part V focuses on the Commandment "Know Your Power Nodes," and presents each of the 12 power nodes in detail with many real-world examples (chapters 12–13).

Part VI (chapters 14–18) provides the practical operating instructions for applying the Four Rules. These instructions are presented in a series of step-by-step templates for evaluating companies and for creating action plans that can be implemented by any business leader or investor who is seriously interested in extraordinary returns. The templates are illustrated with examples of specific strategies that successful competitors have used to achieve greater returns. I also draw lessons from avoidable mistakes.

Part VII explores how investors may apply the Four Rules method to improve their valuation methods and portfolio strategies (chapter 19).

Part VIII is the conclusion (chapter 20).

By the time you finish this book, you will have the tools to create the strategy you need to make the most of the opportunities and challenges that the powerful trend toward transparency will generate.

During my economics-PhD reunion back in 2004, it was clear that neither the profit-seeking heretics in commerce nor the theoretically orthodox in academia had the answers about the full impact of cheap information and unlimited connectivity. That started my thinking about the economics of perfect information and profit power and about how to help executives, entrepreneurs, and investors find new and better strategies for building long term value in the years to come.

As my work progressed, I learned that in transparency perfect information and imperfect markets—and hence extraordinary profitability—can coexist, practically as well as theoretically. *In the light of transparency, the heresy vanished.* A new economics of perfect information emerged and the importance of profit power became apparent.

The transparent economy will offer extraordinary opportunities to business executives, entrepreneurs, leaders of not-for-profit enterprises, and investors. They will come face-to-face with heretofore unseen market dynamics and fierce global competition from a multitude of fronts. However, they also will find that they have new degrees of freedom to shape their destiny, exercise profit power, and create sustainable long-term value. Those who wield their profit power wisely, unapologetically, and ethically will be most likely to reap success.

PART I

The Key to Profit Power

Chapter 1

The Power Node Strategy

Distribution depends on myth and violence (on faith and brigandage)…
                    —Harold Dwight Lasswell and Abraham Kaplan[1]

Profit and Power ought jointly to be considered.
                    —Josiah Child[2]

What do the Industrial and Commercial Bank of China, Intel, and Oprah Winfrey have in common with *Harry Potter*, Harvard, Wipro, and Tata Tea? Why does Coca-Cola earn huge returns, when its bottlers—who absorb the lion's share of hard work and risks—do not? Why is it so difficult for mighty Microsoft to catch up with Google? How did Apple and its iPod manage to run circles around the music industry? Does it make sense for snack company Frito Lay and fashion retailer Zara to own lots of manufacturing plants? What sets the winners apart from the losers? The answer is profit power.

We recognize intuitively that many companies have profit power. Coca-Cola and PepsiCo are known for the source of their profit power, namely their global brands. Wal-Mart is famous, and at times infamous, for deriving profit power from its unrivaled distribution network in the United States.

Many companies have little or no profit power. One might expect the Esselte Corporation to be profitable. It makes a broad range of popular office products, including the famous Pendaflex hanging files. Indeed, Pendaflex is the number one brand in hanging files. It has a reputation for quality products. The private equity group that purchased Esselte in 2002 is expert in lean and flexible manufacturing. Esselte has moved its manufacturing plants to low-cost locations around the globe and added an experienced marketing team.

Alas, the office products business of Esselte is also a company without much profit power. Its admirable attributes do not translate into extraordinary profits and long-term sustainable value. Unfortunately for Esselte office products, its major customers are Office Depot, Staples, and OfficeMax. Esselte must bid against other manufacturers to get onto the shelves of these powerful retail chains. Few of the potential profit improvements from clever cost reductions and marvelous marketing went to Esselte's bottom line. Instead, they accrued to the likes of Office Depot and OfficeMax.

A few years ago, the Boise Cascade Corporation was also a company without profit power. The Boise Cascade name had long connoted "paper," and the company still had some of the world's leading holdings in forests and paper mills. But these assets weren't enough to protect its returns in the face of pricing pressures from the chains like Office Depot, Staples, and OfficeMax. Like other office product manufacturers, Boise Cascade got whipsawed by these distributors and it was unable to protect, let alone build, the long-term value of the company. Boise Cascade took action. It bought OfficeMax in 2003, sold forestry and paper manufacturing businesses in 2004, and changed the corporate name to OfficeMax. As OfficeMax, it has profit power relative to companies like Esselte.

Both Esselte and the entity that was once Boise Cascade were quality companies. They had intelligent managements, strong products, and good reputations. For all of their superiority, however, neither could find a way to defend its margins on office products against more powerful competitors in the same value chain. While Esselte struggles to retain and could not build long-term value, the Boise that became OfficeMax now occupies a more powerful and therefore profitable position in the competitive arena. The fates of these companies illustrate the central message of this book: the deliberate pursuit and shrewd application of profit power are essential for corporations to generate or hold on to profits and build long-term value. Merely being the best is not good enough. As we shall see, this lesson will become critically important as we move further into the competitive environment of the transparent economy.

Many popular recipes for corporate success assert that extraordinary returns will occur as a natural byproduct of managerial excellence. Unfortunately, as Esselte and Boise Cascade and many other companies like them demonstrate, this is not true. A company can make outstanding efforts toward operational excellence, achieve all its benchmarks, gain market share, and still not achieve high risk-adjusted returns.

Why? Once a company has generated a pool of value, such economic profits are up for grabs. Somebody, or some company, will seize that value—but it need not be the company that generated it, even if it exhibited superior management or its employees worked most efficiently or creatively. The world is rougher than that. Something else must be added to the mix if companies are not only to generate value but also to hold on to it. That something is power—or, more specifically, profit power. I define profit power as follows:

> **PROFIT POWER**: The ability to hold on to the value from your own activities as well as to extract value from the activities of others with whom you interact in your commercial dealings, to increase the value available to the entire group, and to optimize the risks for yourself and allocate to others the risks that you do not want

This concept can be expressed as follows:

$$\text{Excellence} + \text{Profit power} \Rightarrow \text{Extraordinary economic profit}$$

Expressing this principle as a formula highlights that maximizing value is a multistep process. First, a company creates the preconditions for value by being excellent in many dimensions, which include corporate skills (to make the product or perform its services), physical assets, employees, reputation, and so forth. Next, profit power is required to make sure that the company can hold on to what it has created. As the formula depicts, profit power will translate excellence into economic profits and therefore into long-term value for the company. Furthermore, profit power is necessary to generate additional value for the entire group of competitors and partners. By working together they can mitigate uncertainty and improve overall performance. Finally, profit power is instrumental in assuring that most of this incremental value from working together accrues to the leading company as well.

Why do I focus on profit and profit power?

Profit is the means to an end, which is for an enterprise to create and build value for its employees, its shareholders, and potentially other stakeholders. The guiding principle of this book is that *the objective of corporate strategy is to create value.* When I recommend or evaluate corporate strategies in later chapters of this book, the key test of merit will be whether a strategy builds long-term value.

Many speak, some eloquently, of other objectives for corporate strategy: greatness, growth, market share. Some search for excellence; others build to last, pursue Six Sigma, or focus on finding the best leadership team. As noted, such pursuits help build the preconditions for value generation. Compared to the ultimate objective of building value, in my opinion, these laudable achievements are intermediate steps. Without profit power a company will not be able to hold on to the benefits of these achievements.

Several authors, including Arie de Geus in *The Living Company*,[3] have pointed out that if companies pursue nothing but the achievement of profits, especially short-term profits, they will not live long because they do not build toward something that is of value in the long run. I agree that companies ought to strive for long-term value creation. They also need tools (or weapons) to ensure that they can hold on to the fruits of this hard work for the shareholders, the employees, and other stakeholders. That is why profit power is indispensable.

Long-term sustainable economic profit is the method by which a business creates value. Therefore the spotlight is on profit and profit power.

This book defines value in financial terms. You maximize the value of a company by maximizing its expected economic profits and you increase value if the risk-adjusted return on your activities or investment exceeds the weighted average cost of capital of your endeavors.[4] A company has three levers to maximize value: its cash flows over time, its stream of investments over time, and the risks inherent in the elements of the cash flow. A company that has profit power has more control over these levers than its competitors.

While we are speaking of terminology regarding value and value creation, please note that in our book I have adopted the definitions and conventions of the book *Valuation*. In our book, "maximizing value" is used as a shorthand for the expression "maximizing risk-adjusted returns,"[5] which amounts to the same as "maximizing economic profits." I will use these terms interchangeably. When I say "profit," the word is shorthand for *economic profit* or *risk-adjusted returns*. And when I say "extraordinary profits," this is shorthand for *sustainable returns in excess of the risk-adjusted cost of capital*. *Sustainable returns in excess of the risk-adjusted cost of capital* are often referred to in economic texts as "rents." As I mentioned in the introduction, this book advocates the building of long-term value, without which no company can persist or can hope to exist in the long term. I do not support the pursuit of short-term profits at all cost, because, as we have seen, this may distort incentives and invite manipulation of short-term results, and is as likely to be detrimental as beneficial for the achievement of long-term value.

The Sources of Profit Power: Power Nodes

Now let us turn to the key question: how do companies get such profit power?

I have studied companies that have generated extraordinary profits over the long term to discover what their source or sources of profit power might be. Most of these companies have something in common: they occupy or use a distinctive position or dynamic to achieve those superior returns. I refer to such a position or dynamic as a *power node*.

I define a power node as follows:

POWER NODE: A source of profit power—that is, a thing, position, skill, dynamic, or process that a company can reliably use to influence the financial outcomes for itself and for other commercial enterprises in either a positive or negative way. Power nodes provide companies with the ability to help or hinder the cash flows, risks, and investments—that is, the inputs to returns—of other players over an extended period of time.

A power node is a leading indicator for value. Companies that make the most of their power nodes have wide latitude for choosing which activities to perform, how much capital they wish to invest, and how much risk they want to assume. Power node companies have the ability to insist that others take on expenditures and risks that they themselves do not want. Therefore, a sound power node strategy is essential to a company's ongoing success. If a corporation's leaders or investors use its power node(s) well, they can maximize risk-adjusted returns and therefore the company's valuation.

I have identified the 12 power nodes, old and new, that will be the most important sources of profit power in the decades to come. Many of the older power nodes are already well known, but we will take a fresh look at their capacity to build returns as the economy changes.

The 12 power nodes are: brand (#1), secret, special, or proprietary ingredient (#2), regulatory protection (#3), focused financial resources (#4), customer base with switching costs (#5), proprietary process or modus operandi (#6), distribution gateway (#7), dominant position in a layer (#8), increasing mutual utility (#9), filters and brokers (#11), aikido assets (#10), and hubs (#12). Power nodes # 9, 10, 11, and 12 are relatively new and relate to a dynamic rather than to a position. The hub power nodes (#12) are notable both for their individual profit-making capacity and for their potential to magnify the effect of older power nodes. I will describe all 12 power nodes and their powers in detail in chapter 13.

Even if we don't know their names, we are well aware of many power nodes. Companies tend to be known for their source of profit power. Consumers may think of Coke and Pepsi as purveyors of sodas that have been embraced the world over. In the beverage world, the two companies are known for using the immense popularity of their soft drinks to drive advantageous arrangements with bottlers.

Similarly, Wal-Mart's power node is its unrivaled distribution network. With a Wal-Mart store within easy driving distance of nearly every consumer in the United States, Wal-Mart has incomparable clout. Wal-Mart holds on to the profits from its own activities—retail sales—and also extracts profits from the activities of the consumer goods companies whose products are allowed onto Wal-Mart shelves. Wal-Mart lays claim to the profits of its suppliers by driving an extremely tough bargain when negotiating for their products, as well as by running a system that is optimized for Wal-Mart's purposes. Its suppliers put up with this because they gain more from cooperating with Wal-Mart and generating low-margin sales volume through its incredible distribution system than they would by resisting. Wal-Mart has extracted so much profit from consumer goods companies that one of *BusinessWeek*'s imperatives for successful brand management is to avoid dealing with Wal-Mart altogether.[6]

In any business arena, sometimes only one and never more than a few companies will have power nodes. Those that do have such sources of profit power, however, may be able to use them to control the ongoing shape of an industry or economic niche. As we can see, a power node is not identical to a core competency. Forest management was considered a core competency of Boise Cascade—but that expertise wasn't enough to preserve the company's bottom line. A core competency is something a company does well.[7] As we noted, being best will not necessarily be good enough to deliver economic profits. Power nodes, on the other hand, are those skills and capabilities that allow a company to earn superior risk-adjusted returns, in part by extracting economic profits from others.

Power nodes should also not be confused with control assets, which are a narrow group of transaction-specific assets, such as pieces of equipment, which supposedly affect one side's ability to enforce the terms of the contract.[8] Power nodes are useful in dealing with the problems that may arise with incomplete contracts as they extend over time. But power nodes represent a much broader and more versatile class of assets and processes than control assets, and they are much more useful than control assets in providing leverage for an uncertain future. Unlike control assets, power nodes have positive sum aspects, and this makes them effective in the inherent multiple-game nature of many business relationships. Power relationships in business go on day after day, year after year, and what goes around comes around. The full benefits of profit power accrue only over the course of multiple games. As a result, power nodes have "disciplining" effects on the behavior of the participants.

Now that we see what profit power and power nodes are and what they are not, let us get to the heart of the matter: understanding why a power node strategy is so essential for business success in the 21st century. As we mentioned in the introduction and will explore in greater detail in future chapters, in transparency, most business arrangements will be forged among autonomous focused companies rather than among vertically integrated entities. These focused companies will compete over profits in a new multidimensional environment.

In such a transparent environment, power nodes will be the key determinants of profitability, competitive success, and the balance of power in relationships with competitors and partners. A power node company will be at the center of a nexus of implicit or explicit contracts. A power node company may dominate its value chain and its multidimensional relationships, but in the long run most independent partners will have the option to walk away if the relationship gets too draconian. Therefore, it is generally in the interest of the power node companies to help the other players improve their lot. The power node company and the "weaker" partners will form relationships that are mutually beneficial and that deal with many of the issues that cannot be achieved by arm's length arrangements that purely rely on markets or pricing mechanisms. This I will discuss at length in chapters 8 and 9.

Power Node Strategy in Action: The Examples of Pepsi-Cola and AT&T

Let us look at two examples to illustrate what I mean by power nodes and power node strategy The first tale, about Pepsi-Cola and (secondarily) its close competitor Coca-Cola, will illustrate what a power node is, how it can be deployed in a power node strategy, how to maximize a company's returns by orchestrating a distributed business arrangement, and how this is related to new multidimensional competition. These leading soft-drink companies provide brilliant examples of how the ownership of a tiny slice of a business enterprise can yield enormous profit power. Since the beverage business is not too complex, we can see readily how this power node strategy operates. We will look carefully at the highly profitable and enduring business arrangements that PepsiCo and Coca-Cola have established with their bottlers. We will see that the parent company can drive global growth without committing huge amounts of its own resources. These are role models for how to pursue an aggressive global expansion while safeguarding the returns of the parent company.

Our second tale, involving AT&T, is not as happy a story, but it is extremely instructive. When we consider the telecommunications industry of the turn of the millennium, we see an example of how changing technology and investments by newly minted competitors combined to severely undermine the longstanding power nodes of the leading companies in the industry. A demise of long-time power nodes can happen to any business at any time. The AT&T example will give us the opportunity to understand how using a power node analysis can point the way to resolving difficult business decisions.

Power Node Strategy: The Example of Pepsi-Cola

Some of the most hands-on experiences to inform my thinking about power nodes came at Pepsi, where I had the privilege of contributing to the building of a global business model from scratch. In the early 1990s, I joined as the head of Strategy and Mergers and Acquisitions for Pepsi-Cola International. PepsiCo's then chairman, Wayne Calloway, wanted Pepsi-Cola International to create and implement a business plan that would enable Pepsi-Cola to enjoy growth and profits from international markets. Pepsi's leaders were clear that they wanted global growth—but which business structures would best accomplish this mission and deliver the highest returns? In retrospect, we can see that Pepsi's actions provide a clear example of an effective power node strategy.

In those days, Pepsi-Cola and Coca-Cola sold only soda. In the United States at that time, Pepsi-Cola was essentially vertically integrated; it owned many of its bottling plants and distributors. It would be very capital-intensive (and destructive to returns) if Pepsi were to own all the infrastructure that would be involved in selling Pepsi products in countries as diverse as Mexico, India, the Czech Republic, and China.

Our chief competitor, Coca-Cola, had formed arrangements with or acquired stakes in bottlers around the world rather than choosing to own all its operations outright. Coca-Cola made brilliant use of its power nodes—its global brand and the secret formula for its drinks. The company supplied its bottlers with its syrup and the rights to its world-famous name; for their part, the bottlers had to acquire filling equipment, buy enormous quantities of glass and plastic bottles, manage workers ranging from plant employees to truck drivers, negotiate with unions, develop relationships with retailers, and handle local government regulations. The bottlers absorbed the lion's share of the risk and the capital expenditures, but Coke's returns on invested capital (ROIC) were a multiple of the bottlers' returns.

Needless to say, we at Pepsi also wanted to eschew ownership of plants and trucks and focus Pepsi's ownership on its global brand. Not only would a distributed arrangement enable Pepsi to earn superior returns by reducing the risks and capital expenditures for the parent company, it would also improve the performance of the overall system because it would align incentives with operational responsibilities and enable the parent to tap into the bottlers' local expertise. Such a distributed system also was likely to be more adaptable to change than an integrated company might be.

But Pepsi-Cola International could not get there in one leap. Over the course of a decade, Pepsi-Cola's global network was built in a whirl of transactions—and after the deals were done, we set up a distributed system step by painstaking step. Often we had no choice but to begin with ownership. This was capital-intensive, but these costly holdings were necessary to set up the operations for making and selling our products. It was a huge task for a relatively small group, but we succeeded, laying the foundation for the thriving worldwide enterprise that exists today. While there were many ups and downs along the way, we methodically pursued our plan of establishing operations around the globe. Sometimes, we made a dash to beat Coca-Cola to buy bottlers or to align with partners. In countries where we could not work out a deal with existing bottlers of beer, soft drinks, or other beverages, we had to start from scratch. Sometimes we bought small companies and built them up, as we did in India and in several regions of China, and sometimes, as in Thailand, we took a stake in an existing bottler and grew it with infusions of capital and closer scrutiny of management. Some bottlers progressed more or less in a straight line, like our operations in India. Others needed to be recapitalized or restarted a couple of times.

Whichever way we set up the bottling and distribution operations in those early years, however, in the end we hoped to get to a global distributed business model in which the bottlers would be able to stand on their own feet. The moves necessary to establish most of the bottlers and distributors (even our largest bottlers in the United States) as structurally and financially independent were largely completed between 1999 and 2003, under the leadership of then PepsiCo chairman Roger Enrico. After the structuring had been completed, PepsiCo controlled a global beverage system that delivered high returns to the parent company. In chapter 16, I will summarize the details of setting up and running the bottler network as a nuts-and-bolts illustration of how one might orchestrate a set of power relationships.

As tables 1.1 and 1.2 show, Coca-Cola's and Pepsi-Cola's returns on invested capital (ROIC) in those days were over 20 percent on carbonated beverages, while most of the bottlers had ROICs well below that.

Since those days, Pepsi and to a lesser extent Coca-Cola have drifted away from this structure, for instance because of the addition of other products that are not as suitable for a distributed bottler network and because of changes in the distribution landscape. As we will discuss later, the optimal business model is not static, and these developments by 2009 caused PepsiCo to review their structure in the United States again.

To be sure, there were significant benefits to the Coca-Cola and Pepsi-Cola bottlers during the last decade from belonging to their parents' networks. For instance, the relationship with Cola-Cola and Pepsi-Cola gives them a stability and legitimacy they might not otherwise have had. One day,

Table 1.1	
2000 ROIC for Coca-Cola and selected Coca-Cola bottlers	
	ROIC**
Coca-Cola Co. (KO)*	**25.4%**
Coca-Cola FEMSA S.A. (KOF)	18.1%
Embotelladora Andina S.A. (AKO)	11.1%
Coca-Cola Enterprises Inc. (CCE)	7.2%
Coca-Cola Amatil	4.9%
PanAmerican Beverages, Panamco (merged with FEMSA in 2003)	4.9%

*Acronyms in parentheses are New York Stock Exchange ticker symbols.
**C. Laboy, in *Company Reports*, Bear Stearns Equity Research (2000).

Table 1.2	
2000 ROIC for Pepsi-Co and selected Pepsi-Cola bottlers	
	ROIC*
Pepsi-Co (beverages only)	**25.3%**
AmBev (InBev precursor)	11.7%
PepsiAmericas Inc. (PAS)	10.4%
Pepsi-Gemex (acquired by PBG in 2002)	10.3%
Compania Cervecerias Unidas S.A. (CU)	7.7%
Pepsi Bottling Group Inc. (PBG)	5.8%

*C. Laboy, in *Company Reports*, Bear Stearns Equity Research (2000).

for example, I sat in on the discussion at an investment bank about whether a small bottler should get financing. It was one of the few privately held independents. Its profitability didn't look very strong, but it was a Pepsi-franchise bottler. The bankers green-lighted the deal based on the assumption that, as a member of the Pepsi family, the bottler would receive support from the parent company in times of trouble. Few bottlers will walk away from that.

When we reflect on Coca-Cola and Pepsi-Cola's business models, we note that the parents had to own only two parts of their business—their outstanding brands and their proprietary recipes for soft-drink concentrate. These were sources of profit and points of leverage. In short, brands and proprietary ingredients were power nodes. These power nodes were so potent economically that independent companies were willing to take on all the work involved in producing and selling the product—for a relatively minor share of the overall profit pool.

When we examine the relationship between Pepsi-Cola and Coca-Cola and their bottlers, we can also understand the dynamics of 3-D competition in transparency. In transparency, the threats to corporate returns won't lie chiefly with look-alike rivals for horizontal market share (in the case of Pepsi's bottlers, with the bottlers of Coca-Cola, Schweppes, or Cott Beverages), but rather with "partners" in a vertical value chain. We can see this very clearly in the relationships between Coca-Cola and Pepsi-Cola and their bottlers.

Competing for the largest share of soda drinkers is important to both Coca-Cola and Pepsi-Cola. They have huge advertising budgets to accomplish this. But as far as returns are concerned, their highest-leverage activity is, in effect, competing with their bottlers. This is how "vertical competition" works. Their bottlers are constantly battling to hold on to their returns in the face of pressure from the very companies whose products provide them with their livelihood.

The bottlers do also face the horizontal type of competition that we are accustomed to. They are slugging away in the marketplace every day to get more shelf space and greater revenues versus rivals like the bottlers of Schweppes or Cott. For the profitability of the bottlers, however, this horizontal market share is of far less importance than their vertical competition with the Pepsi-Cola or Coca-Cola parent companies.

As we saw when we compared ROIC, the bottlers are the comparative losers in this vertical competition—even if the sting is lessened by the ancillary benefits they receive as a result of affiliation with Coca-Cola or Pepsi-Cola.

The structures that Coca-Cola and Pepsi-Cola maintain with most of their bottlers are very different from the sorts of business models that dominated commercial life in the not-too-distant past. Back in the industrial heyday that began in the 1920s and 1930s, vertical integration, as epitomized by Ford and General Motors, was hailed as the gold standard of business models. Indeed, for many decades, Coca-Cola's choice to focus on a very small part of its value chain and to work with bottlers that were independent rather than wholly owned would have been considered a deviation from the prevailing business model. But not anymore.

In the past, many companies would have argued that vertical integration was necessary because it was impossible to effectively monitor or coordinate activities with companies that were independent. In transparency, most of these obstacles will disappear. The rise of perfect information will allow companies to have virtual omniscience about the activities of their partners, which of course means that the opportunities for power node companies to structure their global business arrangements for maximum returns will be greatly expanded. For example, these days, in several markets, Pepsi can track every can and bottle sold under its brand: where it was sold, when it was sold, and at what price.

In summary, we can see that Pepsi-Cola and Coca-Cola provide clear examples of the power node strategy. They focused their corporate activities on the highest-return slice of an industry that is very labor- and capital-intensive. With the advent of transparency, their model becomes highly portable, even to companies whose businesses are a lot more complex than carbonated beverages. In an age of abundant and cheap information, companies will be able to choose among a full spectrum of contracts and other types of relationships that are neither rigid as vertical integration nor as "loose" as pure reliance on markets and the price mechanism. A wide choice among different types of distributed business arrangements can potentially be applied to any company in any industry or market anywhere around the world. With the right kind of power node, deployed in the right kind of business arrangement, any company can sweep up a great deal of profit from the other companies that are essential to making its business run—without having to own them.

Another important lesson that we will discuss in this book (see chapter 16) is that the optimal business model is dynamic. By 2009, for instance, PepsiCo explored changing its arrangement once again to deal with significant changes in the retail landscape (where Wal-Mart had established a powerful power node), an explosion of complexity of running a bottler due to soaring SKUs, and parent company acquistions of drinks that did not fit the bottler model.

The Challenges of a Power Node Strategy: The Example of AT&T

In the late 1990s, I had occasion to think about power nodes and power node strategy once again—this time at AT&T, and as the age of transparency was dawning. AT&T was still vertically integrated, meaning that in addition to owning all the lines, hardware, and software operations required to create, sell, and deliver the "finished product" of phone service to consumers and businesses, it also owned the raw underlying infrastructure, including its long-haul network. Up until the mid-1990s, it was one of three companies—the other two were Sprint and MCI/WorldCom—that controlled almost all the available long-haul network infrastructure in the United States. For many years, while they had this position, these companies were able to charge deliciously high rates for their finished product, the long distance telecommunications services that traveled over the network. The companies' ownership of this network infrastructure amounted to a power node, one that readers will likely recognize as controlling a dominant position in a layer (power node # 8). By the time I arrived at AT&T, however, that source of power had started to dwindle as inexorably as snow on a warm day.

One of the predictions of classical economics is that when a few companies are making huge profits, other enterprises will try to jump in and chip away at the market. The theory is certainly correct about this tendency! In the mid-1990s, this began to happen to AT&T and the other incumbents. Their long-distance networks were the cumulative result of decades of investment. In many cases, AT&T was still running copper wires with circuit switching. Meanwhile, there had been quantum leaps in both fiber-optic technology and switching approaches, and numerous investors thought it wise to put their money in start-up companies that would lay high-speed, high-capacity networks across the country and across the oceans. When the network-building boom was over, the available long-haul capacity far outstripped demand. Indeed, give or take a few factors of ten, potential U.S. capacity was expanded *one hundred million* times. As a result, by 2000, the combined backbone capacity of the three incumbents, which had been close to 100 percent of the total in the early 1990s, amounted to less than a speck of the new total potential capacity.

As we now know, this tidal wave of capacity set off fierce competitive wars. Two other dependable axioms of economics say that when competition by price is fierce, prices have a tendency to approach marginal costs, and that one should not expect to be rewarded for sunk costs. The new companies had sunk—literally—many billions each into acquiring rights-of-way, laying pipes, and buying lasers, glass, routers, and other equipment. What were the marginal costs for a unit of transport on the new networks? Once that equipment was set up, the marginal cost of sending lots of messages in the form of shots of light was about close to zero.[9] Variable operating costs of the new networks were also minuscule. But during the period from 1995 to 2000, the demand from buyers did not expand to keep up with a supply that had exploded by so many multiples. With customers relatively scarce, compared to supply, the new providers began tumbling over each other to offer lots of network capacity for next to nothing. The price of long-haul capacity, and of all the products based on it, fell precipitously.

It is instructive to look at AT&T's situation in those days from the standpoint of power nodes. Once upon a time, the company's beloved and relatively high-cost network had been a power node. But after the massive capacity expansion in the industry, AT&T's long-haul network capacity was no longer able to generate exalted returns.

So what could AT&T possibly have done? Did AT&T own anything or could it deploy anything that still had profit power?

The answer was yes: customers, in particular business customers. While the new rival networks were desperately looking for customers, AT&T and the other two incumbents actually had a strong base of corporate clients that they had built up over the years. For sure, these corporate customers did bargain with the incumbents for price reductions, but ultimately they were likely to stay put even at a significant price differential with the newcomers. It is extremely cumbersome for a company to retool its entire communications and associated computing setup. In other words, these clients represented a power node—a customer base with high switching costs (power node # 5).

If AT&T had been aggressive in pursuing a power node strategy in line with new realities, it might have seized the opportunity to restructure itself and the industry. It might have positioned the customer-base power node at the core of a distributed business arrangement, with the new wave of network providers as its bottler-like partners.

In that case, rather than upgrading its own antiquated systems, AT&T could have managed its customers' communications volume over several of the new, state-of-the-art networks, using the new protocols of the Internet to ensure a seamless product. It could have been the beginning of a distributed business arrangement, and beautiful new power relationships.

But it was not to be, for possibly a number of reasons. As is described in *End of the Line* by Leslie Cauley, AT&T's identity had long been built around its network infrastructure. The network had been its source of profitability, its power node. Corporate fiefdoms were centered on it, too. Possibly, the prospect of working with a modern new network that was not theirs had little appeal to the executives in charge of AT&T's network infrastructure. Or maybe they did not believe it would work. At the time, the capabilities of the new networks were so revolutionary and the drop in prices and costs was so steep that it was almost hard to believe what was happening, even when it was right before their eyes. Maybe that is part of why Internet protocol technology was rejected in those early days. Today, it is impossible to imagine the AT&T network, or any modern network, without that "IP stuff."

Even as its prices and revenues went into a tailspin, AT&T continued to invest billions in its long-haul telecom assets. This new equipment was worth pennies on the dollar the moment it was installed. For this and many other reasons about which volumes have been written and will be written, AT&T foundered. In 2005, after many twists and turns, what was left of this great American icon was sold to SBC Communications, one of the large Regional Bell Operating Companies (RBOCs). SBC was primarily interested in AT&T's remaining power node, its business customers. In the ultimate irony, SBC renamed itself AT&T.

I tell this story in part to illustrate how necessary it is to think in terms of power nodes—not only for profitability but even for the survival of the company. It also serves to warn readers that the implementation of a power node strategy can sometimes be quite painful to accomplish. Even if the correct path seems quite clear to you as a corporate leader or leading investor, you may meet with strong objections. It can be very difficult to develop a consensus in favor of reinventing the company around a new power node.

Profit and Profit Power in an Economic Theory

Now that we have seen examples of profit power and of power node strategy in action, let us briefly discuss how this book's concepts of profit power and power nodes fit in with economic literature about power.

This book's concept of profit power is consistent with the theories of economic power that have been advanced by several thinkers. In his *Microeconomics*, for example, economist Samuel Bowles provides a useful summary of four characteristics that must be present in any "plausible representation of power." This book's definition of profit power bears a strong relationship to the ideas encapsulated by Bowles, which becomes apparent when we compare our definition and discussion of profit power with his. He notes that power is *interpersonal*, an aspect of a relationship among people, not a characteristic of a solitary individual; the exercise of power involves the *threat and use of sanctions*; power is *normatively indeterminate*—in other words, neither automatically good nor bad; power *must be sustainable* as a Nash equilibrium, a condition in which all players in a game are fully informed of each other's strategies, and no player can benefit from changing his or her strategy unilaterally. In other words, to be enduring and relevant to economic analysis, power should reflect best-response behavior.

This book's concept of power nodes and how they function in power relationships is quite similar to Bowles' ideas about how these four characteristics of power emerge in the context of an actual power relationship. Bowles writes: "For B to have power over A, it is sufficient that, by imposing or threatening to impose sanctions on A, B is capable of affecting A's actions in ways that advance B's interests, while A lacks this capacity with respect to B."

In this book, we do think differently about power in one aspect, however. Here, power does involve not only the use of *threats and sanctions*, but of *favors* as well. Profit power involves the use of *carrots as well as sticks*. Profit power companies have the ability to create and grant tangible or intangible benefits

Figure 1.1

Profit power and power nodes: what they are not

> *Profit power is **not**:*
> Monopoly power
> Short-side power
> Bargaining power
> Temporary power
> Zero-sum power
>
> *Power nodes are **not**:*
> Core competencies
> Control assets

to the weaker parties. This is the source of the sustainability of profit power. Profit power is able to endure when it is used to create *positive sums* for all parties to ongoing power relationships. When this happens, the extraordinary profits created by profit power will also be *sustainable over time.*

We can further elaborate our concept of profit power by emphasizing what it is not (see figure 1.1). When Sir Josiah Child commented, "Profit and Power ought jointly to be considered,"[10] he was talking about the military power that was deployed to extract concessions so that the East India Company could impose its profit-making methods on India.

When we discuss the link between profits and power in this book, we are talking about the use of a kind of force to assist in the extraction of profits. But we are not talking about one-sided force without benefits for those subjected to it. Such power is only temporary. Nor are we talking about the power contained in the threats of annihilation that cold-war game theorists have used to map the politics of mutually assured destruction.

Profit power is not the type of monopoly power that economists rightly condemn and that produces net negative sums for society. In monopolistic power situations there are relatively few sellers, and one or more of them decides, and has the ability, to withhold a product or service from the market in order to get a better price.

Monopsonistic power works the same way, except that in this case the buyer is the one exercising the power. Profit power is different, in the first place, because the exercise of profit power largely takes place among companies, and not in final markets between companies and final consumers. Moreover, profit power does not produce net negative sums for society. On the contrary, profit power is maintained through ongoing relationships among independent parties, and these can only be sustained by the creation and distribution of positive sums.

Profit power generally also differs from so-called short-side power. Economists often say there is a "short" side to the market in situations where either demand or supply is quite inelastic in the short term (this means that if the price for a good goes up, more supply is not immediately forthcoming, and vice versa for the demand side). We saw a vivid example of this phenomenon when the price of crude oil ran up steeply in 2007–08 and collapsed in the second part of 2008 and first part of 2009. In the short term, supply was limited. If demand had increased, prices would also have climbed precipitously. When demand fell, however, the short-side advantage disappeared, and the prices dropped.

Short-side power may appear akin to profit power, in the sense that the players controlling the desired commodity have enormous capacity to extract returns from others. Certain sources of profit power are rather similar on the surface—for instance, control over special ingredients and dominant position in an industry layer. Even so, short-side power does not qualify under our definition of profit power for two reasons: 1) short-side power tends not to be long-lasting; 2) short-side power does not lend itself to the kinds of relationships that may be sustained over the long term by a system of carrots and sticks.

Profit power is not bargaining power, either. This is because bargaining power,[11] generally, is about allocating a fixed sum.[12] In most cases, bargaining power is no more than a temporary ability to determine how profits are distributed. Profit power, on the other hand, can continue to grow the overall size of the pie even as it determines the size of the individual slices. Since this happens over time, profit power tends to be a longer-term power.

The profit power described in this book involves influence and even coercive tactics, but it is situated in voluntary arrangements. It must therefore provide benefits for all parties—not equal benefits, but rewards significant enough to keep everyone necessary in the game.

The Impact of Transparency on the Sources of Profit Power

From the examples of Pepsi-Cola and AT&T, we can get a good idea of how a power node strategy can work. Although power nodes have played a role in business life throughout history, in transparency they will emerge as dominating influences. In the coming decades, power node strategies will become the key to survival and profitability.

The rise in the importance of power nodes will be compelled by five primary changes, which we will explore throughout this book.

1. *As opportunities for focused companies increase, power node companies will have even greater prospects for extraordinary returns.* In the old days when information constraints made vertical integration seem like the most logical strategy, the packaging of strong and weak units under one corporate umbrella often dragged down returns. As perfect information allows companies to split into ever more focused pieces, it will be increasingly possible to focus ownership on only the activity with the power node—that slice of the value chain with the very highest return. You can of course choose to buy a company without a power node, but be sure not to overpay, and adjust your price for the lack of profit power. Of all the companies gathered together in transparency to produce a product or service, only one or two will have a source of profit power. The challenge and the reward will lie in correctly valuing businesses for the presence or lack of power nodes.

2. *Power nodes will be the tools to extract the largest share of benefits from new distributed business arrangements.* Focused companies can choose to stand alone. But as vertical integration fades, it will often require interactions among many focused companies to produce goods and services. Transparency will bring fantastic freedom in structuring these relationships, with options including cross-ownership, franchises, complex contracts that accommodate many contingencies over time, and tacit agreements maintained by power relationships. Whatever the format of the arrangement, companies with power nodes will have the most leverage to extract profits from others and enhance returns for the group. Power nodes are the pivotal instruments to orchestrate 21st-century distributed business arrangements.

3. *Power nodes will be the most effective competitive weapons in the fierce and multidimensional battles for profit that will characterize the transparent economy.* In transparency, we will see many more profit battles than in the past, simply because there will be so many more points of contact among focused companies. Perfect information is already transforming the competitive landscape. It hastened the demise of vertical integration, fostering the breakdown of old industry boundaries and eliminating the geographic barriers that once isolated local businesses from national or international competitors. As a result, companies are under siege—they face previously unimaginable competition from companies that come from outside their supposed industry niche, from partners and rivals up and down the value chain, and from companies that may be halfway around the globe but are stealing their business as easily as if they were located right next door. Most of the new competitive battles are about returns, not market share. Consequently, there

will be many more occasions when power nodes will be needed to extract or defend profits.

4. *Power nodes will be required to gain high returns in transparency's new marketplaces, whose dynamics will be dramatically altered by perfect information.* Contrary to many observers' expectations, perfect information is likely to create a culture of influence that will lead to extraordinary concentrations of consumer choices on certain products and services. As a result, the prospects for extraordinary concentrations of profit will actually increase. In such a climate, as we have said, new power nodes (based on dynamics rather than on position) will come into being.

5. *Power nodes will gain greater potency in transparency.* Several older power nodes, when maximized through an effective power node strategy, will achieve even greater potency. This we will discuss in greater detail when we cover power node # 12, hubs, in chapter 13.

While transparency will wipe out a number of traditional ways of earning profits, the occasions for profit power to make a difference will multiply greatly. The skillful deployment of new and traditional power nodes will be essential to deal with the new competitive arena and the new market phenomena. In the future, a sure way to identify the companies with the potential for superior profits and valuations is to hone in on those entities that have profit power and are superior at navigating the emerging transparent economy.

PART II

Understanding the Transparent Economy

Chapter 2

The Star Driver
The Vanishing Cost of Information

Felix qui potuit rerum cognescere causas
[Free translation: "Fortunate are those who understand
the underlying drivers of change."]

—Virgil, *Aeneid*[1]

We are in the midst of one of history's turbulent moments. We are witnessing the birth of a new age of cheap information and an explosion of connectivity—an era in which everyone can instantly access huge amounts of information, essentially for free. The transition began in the late 1980s with the spread of high-speed global computing and communications. Since then, businesses and societies have absorbed an almost inconceivable amount of technological change. And yet, even the information-rich milieu we now inhabit will seem almost unimaginably primitive when we look back at it a few years from now.

In this chapter, I will shortly formally introduce the driver that we have mentioned so often already. This driver is the vanishing cost of information. We will start to explore its predictable consequences for commercial life. We do not need a crystal ball to do such work—only the ability to construct a forward-thinking analysis based on a correct understanding of the inevitable forces underlying present-day business fundamentals. I have been involved in conducting such analyses ever since the early 1980s, when I worked with the strategy group at Royal Dutch Shell in The Hague and London. Our team in those days was developing an expertise in scenario planning, a method of envisioning possible futures for an economy or an industry or a company. First, we identified underlying causes of changes; second, we mapped the inevitable consequences of those changes; third, we developed a scenario of what life would be like for the industry or the company should these trends play out. We also developed an alternative scenario that represented what life would be like under the set of assumptions that reflected the current worldview at the company. Finally, we worked with the company's leadership to think through both scenarios. The objective was to help leaders accept that a new scenario that did not reflect the common wisdom was a possible outcome, so that the organization might make better decisions as the future unfolded.

To understand the new challenges for any contemporary business, it is necessary first to demystify the large-scale economic changes that are underway. Such changes may be technological, demographic, or competitive. Whatever their nature, the key is to focus on those changes that we at Shell called the "drivers of change." Drivers of change are defined as phenomena that are already underway and will, barring a cataclysmic event, continue inexorably on whatever path they are on for a while (in some cases a decade or more, but always long enough to make a difference). Once a driver is identified, the next step is to determine which consequences it will inevitably set in motion. After that, it is a matter of looking carefully at industries of interest to understand the challenges each will face in what time frame. A fundamental shift in industry structure can be a driver of change. In the early 1980s at Shell, for instance, I was able to discern the dynamics that would hasten the unraveling of old structures and trading relationships in the oil industry. On the basis of these dynamics, I could anticipate that an explosion of spot and futures markets for oil would be inevitable. It was difficult at first for the company to envision such developments. "How can you say that the oil price is going to be set by markets? Oil is different!" the Shell supply coordinator in effect barked me. "Oil is not a commodity!" As it turned out, once our group presented this possible path for the industry in a scenario format, we did convince the Shell leadership that they should consider that this commodification story might be a possibility. In the following years, the company instituted a great many changes in operating and investment policies that turned out to be highly propitious. The commodification of oil caused an avalanche of other inevitable changes—including the dramatic swings in the price of crude oil that we have seen in the first decade of the 21st century.

The same approach that we applied in the oil industry can be applied to other industries and even to the economy at large. One clear example of an economy-wide driver is demographics. For instance, the burgeoning of the senior-citizen population is a driver of change. According to the United Nations, by 2100 the proportion of the world population over 65 will triple from 7 percent to 21 percent.[2] This global graying will have consequences for how countries finance retirement, how health care systems are structured, how individuals manage their assets, and so on. If you apply such analysis of underlying drivers in a rigorous way, you may reach some startling conclusions.

A driver of change that will challenge not just one, but most—or even all—industries in fundamental ways I call a "star driver." Star drivers are forces that periodically reshape the economics of the entire world. A dramatic example of such a star driver is the steam engine—the invention that launched the Industrial Revolution. Another is the efficient transmission of electricity, a technological upgrade that exploded old limits on productivity by making it possible to work 24 hours a day. Advances like these shake up every aspect of contemporary business and lead to the creation of a great many new industries. It takes more than minor adjustments to cope with the consequences set in motion by a star driver. Instead, existing business practices must be redesigned, almost from the ground up.

Today, we have a new star driver at work: the rapid and unstoppable decrease in the cost of information, also known as "the vanishing cost of information."

In this book, "information" has a specific meaning, which I define as follows:

> **INFORMATION:** A useful input into decision making, especially decision making about commercial transactions. A piece of information, or input, is useful if it causes a difference in a commercial decision.

This concept of information is consistent with that used in decision-making analysis. As Howard Raiffa taught us in his decision analysis lectures at Harvard, if a new piece of information does not alter your decision, it has zero value.[3] This definition is also consistent with that deployed by economist Kenneth Arrow, who described "the cost of information" as "the inputs needed for the installation and operation of information channels," which are the ways of "acquiring relevant information."[4] Information in this book does not simply describe gossip or the expanding universe of facts and anecdotes, trivial and significant, that we can sample through access to technology. It is also not reams of data. Data are raw, unanalyzed facts that may or may not be useful. Information is also different from knowledge—which is sometimes referred to as information about what to do with the primary information and which is a subject that has been discussed at length by other authors.[5]

It is worth noting that under our definition, the inputs that affect our decision making may be true as well as false, and our resources may not allow us to instantly tell the difference. But if high connectivity at low cost enhances our ability to disseminate information that is inaccurate, it also greatly enhances our ability to refute falsehoods and search out what is true.

(I will talk more about transparency's role in undoing asymmetries of information in chapter 3.)

It is also important to note that when I refer to the cost of information, another critical term, we are talking about expenses incurred in a wide spectrum of activities: everything from calling customers to storing design specifications to accessing financial data to monitoring the productivity of an assembly line. The explosion of connectivity—of people being able to communicate with other people and with myriad devices all over the world—is a subset of the declining cost of information. This book's definition of the cost of information is a broad one:

> **COST OF INFORMATION:** Shorthand for a set of related costs, including the cost of computing, storing, recording, processing, analyzing, and displaying information in myriad forms; the cost of communicating, including the cost of connecting to any other economic actor and exchanging information; the cost of finding and passing on information; and the cost of coordinating, monitoring, and assessing financial, business, and economic activities.[6]

Thanks to plentiful computer power and connectivity, and advances in a host of technologies, these costs are *all* rapidly dropping. It is becoming quick and simple and cheap to fish for information, sort through data and archives, transmit information across previously insurmountable geographic barriers, and connect large groups of people without actually moving anyone physically. The bulk of the world's information will no longer be invisible or beyond reach, either to those who are directly concerned with it or to outsiders. Except for a shrinking subset of information that can still deliberately be kept hidden (for example, classified information and trade secrets), it is not only possible but also practically effortless to have access to information about everything. The vanishing cost of information is driving a tremendous decline in the amount of asymmetrical information.

When we talk about the information whose cost is being reduced, we also include *future information*. We don't need to guess about what will happen down the line; we can now afford to gather information about everything as it happens, and we can construct contracts that contain provisions to respond to a huge range of possible future contingencies. (I will talk more about the implications of cheap information for contracts in chapter 3.)

This cost of information has plunged by several orders of magnitude since the late 1990s and is still continuing to fall. By now, the effects of this decline are everywhere to see. Whether they know it or not, everyone who sends a text message on a cell phone or calls up real-time assembly line information from a distant factory has the star driver to thank. But these changes are only the beginning. In the coming decade, the star driver will cause dramatic revisions in corporate structures and reshape the most basic patterns of economic life.

In order to understand what is yet to come, it is worth retracing the path of what has already occurred. The changes are so revolutionary that already it is difficult to imagine how we used to manage in the old days. As recently as the early 1990s, telephone connections were still scarce in many places. This scarcity manifested itself in Rio de Janeiro, for example, in a lively black market for telephone numbers. In London, around the same time, folks had to wait in their homes for a day to have the phone company install a line. Obtaining financial information used to be cumbersome. When I was an investment banker at First Boston in New York in the mid-1980s, our entire group, which was then one of the world's premier mergers and acquisitions teams, shared two Telerate terminals to look up vital information about companies and securities. The terminals seemed frozen more often than not. Even so, worldly senior managing directors and dog-tired analysts alike took turns at the precious Telerate terminals. Nowadays we pull up this information for free from Yahoo! while moving about.

As transformative as such devices and services may be, they are only the most visible manifestations of a much larger economic shift. When we look deeply, we will see that many aspects of business life that seem to reflect natural laws of economics in fact came about because information was costly and difficult to obtain. As obstacles to acquiring information fall, businesses will find themselves operating according to an entirely different set of principles. In the immediate future, many business relationships and practices will change or disappear, because the hurdle they served to overcome—expensive, scarce information—is being swept away. Commercial enterprises are being organized and will operate in entirely new ways, and the dynamics of marketplaces will be very different from what current textbooks describe.

To understand why this is so, it is important to understand that all societies—and their economies—run on information. This has been so throughout history, as we find illustrated in literature and lore. In Greek tragedies, major disasters often happen because the decision makers do not have a vital piece of knowledge. Had Oedipus been aware that his wife was also his mother, for example, there would have been no play. Romeo and Juliet had a similar type of problem; with full exposure of the facts, they both might have lived happily ever after. What is true for star-crossed lovers is even truer for businesspeople: for as long as human beings have been engaged in commerce with each other, having the right information at the right time has been a source of great advantage. Julius Paul Reuter built a first successful business by using carrier pigeons to fly stock prices between Aachen and Brussels, for example, and then moved to London to found his

Reuters financial news service in 1851.[7] Andrew Carnegie started his career as a telegraph boy, and his insistence on getting and disseminating information rapidly was one of the cornerstones of his companies' success. As his story illustrates, it is very hard to make correct financial decisions without access to pertinent information.

The declining cost of information is earning its status as a star driver not just because it affects companies in every industry around the globe, and not just because a vital component of every business endeavor will soon become free. The vanishing cost of information is a star driver because ultimately it will change the way all economic actors make decisions as well as the decisions they make. We will examine the two inevitable trends that the star driver will set in motion. The first is the trend toward perfect information; the second, an outgrowth of the first (i.e., of the trend toward perfect or near-perfect information), is toward interdependent decision making. These two trends are the subject of my next chapter. They are the most significant consequences of the declining cost of information, and they represent the defining characteristics of the new economy of transparency.

And what is transparency? We have used this term loosely so far. Transparency in this book denotes an environment in which we are able to connect with anybody, and can access any source of information, anywhere on earth, instantly and essentially for free. I define this environment as follows:

> **TRANSPARENCY:** A state in which the cost of information (as we have defined it, including the cost of computing, processing, communicating, searching, coordinating, and monitoring) is approaching zero or, equivalently, in which cheap connectivity is so abundant and easy, one might consider it infinite.

My use of the word *transparency* is meant to emphasize the fact that information will travel instantly and without obstruction, equally clear and perceptible to everyone. I am not describing the sort of transparency that is demanded when critics insist that windows into business or government operations be held open in order to enforce accountability.

The world may never quite get to the extreme transparent state of zero information cost and infinite connectivity. Practically speaking, however, we are already living in a stage that we might call a "transition to transparency." In some markets, there is so much information available instantly that we might say they are already in a virtual state of transparency. The markets for books or recorded music or for Treasury bills come instantly to mind—but we can see that many more are on the way.

In the next chapter we will see what commercial life in transparency will be like.

The final element that permeates all considerations about drivers of change is the question of inevitability. Is this great rush toward ubiquitous and cheap information likely to continue? Are there forces at work to guarantee that a star driver will be unstoppable in generating other unstoppable changes for the foreseeable future? In the case of our star driver, the declining cost of information, the judgment is obviously yes, and for two reasons: technological progress and human nature.

Regarding technological progress, some predict that, thanks to Moore's Law (the doubling every eight months of computer power per dollar) and other fantastic growth rates, a computer that may cost as little as a dollar will one day be as powerful as the human brain. This seems a daring forecast, but the comparison does provide some indication of how cheap computing truly will be. With all that additional computing power at our disposal, moreover, the human brain is likely to seem more remarkable than ever. As Ray Kurzweil puts it, "Information technology's exponential curve will fuel advances in biology, robotics, nanotechnology and artificial intelligence— with world-shattering results, including...practically omniscient...abilities for humans."[8]

Many credible predictions insist that the pace of technological change will continue to accelerate, with each new innovation driving others. To be sure, it is possible that Moore's Law could be exhausted; the ability to build smaller, less expensive, more powerful computers may be constrained by the laws of physics. The path of technical progress is never certain. Even so, in the near term at least, it seems reasonable to surmise that technological advances will continue, and that their implementation will continue to drive information costs downward.

In the end, however, human nature is the factor that is most likely to sustain the driver and to make information costs drop further and further. True, the immediate cause of declining information costs is science and engineering. But the vast majority of people don't get excited about technology for its own sake. The underlying impetus for technological development is actually an age-old set of human desires: we not only want to know and communicate with each other but also to use the information we gather for commercial, military, humanitarian, or political advantage. No wonder, then, that people at every stage of history have been willing make whatever investments are necessary to boost access to information and facilitate faster communication. People have pushed, pulled, and rewarded the scientists, entrepreneurs, and companies who have made it possible.

In our own time, individual industries, markets, economies, and even societies will march toward transparency at differing rates. In some places transparency is effectively here; in others it is coming soon. The march of progress always brings turmoil and uncertainty, and this period is no exception. Largely unforeseen changes have roiled companies, industries, global economies, and financial markets, and more than a few business leaders and investors may feel beset by the turbulence.

While we can only speculate about the trajectory of technological innovation, we can be quite sure about the larger human motivation. In a world of continual change, the hunger for information is one of the few constants. For this reason alone, it is entirely logical to predict that a progression toward transparency is inevitable.

Chapter 3

The Two Trends of Transparency
Perfect Information and Interdependent
Decision Making

As the cost of information continues to plummet, I believe that it will drive
two inevitable trends, one arising from the other. The first is a trend toward
information that is abundantly and equally and instantly accessible to all—in
other words, toward what economists have described as perfect information. Perfect information will itself drive a second inevitable trend—the rise
of what I call interdependent decision making. This is the ascent of a culture
of "know-everythings" and an increasing tendency by consumers and others to think in an interconnected fashion and to act in herds.

As mainstream theorists have predicted, the trend toward perfect information is well on its way to erasing many marketplace imbalances and other
economic inefficiencies. Contrary to predictions, however, the trend toward
perfect information will also create a new set of market failures. When interdependent decision making and its dynamics are added to the mix, previously unforeseen inefficiencies will result. These will permit the creation
of new market dynamics that will promote extraordinary profits and new
sources of profit power, as we will see in chapter 4, and that will necessitate
the formulation of a new economic paradigm, as we shall see in chapter 5.
As the two inevitable trends play out, the current structures of companies
and industries and the old dynamics of competition and marketplaces will
fall away, and the new forms and dynamics of the transparent economy will

emerge, as I will discuss in part III. Naturally, these developments call for a new set of strategies for maximizing value, which I will articulate in part IV.

The depiction of the evolution of these two trends and of their consequences that you will find in the following chapters is a scenario. These developments are not cast in stone. What I will present is a possible path for these trends to follow and a picture of what business life might become. The objective is not to make you accept that this is exactly what will happen. The objective is to have you consider that this sketch of life in transparency is a possible outcome.

I believe that there is compelling logic to the proposed flow of events that is presented in the following chapters. But you and your organization do not have to accept this logic to benefit from this book. You may believe that the underlying driver of cheap information and the two inevitable trends will take you in a different direction. You will derive maximum advantage if you contrast the future that is painted in this book with the set of assumptions and implicit scenarios that currently prevail in your own organization or company. As we learned at Shell and at many other organizations, the greatest benefit is derived from considering the sketched scenario as a possibility, and letting that prime your own thinking, analysis, and preparations.

Perfect Information and Its Consequences

The first inevitable trend is toward perfect information. For the purposes of this book, perfect information is defined as follows:

> **PERFECT INFORMATION**: The immediate availability of, and connection to, all existing information regarding anything and anybody, at extremely low cost.

In the previous chapter, we defined this book's concept of information and drew the distinction with knowledge.

Only a decade or so ago, any suggestion that perfect information might actually become reality might have been greeted as completely farfetched. In the view of classical economists (and everyone else), as I explained in the introduction, perfect information was a purely theoretical construct. Needless to say, humans have never before experienced a world of completely accessible information; it is an extraordinarily exciting development.

When perfect information prevails, every human on earth will be granted "inherent omniscience"—a term that is widely defined as the ability to know anything that one chooses to know and that can be known. ("Inherent" omniscience is distinct from "total omniscience," which means *actually* knowing everything that can be known.) Despite its name, perfect information may not always be true. The desire to manipulate information to produce desired results—whether it's by casting multiple All-Star ballots for your favorite baseball player or planting malicious rumors about business rivals—is as old as human nature. In an age of perfect information, happily, the ability to spread and detect corrective information will be greatly enhanced as well. If someone has done wrong, word of the misdeeds can travel fast and far. Absolutely perfect information will of course remain a theoretical construct, although we are on a continuous trend toward it.

As the first inevitable trend toward perfect information advances, obtaining information about prices, quality, and quantity of goods and services—even at the farthest corners of the earth—will become increasing faster and cheaper.

Many distinguished writers have already elaborated the ways in which imperfect information and asymmetrical information have so far shaped the parameters for our commercial life. Over time, there has arisen an entire field of economics devoted to examining the effects of imperfect and asymmetrical information and showing all the ways that they create pockets of inequity in the marketplace. My discussion in this chapter—about the depth and breadth of the changes that our first inevitable trend will make possible—is based on this very large body of research.

Here I highlight seven of the most important ways in which perfect information will significantly alter economic interactions. Obviously this list is not exhaustive, but it does highlight some of the significant changes that we will be considering over the course of this book. The list itself provides a sort of snapshot of commercial life in transparency.

The benefits of the emergence of conditions approaching perfect information include:

- The reduction of search costs will enable markets.
- Wage and price competition will be global.
- Coordinating activities far and wide will be cheap and easy.
- Monitoring of people and processes will be cheap and easy.
- Asymmetries of information will be difficult to maintain and exploit.
- Transaction costs will fall.
- Intricate contracts, options, and conditional deals, including those that prepare for an almost infinite range of possible future outcomes, will be increasingly feasible.

Each of these items is discussed in more detail below.

The Reduction of Search Costs Will Enable Markets

Perfect information puts an end to high search costs and other information obstacles that have been limiting the feasibility of markets for many goods and services. Each day it gets easier for buyers and sellers to find each other. People who have never met can trade with confidence as well, since at the push of a button, any potential customer can check out what others think of a producer, a product, or a seller. Similarly, buyers can compare prices and specifications. If there is a better deal, people will find it.

A TV advertisement for banglalink, a Bangladesh-based mobile-phone company, provides an excellent illustration of the trend toward perfect information and its potential to improve economic efficiency. This ad, which aired on Bangladesh TV in the winter of 2006, became very popular, and several people told me about it. Indeed, the storyline got better and more elaborate each time I heard it; it was embellished beyond the original script. Obviously, something about the story, which concerned the benefits of cheaper information and greater connectivity, resonated with the Bangladesh audience—and it resonated with me, as well.

The commercial, as I heard it described, starts with a flashback to the narrator's childhood. At dawn, a smart-looking five-year-old boy greets his father as he comes in from the sea. His father is a fisherman, and he has just returned from a long night's work with a big, lovely-looking catch. Together, the boy and his father struggle to haul the fish off the boat. They present the load to the fish buyer, a shifty-looking middleman who tells the father: "Too bad, the market for fish in Dhaka is very bad today." The poor, tired fisherman has no choice but to accept a pittance for all his beautiful fish. We learn that the boy yearns for a bicycle—but given his father's circumstances, there is obviously no money for such luxuries.

The next sequence takes us to the present day. The little boy has grown up to become a fisherman as well. He is now a smart-looking young man, and he is driving a truck full of freshly caught fish. When he enters the yard of another shifty-looking middleman, he hears a familiar line: "Too bad, fisherman, the market for fish in Dhaka is very bad today." The young man doesn't argue or look downbeat; instead, he pulls out his mobile phone and gets right through to a big fish shop in Dhaka. Thanks to the low cost of information, including cheap connectivity, the tables are turned. "OK, OK," he says with a big grin, making his deal directly with the shop. Then he turns to speak to the middleman. "Too bad," the young fisherman says, "at my customer's in Dhaka, the market is very good today." He drives off to town to deliver his catch. Of course, the final shot shows him, a few days later, taking his children to a gleaming store where they each get to choose a new bike.

Obviously, only one party in this advertisement has stepped into the world of transparency, and that is the fisherman. If the middleman had realized how the world had changed around him, he might not have bothered trying to deceive the young man. As you can see in this commercial, perfect information is an *equalizing trend*, and obviously one whose effects will extend well beyond fishermen in Bangladesh.

This ability to discover prices and counter parties readily, to undo asymmetries of information (those imbalances that often result when one party to a transaction withholds or distorts information for personal gain), is one of the positive transformative aspects of perfect information.

Thanks to perfect information, everything from unique software programming skills to hand embroidery can be priced globally. Even exotic, one-off, or highly specialized products can find all potential buyers. More and more, we will see markets for intermediate goods—those raw materials or components or semi-finished parts that go into a final product. As we shall see, this is one of the factors that is likely to facilitate the movement away from vertical integration. If a company can maintain quality standards by establishing relationships with suppliers that have been vetted by the open market, and obtain inputs (e.g., components) at the best prices globally available, there will no longer be a need to own a component manufacturer outright.

The emerging system of perfect information also reduces the need for intermediaries, who have traditionally inserted themselves in transactions to help one side gain access to the other. Many companies that earn their keep by bringing buyers and sellers together will be challenged by electronic trading or matching systems. Already, local flea markets have taken a pounding from eBay, matchmaking firms have lost hearts to online dating services, travel agents have given way to Web-based booking systems, and headhunters have lost prospects to online job search sites. Local real estate brokers no longer have a monopoly on what is for sale in their towns, and with interesting results. In the Netherlands, as in other locales, for example, the housing market used to be a fragmented, local, and secretive affair. The Web site funda.nl put an end to that. Funda lists properties for sale by hundreds of different brokers and lets prospective buyers search for and comparison-shop among properties nationwide.

Wage and Price Competition Will Be Global

Perfect information also implies that price signals can be observed more easily the world over. Markets will be more global than ever before. Perfect information will result in global wage and price competition, even for goods, services, and labor that do not cross borders. This is because perfect information lets companies compare prices and wages for goods, services, and workers from anywhere in the world—to get whatever the world's best price or wage may be. The wages of jobs and the prices of services that can be delivered electronically from anywhere on earth will be especially vulnerable to downward pressure.

Contrary to what has happened in past cycles, it is not just the low-skilled jobs that will face competition from foreign labor. Knowledge workers will see their wages adjust to the wages of similarly qualified people in faraway countries. The trend toward transparency may even have a disproportionate impact on skilled workers such as lawyers, accountants, computer specialists, medical researchers, and financial analysts. Even if they don't actually lose their jobs to overseas workers, skilled workers' compensation will be affected. Closing borders to trade will not make any difference, since price information can fly across any border. With the advent of perfect information, almost every single component, ingredient, or service becomes de facto tradable. Only the most local, personal, and time-sensitive of labor or services—a plumber on a remote island receiving an emergency call on a Sunday morning, say—is likely to escape global price competition at any given moment.

Coordinating Activities Far and Wide Will Be Cheap and Easy

It will become easier to coordinate activities across independent companies and do things well without shared ownership. Falling coordination costs are already allowing businesses to reach beyond traditional limits of all kinds. Thanks to the proliferation of cheap communication and computing, for example, companies can surmount geographic boundaries to manufacture in cost-effective ways without sacrificing efficiency. "As soon as Motion Computing Inc. in Austin, Texas, receives an order for one of its $2,200 tablet PCs, workers at a supplier's factory in Kunshan, China, begin assembling the product. When they've finished, they individually box each order and hand it to a driver from FedEx," *BusinessWeek* reported. Five days from the day the order is placed, a new personal computer is in some U.S. customer's hands. "Motion's inventory costs? Nada. Zip. Zilch. 'We have no inventory tied up in the process anywhere,' marvels Scott Eckert, Motion's chief executive."[1]

As we learned from the example of Motion Computing Inc., a computer manufacturer in Texas can buy all needed components from third parties and still run a just-in-time assembly plant in China. Similarly, low or practically nonexistent coordination costs will enable many focused and independent companies to work together and be coordinated as if they were part of one large company.

Monitoring of People and Processes Will Be Cheap and Easy

Thanks to the trend toward perfect information, companies will be increasingly confident that they can cheaply keep tabs on the performance of partners over the course of contracts and manage surveillance over employees to ensure that they work hard and honestly. Lower monitoring costs and improved monitoring capabilities will reduce the need for shared ownership among companies that need to cooperate.

About a dozen years ago in Tokyo, I marveled when I saw that a Pepsi delivery man could ascertain what had been sold in any given downtown vending machine without even leaving his truck. Such tricks are now common. Gillette, for instance, can track every package of razor blades it sells from factory to checkout register. Rising numbers of companies now have the capacity to tell exactly which item is getting sold at which retail outlet for which price. But that's only the first step. Many companies are working out the kinks in using RFID chips—inexpensive radio transmitters that give off a unique identifying signal—to provide supply-chain managers with the location of all their goods.[2]

Transparency is offering previously unimaginable options for monitoring people too, whether they are customers or employees.[3] All around the world, an unprecedented amount of information about people is being collected, analyzed, and stored. In urban centers, surveillance cameras keep an unblinking eye on the populace;[4] if you live in London, you are likely to be on camera 300 times per day.[5] In advance of the 2008 Summer Olympics, China geared up to install some 300,000 cameras in Beijing.[6] We can check out our own homes on Google Maps' detailed Satellite and Street view photos. We can implant RFID chips containing our medical records under our own skins,[7] or mark our pets with RFID chips to help us reclaim them when they are lost. Soon we may be able to do the same for our children. A school in England is conducting a test of RFID chips in school uniforms, so they can make sure the students come to school and make data entry easier for teachers when they do.[8]

All of us can cheaply monitor and report about events from all walks of life. We can report from crime scenes with cell phone cameras and share the news with friends on Facebook, monitor stock markets on our BlackBerrys, catch up on outrageous videos with YouTube, keep tabs on sports events the world over, and then see what our colleagues in Russia are up to by checking their blogs.

Asymmetries of Information Will Be Difficult to Maintain and Exploit

As we saw in our example of the Bangladeshi fisherman, many forms of cheating rely on asymmetries of information—that is, the withholding of useful information by one party in a transaction from another. Counterfeiting is an example. At best, companies and governments will be able to prevent fakes entirely; at least, they will have many new tools for tagging and monitoring authenticity. Philip Morris, for example, has added scannable bar codes to cases of cigarettes. An article in the *Wall Street Journal* noted in 2005 that for the first time, the company can "afford procedures to fight counterfeiters in faraway places by tracking its products in other parts of the world."[9]

In a world of perfect information, there will also be innumerable mechanisms for evaluating the reputations and performance of individuals and companies. Whether a buyer or a seller cheats before the deal or after it, perfect information ensures that everyone will know—instantly.

By undoing this kind of asymmetry, cheap and fast information will mitigate two types of market failures in particular. These are the problems of "lemons" and of "moral hazard." Lemons—a name that derives from the well-known epithet for unexpectedly unreliable cars—refers to a problem of cheating before a deal is done. When used-car dealers develop a reputation for being dishonest, buyers tend to believe that every used car offered is overpriced. As a result, buyers refuse to pay the market price. This makes the price drop, and the dealers respond by cutting corners and trying to deceive customers even more. As the cycle continues, the market simply unravels.

But as the success of eBay's used-car market attests, low-cost information can eliminate the lemon problem. eBay's system of feedback and ratings permits users to evaluate both the reputations of the sellers and the provenance of their cars, and thereby makes the market more viable. In the future, this type of process will become feasible for many other products.

In a "moral hazard" problem,[10] as it has been traditionally defined by economists, parties cheat after the deal is done. The resistance of insurance companies to paying out legitimate medical or accident claims is an example. In such a case, perfect information ameliorates the problem by giving consumers an increased ability to check claims, to broadcast the shortcomings of illegitimate insurance companies, and to switch. Already, online bulletin boards for freelance workers openly compare health insurance plans, warning people away from those that advertise heavily but resist paying benefits.

Another variation of the use of the term moral hazard became a hot topic of conversation in the spring of 2008, when the U.S. Federal Reserve stepped in to deal with the credit crisis on Wall Street. In this context, the moral hazard comes from the danger that offenders will continue to act irresponsibly if they know that they will be bailed out. Risky behavior is encouraged because risk takers have been shielded from any punitive consequences for their actions.

Transaction Costs Will Fall

Already, the costs of executing financial transactions have been reduced greatly. In 2006, the *Wall Street Journal* noted "a shift by big institutional investors toward cheaper electronic and direct-access trading."[11] At the time, big investors were paying four to five cents a share for trades executed by the trading desks of the large Wall Street firms, while direct-access venues allowed them to trade for less than a penny a share. "The result is that the effective 'blended rate' for both electronic and non-electronic trades by institutional investors had fallen to 1.45 cents in mid-2005 from 4.82 cents in 2002," the article reported. These days, even those shrunken rates appear astronomically high.

It's not just corporate transactions that have become cheaper. There are savings in countless activities that involve the consumer as well. By now, many Americans and Europeans are accustomed to calling consumer help lines and talking to customer representatives based in India. But even the simple process of transferring a hamburger from a grill to a nearby car window may actually be cheaper if you involve workers half a world away. Consider the example of Julissa Vargas. "Like many American teenagers, Julissa Vargas, 17, has a minimum-wage job in the fast-food industry—but hers has an unusual geographic reach," the *New York Times* reported.[12] " 'Would you like your Coke and orange juice medium or large?' Ms. Vargas said into her headset to an unseen woman who was ordering breakfast from a drive-through line. That customer was not just outside Ms. Vargas's workplace here on California's central coast. She was at a McDonald's in Honolulu. And within a two-minute span Ms. Vargas had also taken orders from drive-through windows in Gulfport, Miss., and Gillette, Wyo."[13]

Intricate Contracts, Options, and Conditional Deals, Including Those That Prepare for an Almost Infinite Range of Possible Future Outcomes, Will Be Increasingly Feasible

Cheaper information enables companies to structure and enforce a wide range of types of contracts across company boundaries and many possible outcomes. Very complex deals can be worked out in a transparent world because so much can be monitored, measured, calculated, and programmed. This makes moot what the economists call "the problem of bounded rationality"—the inability to design models or contracts that can accommodate every possible future outcome.

Real-world dealmakers have already found ways to be far more innovative than the bounded-rationality theory would suggest. We have seen numerous examples of very creative structures that take advantage of cheaper information and connectivity to do such things as split rewards and investments, allocate risk, and manage relationships. Compared to what these arrangements make possible, traditional corporate structures—including vertical integration—are but crude instruments.

For example, in his book *Creative Industries*, economist Richard Caves describes the multifaceted contingencies spelled out in contracts between movie producers and Hollywood stars, painters and galleries, musicians and agents. If this could be accomplished in the past, under conditions of far more limited information, we can imagine that there will be few limits to possible commercial arrangements under conditions of transparency.

Companies in the soft drink and retail industries are already making good use of cheaper information to structure and implement contracts that accommodate multiple potential outcomes. In several markets around the globe, Coca-Cola's computer and telecom system tracks every can, logging many details about its sale: from which specific store or vending machine, on which date, at what temperature, time, and price. On the basis of that information, noted the *Wall Street Journal*, Coca-Cola can theoretically determine how much to charge bottlers on a can-by-can basis and fine-tune marketing incentives.

This marks a big change in the beverage industry. When information was hard to come by, the *Journal* article explains, Coke "sold its beverage concentrate to U.S. bottlers at the same price no matter how its soft drinks later were packaged and sold to the consumer. As a result, Coke's profits [were] tied to volume growth, while bottler profits [were] driven more by the margins [they got]." Retail pricing for soft drinks does vary by specific package and by the outlet where drinks are sold. A single ice-cold can at a gas station may be more expensive than a box with 24 cans from an oversized supermarket. With the advent of this new level of information, Coca-Cola has the capability to vary its concentrate price by package or sales channel as well, instead of charging a leading bottler a flat price for all concentrate. Such flexible pricing is known as "incidence pricing." Coke has already used this method in some markets outside the United States.[14]

Similarly, Wal-Mart uses a sophisticated algorithm that takes into account exact delivery times, exact moments of sell-through, and exact costs of production to calculate how much to pay its vendors.

As this list of consequences highlights, perfect information will erase many market inefficiencies. In conclusion, perfect information will enable new markets, create new kinds of global competition, and allow businesses to establish a wide array of previously unthinkable business relationships. It will free us from structures and processes that have evolved to deal with imperfect information.

The Second Inevitable Trend: Interdependent Decision Making and Its Consequences

As we just saw, perfect information can be a liberating and equalizing trend. If it were the only force unleashed by the vanishing cost of information, the result would be the leveling of playing fields. But it is not the only force: as information gets faster and freer, a second inevitable trend kicks in. This is the trend toward interdependent decision making.

As transparency arrives, it will be impossible to make any choice without holding at least some knowledge of what others are choosing. When economic actors—whether people or companies—make decisions based on information about how other economic actors are behaving, they may come to different decisions than the ones they would have made if they had not known what others were doing. When decision making becomes interconnected, things change. Interdependence of decision making will *change the outcomes* of decision making as well as *change the types of decisions* that are made.

Hence this definition:

> **INTERDEPENDENT DECISION MAKING:** A description of a process whereby economic actors make decisions based on a set of inputs that include the decisions of other economic actors, or make decisions based on a set of (decision) functions that have been shaped by the decisions of others.

Research studies, as well as our own observations, tell us that people are influenced by what others do. Studies of buying trends, for instance, have found that "67% of all purchases are influenced by word of mouth."[15] In leisure products, such as movies, music, television and books, this figure is close to 90%.[16]

Most of us know at least a few people whose opinions can sway our own. When information flows freely, however, the numbers of influential "others" can become very large. A peer group, for instance is no longer limited to the people we've encountered in person. Instead, it could encompass the entire universe of people who share a common interest. The opportunities for social engagement on the Web are enormous, even on sites that aren't directly concerned with fostering relationships. People turn to sites like Facebook and Amazon to find out what other people like, and then adjust their tastes and choices accordingly. A company like Covestor even takes any thinking out of following the decisions of others. Covestor publishes the returns achieved by individual investors based on actual trades in their brokerage accounts. Other investors can copy the trades one by one, or they can instruct their funds manager or their Covestor program to copy instantaneously every trade of one or more other investors that they have specified.[17] How's that for instantaneous interdependent decision making?

Even those of us who try to avoid following the crowd may notice that our choices are influenced by others. Information and connectivity are becoming so ubiquitous that we can't help but absorb what others are up to.

On Amazon, we learn what books others have preferred. On Netflix, we discover which films others have rented. Nearly every Web site we look at uses links to echo recommendations of others. When we do a Google search, the results are weighted based on what others have found worthwhile to link to. Nowadays, it is tricky even to pull up a stock quote without seeing third-party commentary. Information about others is constantly before us, even when we do not want to look for it. It is flashing from newsstands, workplace bulletin boards, mobile-phone screens, and TV monitors in elevators and taxis: "The top ten most read stories on FT.com," "The most e-mailed NYT stories," "Top five rising Google searches."[18] Whether we like it or not, almost every choice we make is measured, monitored, and looped back into the collective feedback machine.

As you can imagine, this information-surround will wreak havoc with many accepted economic "truths." We will discuss perfect information's undermining influence on theory in our next chapter, but it is worth noting here that when there is interdependent decision making, distributions of choices, votes, and so on tend not to be normal. In such instances, the law of large numbers, or regression toward the mean, cannot be assumed to apply. The convention about the wisdom of the crowds also depends on the underlying distributions being normal. The axiom is meant to convey that if opinions are formed and expressed independently (i.e., without participants knowing what their fellow participants are saying), these opinions will be randomly distributed around a correct answer. In such a situation, the average of a lot of answers has a higher probability of being close to the right answer than any individual answer. Thus, when the law of large numbers does apply, the crowd is "wiser." Clearly, this does not hold true for distributions in which errors do not average out. The last place you will find "wisdom" is in a crowd of people who instantaneously know what others are doing and saying.[19] As we shall see, regression toward the mean is not a meaningful concept in the context of interdependent decision making and when underlying distributions are bound to lack a stable mean.[20]

In transparency, we will all be running with the herd, all the time. Often, this stampede of communal information and collective activity will feel like fun—interdependent decision making, after all, is the underlying force behind a ceaseless progression of fashions, manias, and fads. But there is a dark side to herd behavior as well. At times, interdependent decision making may result in what Steven Strogatz has labeled the "brutal stupidity of mobs."[21] Think back to *12 Angry Men*[22]—the movie in which one juror convinces 11 others that a person on trial is innocent. In this case, the persuasion serves the cause of justice, but of course the opposite might also be true. The real message of the movie is about how easy it is to succumb to the groupthink that often comes with interdependent decision making.

Similarly, Graham Allison's well-known book on the Cuban missile crisis[23] shows how groupthink might have led the world to nuclear war.

Our contemporary experience is already rife with examples of interdependent decision making in action. Consider, for instance, the tremendous speed and volume of early iPod (and more recently iPhone) sales. "The most powerful factor working in Apple's favor," commented the *Economist*, "is peer pressure: what friends and relatives have to say about products is now the most trusted form of consumer advice, and to be seen with something different can be almost taboo. That is why millions of people said they wanted an iPod for Christmas, and not a digital-music player from another manufacturer—even though rival players are often cheaper than iPods, and generally have more features."[24]

In transparency, phenomena like the off-the-charts response to iPods, which may still seem unusual, will become a familiar feature of the economic landscape. Over time, as we will explain throughout this book, marketplaces will come to function quite differently from the classical model of efficient markets, and we will offer new models to explain them. Already, we can see how interdependent decision making is shifting relationships between business and customers, and even forcing philosophic changes in the way some institutions do business.

For many economic entities, the rise in interdependent decision making will greatly enlarge the ripple effects of any successes or failures in attracting key customers. Ivy League colleges, for example, are experiencing a rising sense of urgency about recruiting elite students to their schools. "Top-scoring students are an asset whose value has been appreciating more rapidly than Manhattan real estate," reported the *New York Times* in 2005.[25] "If success in attracting these students tends to be self-reinforcing, so does failure. Losing even a few of them to a rival university can set off a downward spiral, making a university less attractive not only to other top students, but also to distinguished faculty who prefer working with such students."

In transparency, people will increasingly forge their own paths to information rather than passively wait for information to come to them. It is ironic that the ways in which they each follow their "own" paths will turn out to be interconnected and predictable. Consider, for example, the telephone tree, a venerable method of communication that is frequently used to spread the word about school closings among parents of schoolchildren. On the morning of a severe snowstorm, each family has instructions to await a call from the family ahead of them on a phone list, then to pass on whatever news they have learned to the family after them on that list. The phone tree is in fact a chain-network protocol, a command-and-control structure organized to direct information along a well-defined route. These days, however, the official chain often ends up being irrelevant. Most parents go online long before the call from the tree reaches them. If they can't get the updates they need from the school's site, they e-mail or call their friends, particularly those friends who always seem to know everything. Parents will focus their search efforts on the people who are most likely to help them get to the information most efficiently.

This telephone tree example is worth noting because it beautifully illustrates the patterns of information flow and decision making that we can expect will be dominant in a transparent economy. First, in transparency, economic actors actively seek information. They will not wait for information to be passed to them; they will not be "fed" information; they will refuse to respect any superimposed structures or rules about how to access information. Second, when they are reaching for information, they go first to the places or people they think are most likely to have it. When people look for information on the Internet, for example, they gravitate to what are called "hubs" of information (the Web equivalent of "know everything" parents) to maximize the efficiency of their search, even though casting a wide research net has never been cheaper. It is important to note and remember that the more a source gets queried, the more people consider it a go-to point for search.

To be sure, a few people disdain the strategies of the crowd. But statistically, most agents appear to look for information in the same places where others go to look for it too. In other words, they query the hubs first—they go to Amazon to find a book, to Wikipedia to find a fact, to Google to find a Web site, to "know everything" parents to find out about the school closing. They don't send a query to every site on the Internet or e-mail every parent in the school.

In the global transparent economy, we will see the phenomenon of the concerned parents reaching out for information reenacted on a scale involving hundred, thousands, millions, and even billions of people. In May 2008, a devastating earthquake struck in China's Sichuan province. China has the world's largest population of Internet and cell phone users, and according to the *Wall Street Journal,* many turned to technology instead of waiting for the Chinese government to spread the news. The result was some extremely swift on-the-ground reports such as by the video-sharing site Tiana.cn.[26]

To understand the dynamics of our new era, we have to shift our perspective from the message (or the information) to its receivers. We have to flip our line of thought about how information travels by 180 degrees. In transparency, the statement "information wants to be free"—a well-known hacker refrain[27] first articulated by Stewart Brand[28]—does not apply. The energy in transparency does not derive from information wanting to go somewhere. If information wants anything, it can only want to be found. In transparency the energy derives from the actors. It is the actors searching for what they want or need who provide the energy in the system; it is they who *reach out* for the information. The actors are not passive recipients of messages. They are active seekers.

In conclusion, although perfect information will erase many market inefficiencies, it will also foster the second inevitable trend of interdependent decision making on an unprecedented scale. That will create major new inefficiencies. I will discuss the ramifications of this in the next chapter. In the meantime, it is important to remember that the economic actors who are creating these market failures are not monopolists or other nefarious characters. Multiplied by dozens, hundreds, millions, they are simply the equivalent of those concerned parents—reaching out to their friends to find out what they know.

Chapter 4

Perfect Information
and Imperfect Markets

You couldn't advance in a finance department in this country unless you taught that the world was flat.
—Warren Buffett[1]

As we saw in the previous chapter, perfect information and interdependent decision making are the twin faces of transparency, but from the perspective of classical economists, they may resemble Dr. Jekyll and Mr. Hyde.

Perfect information enables new markets, makes existing markets appear to work better, and removes many of the problems that arise when information is expensive, incomplete, or asymmetrical.

Interdependent decision making, however, is the source of a new category of market failures. Unlike the market imperfections highlighted in conventional economics, these failures can't be attributed to underhanded tactics that exploit imperfect information or to monopolistic schemes. Instead, they are caused by the behaviors of large numbers of individuals who display a very human tendency to adapt their own choices to what they know about the choices of people around them.

In this chapter, I will discuss why interdependent decision making will destroy one of the bedrock notions of mainstream economics, namely the theory that the market is always "right" when information is perfect. Interdependent decision making will also affect the distributions of economic choices, events, prices, etc., so that they will *not* tend to fall into a random or normal pattern. Normal distributions are a common simplifying assumption in many financial models.

We know that markets fail under conditions of imperfect information. Now we will see that *markets can fail just as spectacularly under the conditions of perfect information.*

This is a key insight in our exploration of the impact of cheap information on the prospect for extraordinary profits and on the sources of profits. If market failures are a predictable and inevitable consequence of interdependent decision making, then extraordinary profits and profit power are feasible, legitimate, and sustainable.

As you may remember, the classic theory posits that, in a proper economy with free markets and free competition (and an absence of monopolies and other obstacles), when people, companies, and investors have equal access to information (when there is "perfect information"), markets will successfully set prices for goods, services, and all sorts of assets at the right level.[2] The actions of the price mechanism in a given market will bring aggregate supply into balance with aggregate demand and allocate resources in the most efficient manner. In other words, a market will move toward equilibrium. This outcome is typically represented by the graph depicting an aggregate demand curve crossing an aggregate supply curve.

When this happy outcome occurs for one particular product or service, economists call it a *market equilibrium*. A *general equilibrium* occurs when all markets for all goods and services get to their equilibrium. As you will recall, this alignment process has been referred to as the working of the "invisible hand." Markets that work this way develop an efficient exchange of goods, services, and workers without a need for ongoing government command.

Naturally, this is a highly simplified depiction. Equilibrium in a market is not something that happens at 2:45 p.m. Nor is it static. It is a conceptual depiction of an allocation of resources that is predicted to prevail when no actor wants to change his or her choices based on what the price mechanism tells that actor about the choices of the others. Even theoretically, we are never supposed to see this static result because of continuous adjustments. But the idea is that there is in principle an equilibrium for a given market at any given time, and that the price mechanism is continuously at work to move markets toward such an efficient allocation.

From the perspective of classical economics, individuals and individual companies are participants in an equilibrium-seeking process whose outcome cannot be influenced by their actions. Consumers and manufacturers make changes in how much they buy or produce only in response to price changes. The price at any given moment is supposed to reflect all the information available in the markets. Individuals or individual companies have no ability to affect market outcomes or sway special deals, nor can they cajole or use their influence to grab profits.

Also, according to mainstream classical economics, when markets work perfectly, they don't provide extraordinary profitability to the companies that participate in them. An individual or company can earn sustainable extraordinary profits only when there is something amiss and a market cannot move toward its equilibrium.

So far, so good.

Interestingly, if one inspects the theoretical conditions that must be met in order for a theoretical equilibrium to exist, one finds that there are actually two necessary conditions, not just one. The first is perfect information. The *second condition*, which has been rather hidden from sight, is *independence* of decision making. The classical model assumes that, left to their own devices, companies and individuals will base their decisions on what to buy or sell only on price and their *own* production or utility functions. According to theory, they are not influenced by the choices of other people, except through the price mechanism. They are not supposed to act like the interconnected herds that we described in the previous chapter.

In transparency, however, this is bound to be far from the case. As we saw in chapter 3, perfect information creates conditions in which it is very difficult to make decisions independently. In transparency we cannot assume that decisions will be unconnected. The two necessary conditions for an equilibrium, *perfect information* and *independence of decision making*, can not coexist in transparency. When there is perfect information there is likely to be interdependent decision making, and then there will be no market equilibrium. Therefore, we can rule out the general case of the existence of a general equilibrium in transparency.

We can also demonstrate this point using a simple practical example:

> At a price of $10, according to my own demand (or marginal utility) function, I was only going to buy one basketball, but then my best friend said he had purchased a few and as a result I bought ten instead. At $10 per basketball, my neighbor was only going to buy two, but after she saw what I was doing she bought four. I was rather pleased with my purchase, but when I learned that my neighbor bought some balls, I returned all of mine even though their price is still $10.

Obviously, this situation wreaks havoc with the classical economic picture of demand. How can you possibly plot the demand curve for the person in the example? What function (with a one-to-one relation between quantity as the dependent and price as the independent variable) can you come up with that has the same person buying one, ten, or zero basketballs at $10 per ball? Or that has her neighbor similarly buying either two or four balls at the same $10 price? Even worse, how can you "add up" these individual demand answers to arrive at the aggregate demand curve? The answer is: you can't.

If we wish to develop a representation of a market as a whole, we do need to "add up" the demand of individuals into an aggregate demand, and to add up supply curves of individual companies into an aggregate supply curve—which is to say, express the aggregate quantity demanded or supplied in terms of a function of price.

But this method doesn't work in transparency. If decisions about quantity are influenced by others' behavior and not just by independent considerations of the price and one's own production or utility functions—in other words, if the economic actors move in herds—you cannot "add up" the demand functions of individuals into an aggregate demand, nor, similarly, can you add up the supply functions of individual companies into an aggregate supply curve. The curves will keep pulsating, the variations due to others' decisions. When you add them up, you learn nothing at all. If my best friend changes his mind because his girlfriend changed her mind, I will change my mind, and so forth. If the invisible hand insists on "crossing" these pulsating aggregate supply and demand curves anyway, the price mechanism will not be able to bring about a stable resting point. Price cannot work its equilibrating magic because quantity decisions have been moved by non-price inputs, such as what my best friend likes. No single stable resting point for the intersections of the aggregate demand and aggregate supply curves means no equilibrium.

In transparency, the decisions and the decision making processes of economic aggregates (such as groups of buyers and sellers) are interconnected. Thanks to these interconnections, these groups behave like networks. One cannot add up individual functions to capture their aggregate behavior. Instead, one has to try to capture the behavior of a network in continuous motion.

In transparency, there will be lots of people acting as if they are part of an interconnected network. They won't be thinking only about price or their own utility: they will also weigh the opinions of their friends—or their online acquaintances, or some blogger on the Internet, or a list they half-noticed in an elevator. In many instances, the friends' views of a particular product may trump an individual's initial judgments about price and quantity. In the case of the portfolio-sharing service Covestor, customers actually hardwire their investment decisions to completely copy a group of designated others.

The conflict between theory and real behavior has always existed, but it wasn't sufficiently in evidence in actual marketplaces to derail economic models when information was scarce. In the past, even if people wanted to take others' decisions into account, they weren't able to. The information used to be too hard to come by.[3]

In the past, mainstream economic theories have been very helpful; they have demonstrated the benefits of market forces and drawn attention to trade-offs involving marginal costs and marginal benefits. But they are already at odds with many real business phenomena,[4] and this gap between classical theory and reality will only get wider in a transparent economy.

As I have said, I am not alone in questioning the theory of equilibrium. It continues to have strong defenders, but there are growing numbers of cutting-edge researchers and economists who are willing to challenge the old thinking about the concept. This book's analysis has benefited from the extensive research in this area.

For instance, scholars like Robert Axtell have used computational science to model various social conditions. In one notable experiment at the Santa Fe Institute, Axtell and others tried to simulate the dynamics of large groups of actors who make interdependent decisions. They found that equilibrium usually fails to materialize. Rather than discovering any easily aggregated patterns, they found that the analysis was so complex it could blow up the models or exceed their available computing power.[5]

In his book *Origin of Wealth*, Eric Beinhocker surveys a number of research efforts pertaining to "complexity economics." Many of these explorations involve "complex adaptive systems" consisting of agents who process information and then adapt their behavior. The dynamics of a system of "know everything" actors who make interdependent decisions are a subset of the dynamics that can be found among this large family of complex adaptive systems. Complex adaptive systems generally do not achieve a general equilibrium.

Investor George Soros is another critic. "The global financial system, as it is currently functioning, has been built on a false paradigm," he told reporters in April 2008. "The false paradigm is that financial markets tend toward equilibrium, and that deviations from that equilibrium are random, and therefore markets are self-correcting. This has led directly to regulators abandoning the role they ought to play—which is to prevent excesses from going too far."[6]

Now we have license to view our corporate strategies in a new and more positive light, because if it is okay to expect persistent market failures, then it is possible to contemplate the achievement of sustained and extraordinary profits as a legitimate end. Furthermore, whenever there is a pool of extraordinary profit, there is quite understandably going to be a struggle between companies to gain control of it. This is where profit power enters in.

In the new economics of transparency, the successful manipulation of power will be neither a symptom of market failures with negative consequences nor an expression of anticompetitive self-interest. Instead, profit power will be accepted as a legitimate, high-level management tool, and one that is ideally suited to the emerging business conditions of the 21st century. Our discussion of economics provides the intellectual underpinning for a wide array of power-based strategies aimed at achieving extraordinary profitability. We will talk about these strategies in much of the rest of this book.

Why the Random-Distribution Assumption Is Wrong and Dangerous

Cheap information also brings into question a well-known simplifying assumption of economic and financial models that many distributions (of prices, of deviations from equilibrium, of people's choices, and so on) are *random* or *normal*. Such distributions can be conceptualized by thinking of a bell curve.

When distributions are normal, there is a stable mean (or correct answer) and any subsequent observations, choices, etc., will be independent from previous observations. Errors in observations (deviations from the true mean) will also be random. If a distribution is random, your best guess of the actual mean (or the correct answer) is the average of your observations.

A well-known example of a normal distribution is the height of adults in a country like the United States. If you took the individual heights of all 300 million adult residents and plotted them with height on the horizontal axis and number of people per height in the vertical axis, the bell-shaped result would indicate that there is a mean height (what we ordinarily think of as the "average" height), which is around 5' 9" (175 cm) for men and 5' 4" (163 cm) for women. Most of the data cluster around the mean; only a few outliers fall a great deal above or below the mean. In the case of heights, there is a natural limit to the extremes of the curve. No grownup is shorter than one foot; no one is ten feet tall. The extremes are often called tails. Heights and other normal distributions have very few observations at the tails. Their tails are skimpy, not fat.

The normal distribution is very well known. Many forecasting models, financial risk management models, and pricing models (for instance, the original Black-Scholes option pricing model) assume normal distributions.

The key requirement for normal distributions is that the errors (the deviations from the mean or from the true answer) are also randomly distributed. For this to happen you need events, choices, etc., to be independent from one another. When decision making is interdependent, of course, the choices will not be independent, and the errors won't be either.

Hence, in transparency, when virtually all choices will be made in the context of interdependent decision making, it will no longer be safe to assume that distributions of votes, choices, price variations, and so forth will be normal. The key requirement of independent errors will not apply.

Already, an overly rigid reliance on the bell curve has at times been hazardous. This approach was said to be partially to blame for the collapse of Long-Term Capital Management, a hedge fund that famously lost $4.6 billion over four months in 1998 and finally folded in 2000, and whose founders included two Nobel Prize-winning economists. LCTM[7] sank in part because its models underestimated the degree of interdependence among market events and therefore failed to correctly anticipate the non-normality of financial-instrument distributions.

A part of the blame for the collapse of the global financial system in 2008–2009 may lie with the interdependent decision making of actors and a generally poor understanding of the interconnectedness between investment strategies and the behaviors of asset classes, which led to a poor modeling of risks.

As transparency approaches, we will see many more examples of non-normal distributions. Consider the pattern of hits among search engines, for instance. It wouldn't be at all strange to imagine that they follow a random distribution—all search engines have the same price (they're free) and all the major ones are of comparable quality, so why wouldn't they get the same average number of hits? They do not! In December 2007, as comScore reported, 62.4 percent of the 66.2 billion searches worldwide went through Google. Google received 41.3 billion searches worldwide that month. Yahoo! was second with 8.5 billion, Chinese Baidu was third at 3.4 billion, and Microsoft sites followed at 1.9 billion searches.[8] The top four search engines got about 83 percent of the searches that month. The remaining hits were scattered among thousands of search engines with few hits. When the same survey was repeated in December 2008, the results showed the same pattern, but had become even more concentrated.

How does this distribution differ from a normal one?

To begin with, it does not have a mean. It can't be used to draw any conclusions about a "typical" search engine. If you insisted on calculating an average of hits across all search engines, the resulting number would be of little use. It would tell you nothing of value about the expected number of hits for any given engine. There is no meaningful mean of hits per search engine. Therefore, the curve for this distribution would not look at all like a bell. It would look like a like a great flat plain with a few tall spires—with the spires representing the few leading search engines that get the vast majority of the hits.

Why are those four top search engines so far ahead? One reason, as we are now aware, is that people looking for information tend to follow the crowd to the sites that seem most "in the know." Looking further at these search numbers, you may also wonder how Google is able to maintain such a huge lead. Why hasn't the mighty Microsoft risen closer to the top? This is because sites that are ahead tend to stay ahead. In 2009, Microsoft and Yahoo! joined forces. Will their combined effort be able to overtake Google? There's an expectation for this, too, and it has to do with a common feature of network math and the dynamics of marketplaces in transparency that we will discuss further in chapter 5.

Chapter 5

The New Paradigm
Powerlaw Economics

In previous chapters we have learned that with the advent of cheap information we cannot rely on such core concepts as market equilibrium and normal distributions. This, of course, raises the question of what tools we *can* use.

We need a paradigm that can accurately describe the behaviors of participants in a marketplace and guide us in constructing our profit-making strategies. The emerging complexity models help to describe the new world, but so far they have given us little concrete advice about how to navigate it. From a practical perspective, we urgently need a tool that will allow us to cut through the dynamics of complex adaptive systems. Is there any possibility of anticipating the behavior of groups that make decisions interdependently? If we don't believe markets will tend to equilibrium, is there another way we can predict their patterns?

When I began my search for a new paradigm for transparency, I asked myself this question: Are there any guiding mathematical principles for networks that will describe the behavior of large economic aggregates that, thanks to perfect information and interdependent decision making, have begun to function like networks in their own right?

The answer is yes.

In general, if information becomes abundant and cheap and approaches perfect information, we should expect decision making to become interdependent. When decision making becomes interdependent, the choices of shoppers and voters (and of aggregates, in general) will not be distributed randomly (see table 5.1). What will the new distribution look like? Will it be chaotic and utterly unruly?

Fortunately, large economic aggregates in transparency will often display patterns and behaviors that follow the rules of a statistical distribution called a powerlaw distribution. This means that while perfect information and interdependent decision making may derail the notion of market equilibrium, they will not create a situation in which the behaviors of "know everything" market participants in transparency will descend into indecipherable chaos. Quite the contrary: the closer we get to transparency the more predictable those behaviors will be.

In this chapter I will describe why and when power laws will be a dominant feature of markets and economies in transparency. In later chapters, and particularly in chapters 10 and 18, I will show how you can profit from this insight.

The simplifying assumption for transparency is this: under conditions of perfect information and other conditions that are satisfied in transparency, distributions of economic choices in interconnected groups will tend to obey power laws. We have already had a preview of what the new world will look like: the distribution of hits among search engines, which we have

Table 5.1			
Perfect information, interdependent decision making, and aggregate behavior			
		From:	To:
If			
Information	:	scarce →	abundant and cheap; perfect
Then			
Decision making	:	independent →	interdependent
And then			
Distribution of behaviors of aggregates	:	random →	not random

just described, is a powerlaw distribution. Such a distribution is very understandable, and behaviors that obey this distribution are predictable.

What are power laws, and how did I reach the conclusion about their prominence in transparency? First, a definition:

> **POWERLAW DISTRIBUTION**: In general terms, an 80–20 distribution, or one in which a few events, products, players, or ideas account for most of the action. In a network, a powerlaw distribution of links is one in which the great majority of points have very few links but a small number of points (hubs) have a lot of links. Powerlaw distributions may be precisely described using mathematical formulas (see the "powerlaw distributions" entry in the glossary for an example).

The topography of networks with powerlaw distributions is very different from the topography of networks with random distributions, as we can see in figures 5.1 and 5.2.

Powerlaw dynamics are understandable and predictable. When we observe Microsoft's difficulties in catching up with Google, for example, we are watching powerlaw dynamics in action. As we look at our economic experience through the lens of power laws, we will increasingly be able to discern the orderly patterns that underlie the apparent tumult of transparency. Along with the other strategies for profitability in this book, this understanding is one of the foundations for prosperity in our future.

Figure 5.1

A powerlaw network

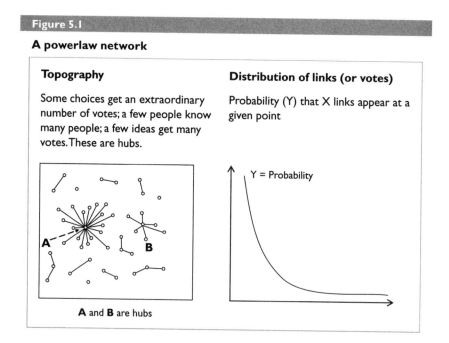

Topography

Some choices get an extraordinary number of votes; a few people know many people; a few ideas get many votes. These are hubs.

A and **B** are hubs

Distribution of links (or votes)

Probability (Y) that X links appear at a given point

Y = Probability

Figure 5.2

A random network, also known as a mesh network

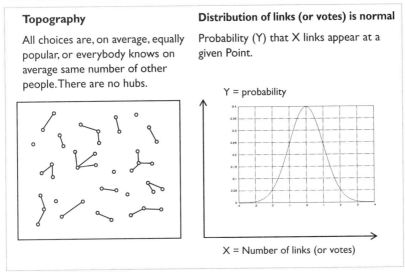

Topography	Distribution of links (or votes) is normal
All choices are, on average, equally popular, or everybody knows on average same number of other people. There are no hubs.	Probability (Y) that X links appear at a given Point.

Y = probability

Y = probability

X = Number of links (or votes)

In transparency, powerlaw distributions are likely to rise to the same level of prominence as a practical simplifying assumption that normal distributions have enjoyed in economic models of the past. A powerlaw distribution is as useful in transparency as the normal distributions would be in random environments. Transparent marketplaces will move in dynamic disequilibrium, in the predictable and orderly pattern of power laws. This is the new economic paradigm for transparency. We may think of transparency, therefore, as an age of powerlaw economics.

There has been a great deal of new research on power laws and networks in recent years, and the distributions themselves have long been familiar to mathematicians and others. Power laws have been found at work in computer and social networks, neural networks, and in the spread of disease. Benoit Mandelbrot and others have reported that power laws are common in nature and in social settings. Mandelbrot writes:

> In economics, one classic power law was discovered by Italian economist Vilfredo Pareto a century ago. It describes the distribution of income in the upper reaches of society. That power law concentrates much more of a society's wealth among the very few; a bell curve would be more equitable, scattering incomes more evenly around an average.[1]

As you may have noticed, we have not yet backed up our assertion that power laws are likely to be a dominant feature of transparent markets and economies. Now let us see why I think this is so. This book's insights about power laws in large economic aggregates in transparency are inspired by the work of a number of researchers who have written lucidly about the mathematical properties of networks and about the behavior of individuals and the paths of information in networked groups, for instance: Albert Laszlo Barabasi,[2] Steven Strogatz,[3] Duncan Watts,[4] Robert Axtell, and Bernardo Huberman.

Not surprisingly, these researchers have found that networked groups and their information behave differently depending on how easily information can travel, how large the groups are, and how the members of the groups are connected to each other and to other groups. For example, teams led by Huberman[5] have used mathematical simulations to test many hypotheses about the relationships between various conditions and the behaviors of networked groups.

For our purposes, it is worth noting that not all groups are networks. (The term *network* is often very loosely applied.) When decision making is independent, a simple group (or aggregate) can be reasonably imagined as individuals in a two-dimensional queue without any communication between them. This is what classical economists are describing when they refer to aggregates—an aggregate of buyers, say, is a large group of buyers in which choices about purchases are made independently. Whenever decision making shows even a hint of interdependence or interconnectedness, however, a group can better be imagined as individuals arranged in a multidimensional structure with connections or information channels between them. Groups with such links are often called networked groups or simply "networks."[6] Note that under conditions of interdependent decision making, an economist's *aggregate* suddenly looks and acts like a *network*.

One of the pioneers in network research is Barabasi, who in the late 20th century was among the first to map the connectedness of the Web and discover that the patterns of hits to Internet search engines, as we saw in chapter 4, do not at all fit the expected model of random distribution. Barabasi was one of the first to discover that those hits fell into powerlaw distributions. Barabasi also studied the patterns of relationships involving Hollywood figures. His tallies of the links among these personalities did not conform to random distributions, either.[7] Barabasi and his colleagues have applied the term *scale-free network* to describe the large complex networks that express power laws. I call such network *powerlaw networks*.

Although powerlaw and scale-free networks may be considered synonymous, I will henceforth use *scale-free network* to refer to the networks studied by researchers, and *powerlaw network* to refer to those real-life groups (like commercial aggregates or voters) or those expressions of consumer choices (or votes) that begin to express the dynamics of scale-free networks.

The behavior of powerlaw networks is orderly, and the distributions of their links can be predicted using established mathematical formulas for powerlaw distributions

> **POWERLAW NETWORK:**[8] A multidimensional aggregate or structure consisting of points (buyers, sellers, companies, products, etc.) with links between them (family ties, tastes, votes, etc.) in a transparent environment of perfectly fast and free information with no constraints to connectivity. These links are distributed according to power laws.

As I studied the empirical results and the simulations of the distinguished researchers, I identified the four conditions that are required for networks to be scale-free or powerlaw networks by combining the learning across the work of a number of researchers (Barabasi, Watts, Huberman, and Strogatz had each identified one or two requirements for networks to be scale-free networks). I compared these four conditions to those of the transparent environment.

Much to my excitement, the four conditions necessary for networks to be powerlaw networks corresponded *exactly* to the four conditions that will characterize the transparent economy. Though the language differs, the substance is the same.

The list of four conditions that need to be satisfied for networks to be scale-free and to express power laws is as follows:

Four Requirements for Networks to Be Scale-Free
Zero search cost
Preferential attachment
Growth and change
Infinite size

The first two conditions of preferential attachment and growth are consistent with work by Barabasi.[9] Watts has pointed out the importance of the infinite size criterion[10] and the importance of zero search cost networks.[11] Strogatz also stresses the critical condition of zero search cost.[12] Separately, Axtell has summarized research showing that power laws are incompatible with static equilibrium and that skewed distributions, like power laws, will result when agents are constantly adapting to each other.[13]

How do these four conditions relate to the economic realities that we will experience in transparency? As you know, transparency is characterized by the following conditions:

Four Conditions Present in Transparency (for Large Aggregates)
Perfect information
Interdependent decision making

Lack of equilibrium,[14] not a stable mean
Large groups, expanding connectivity

These conditions correspond to the conditions that are necessary for scale-free networks.

The list of conditions for scale-free networks that express power laws is satisfied in transparent markets and in a transparent economy. Therefore, we will increasingly observe power laws as we approach transparency. This, of course, also helps us to understand and predict the behavior of groups in transparency, namely that they will exhibit powerlaw dynamics.

Here are the four conditions for scale-free networks and their equivalents for markets in transparency, side by side:

Conditions for a Scale-free Network		*Conditions in Transparency*
Zero search cost	=	perfect information
Preferential attachment	=	interdependent decision making
Growth and change	=	lack of equilibrium[15]
Infinite size	=	expanding connectivity, large groups

Every day, as the cost of information keeps falling, we can find more and more circumstances in which the four conditions are met and power laws hold. Although there are some areas of the economy in which perfect information will lag and distributions will continue to be more or less random, transparency is busting out all over. In a fully transparent world, almost all large, linked commercial aggregates—including consumer choices, stock market prices, votes, preferences, and popularity—may be expected to behave like scale-free networks.

The Structure and Dynamics of Powerlaw Networks

In order to appreciate what we can do with this understanding, let us take a moment to familiarize ourselves with the structure of and the dynamics in and on powerlaw networks.

A well-known example of a distribution that follows power laws is the population of people across cities. In most countries we can observe a small number of very large cities, plus a large number of smaller cities and towns. The size, or number of inhabitants, of those few large cities is many multiples of the mean city size. In other words, the probability of a city being many standard deviations more populous than the average city size is much larger than the probability would be if the distribution were normal.

Powerlaw distributions have very large and sometimes even infinitely large standard deviations. If you were to plot the distributions of cities, the tail would look "fatter" than the tail or end of a normal distribution. In general, relative to normal distributions, powerlaw distributions have fat tails. If a distribution were normal, the chances of a fat tail—that is, an event very far (many standard deviations) from the mean—would be extremely remote.

As by now you know, powerlaw distributions are not like random distributions, in which you could expect that all points will have the same average number of links. Powerlaw distributions do not have a mean: no confidence can be placed in a prediction of the number of links at any given point based on the number of links present at any point sampled at random. Remember the distribution of hits per search engine? Powerlaw distributions do not settle down;[16] they do not as a rule have equilibrium. Sound familiar? Many of the "tall spires on a flat plain" distributions that we said would come about as the result of interdependent decision making will in fact express power laws if the other three of the four conditions are present as well.

If you plotted popularity—in a network, this would be equivalent to the number of links to a point—vertically (either in absolute terms or expressed in terms of probability) and rank-ordered the points horizontally, you would get an asymptotic-looking graph. You can do this for cities (points) and their populations (links); or potato-chip types (points) and their volume sales (links); or words in the dictionary (points) and their frequency of use in English text (links).

The exact features of powerlaw distributions can be clearly defined in mathematical terms. There are a number of well-established formulas for powerlaw distributions that will allow us to estimate the probabilities that the next customer will go to one point in a network as opposed to another.

In everyday speech, a powerlaw distribution is often referred to as the "80–20 principle." This shorthand conveys the notion that when power laws are in operation a few events, products, or players account for most of the action.[17] When the 80–20 principle plays out in the real world, connections and influence will flow disproportionately to a relatively small group of people.

To some extent, the representation provided by a powerlaw equation will always function as an ideal. As transparency approaches, the four conditions that are required to generate true powerlaw distributions are likely to be met more often—but certainly not always perfectly. Just as we could observe traditional markets tending toward equilibrium even in the absence of perfect conditions for equilibrium—when high prices created a rush of products to market that led to lower prices, for example—so we will see powerlaw *phenomena* emerge even if the conditions of powerlaw math are not purely satisfied. For example:

- *Open-source contributions:* Wikipedia's online encyclopedia is open-source, which means that anyone can write or modify its entries. Typically, only 5 to 10 percent of Wikipedia's contributors produce 80 percent of the product.[18]
- *Business books:* According to *The Economist,* there are approximately 3,000 business titles published each year in the United States, the world's largest market, but a mere 50 of these titles account for roughly half the total sales—more than 4 million of the 8 million to 10 million business books sold in total each year.[19] As you can imagine, I read that with interest!

Powerlaw phenomena that look more or less like this have always existed in business contexts, but they have never occurred with enough frequency to attract particular attention. As the four conditions for powerlaw networks are increasingly met, we can expect to see many more powerlaw-type distributions. Powerlaw phenomena will need to be dealt with specifically in strategy, as we will do later in this book.

Now that we have established that aggregates in transparency behave like powerlaw networks, what do we know about how they behave? How do they choose? Here we can piggyback on the findings of network mathematicians—especially if we make one important shift in our usual perspective on how people and information come together.

Many social-network theorists have tried to decipher the mechanisms of how messages travel from one person to the next. Following the messages around, however, did not yield repeatable methodology.

As I contemplated the overlaps between the conditions that are necessary for scale-free networks and the conditions that are likely to be present in a transparent economy, however, it occurred to me that you could solve this problem of information flow in transparency if you *flipped your perspective.*

In a world of perfect information and interdependent decision making, rather than thinking about *people* as being the points, one should think about *messages* (or products or services or candidates or ideas) as being the points, and think about their links as the messages. It is people (or their choices or votes) that converge on messages,[20] and it is their votes or choices that follow the pattern of powerlaw distributions. This makes sense, because it is choices that are affected by interdependent decision making.

When you look at it this way, the question of how information travels becomes a side issue. You don't need an elaborate diagram to parse it out: people go to the message. The product is there; *decisions go to the product.* Simple though this concept may be, it has great benefits for understanding modern marketplaces. *How do you influence the hearts and minds*[21] *of consumers when THE CONSUMERS are the ones doing the reaching for information, rather than waiting to be reached?* As I will argue later, the answers to these questions will require a variety of innovative tactics and a fresh strategic mindset.

Before we get to the new tactics, we need to review a few of the distinguishing attributes of powerlaw networks. The most significant structural features of powerlaw networks are the hubs, which are created by the phenomenon of links reaching out to points. Hubs may be defined as follows:

> **HUB:** A point that has an extraordinary number of links; in a network operating according to power laws, hubs are the points with the predominant number of links.

As a powerlaw network grows, the fastest growth of connections (links) occurs at the most connected points (hubs). As new links arrive, they are more likely to form connections with points that already have relatively higher numbers of links—in other words, with existing hubs. This is what is meant by *preferential attachment*,[22] which is the condition that corresponds to interdependent decision making. Hubs that are ahead in terms of links (or votes or market share) will tend to get ahead even more. The dynamics in a network are dictated by the attraction of the hubs.

It's important to note that in a consumer market, links don't coalesce only around companies and services; hubs can also be products, product features, or even people, like movie stars or star hairstylists. All hubs have in common the attraction that comes from being highly connected, or popular, and visible in a world where consumers can easily "see" what other people look at and choose or do.

The appearance and behavior of powerlaw networks are closely intertwined. The structure of a powerlaw network is a direct result of its dynamics. A fascinating example of a powerlaw network that has formed "naturally" is the U.S. Internet data communications infrastructure. The distributions of Internet router equipment and physical linkages among them appear to follow power laws.[23] This is remarkable, since the original Internet infrastructure was deliberately set up as a random mesh, in which all hubs were seen as equally important and were expected to have the same average number of links. Random mesh networks are much more robust to disruptions and attacks than powerlaw networks, which have many more links clustered around a few points, and therefore would be far more vulnerable to terrorism or any other kind of threat. With security and reliability in mind, one would not design the current Internet infrastructure. But over time, capacity had to be added to the mesh-designed network in ways that supported people's patterns of use. These patterns of communications, Internet search, and so on began to concentrate in ways that expanded some hubs of electronic activity.

As a result, the physical infrastructure was transformed into a design that resembles a powerlaw network.

One of the significant attributes of powerlaw networks, as I have noted, is that once a network point—whether it is a search engine or a city or a snack or an investment bank—is ahead in terms of the number of links, the harder it is for another point to catch up with that hub.

For all of this activity, it is difficult to exert a strong influence on the dynamics of a powerlaw network. This is because it is very difficult to weaken points that have achieved hub status. If two hubs are equally attractive on quantitative measures—for example, if there are two equally useful and comparably priced college guides—the one with more links is likely to remain ahead, garnering more links or votes or market share. Only if the lagging guide has substantially more *fitness* (the term used to describe the innate power of attraction of a hub)—for example, if it cuts its price in half—can it increase its probability of attracting the next link.[24] Attributes such as lower price or higher perceived quality play a role in consumer purchases, for instance, only indirectly, by contributing to the fitness of a product against competitive products.

There is the potential for continual waves of popularity. These may indeed be caused by the arrival of new points that surpass the existing points of interest in terms of fitness. In the period of transition to transparency, it may be possible to engineer such a wave.

Finally, it is by definition impossible to cause a powerlaw network to "tip"—that is, to make all its votes land on one choice—because that is not consistent with powerlaw dynamics and hub formation. In powerlaw distributions there will be several major hubs as well as several minor hubs in addition. *There is no threshold and there is no tipping point.*

As conditions change, the kinds of distributions we most commonly see among economic choices will change as well. The conditions that tend to prevail in transparency will satisfy the four requirements for power laws.

The closer markets are to transparency, the more likely we are to observe powerlaw distributions. In the years ahead, strategies based on the random walk or efficient market hypotheses, along with other theories that rely on the idea that the broad stock market is distributed normally, will need to be in doubt, as many financial market practitioners are aware. Risk management and forecasts based on normal distributions may be at best unhelpful and at worst dangerous. Concepts of risk aversion will also need to be reformulated in light of nonnormal distributions caused by interdependent decision making. The conventional wisdom tells us that people who do not accept apparently even odds are "risk-averse." In reality, they may simply be wise; they may already understand that the distribution of possible outcomes is not normal.[25]

In summary, whereas the simplifying assumption in classical economics most frequently has been the normal distribution, the simplifying assumption for transparency is the powerlaw distribution.

Furthermore, we may consider powerlaw dynamics and the *pattern* of hubs and links as the equivalent of a dynamic equilibrium. *What is sustained in transparency, is the powerlaw distribution, not a single fixed point of general equilibrium.* Nevertheless, even if the pattern of hubs represents a form of equilibrium, powerlaw networks are not static. New links are constantly arriving in networks and making connections with existing points.

On the Road to Transparency

It is helpful to distinguish the types of behavior that may develop once we get to a fully transparent world (namely, powerlaw dynamics) from those that may be encountered during the transition stage. Amid the transition to transparency, we may well encounter *a spectrum of dynamics* resulting from linked networks. Some markets or groups will approach conditions of transparency and behave like powerlaw networks, others may have a normal or random distribution of prices and quantities, and some may be in between or "unruly." Table 5.2 summarizes the key attributes of random mesh, unruly, and powerlaw networks.

These lagging and "in-between" groups, marketplaces, and networks will evolve toward transparency at varying speeds. Information will be widely available in transition periods, but still not quite perfect. Marketplaces will consist of customers who know of others' choices to some degree; they will make decisions within self-forming groups. As a result, these marketplaces will be experienced as unpredictable, wild, difficult to control, and lacking governance—in short, unruly.

When interdependent decision making occurs before all the conditions for power laws have been met, the result is a battleground that is genuinely difficult. Because customers, employees, voters, and suppliers are making decisions with awareness of each other, we cannot add up their demand curves. We also cannot expect that the distribution of their choices will display a normal distribution. And because information is still sometimes blocked, the predictable patterns of powerlaw distributions are not yet fully in evidence, either. We say that the result is an unruly distribution.

The appearance of unruly distributions has been supported by findings of network researchers. Zero search cost, or free information, is an extremely important condition, as analyses by Huberman and others have shown.[26] If there is preferential attachment, but no growth (i.e., a completely static model), we will not see the generation of power laws.[27] If there is growth, but

Table 5.2

Comparison of the characteristics of mesh, unruly, and powerlaw networks

Characteristics		Network Type		
		Mesh	Unruly	Powerlaw
Network	Distributions of links among points	Random distribution	Spectrum of distributions	Powerlaw distribution
	Points	Points have identical distributions of links	Some points are more connected than others (e.g., local hubs in cliques or small worlds)	Hubs have the bulk of links
	Robustness against random attack	Medium	Depends on structure	High
	Robustness against targeted attack	High	Depends on structure	Low
Marketplace	Economic Phase	Efficient markets (theoretical)	Transition to transparency	Transparency
	Dynamics on aggregate		• Messages can get blocked • Starting point matters: near local hubs is best • Information decay	• Messages go fast, everywhere • Entry point is irrelevant • No information decay
	Dynamics in aggregate			• The network votes • Hubs tend to stay ahead • Preferential attachment • Efficient searches query hubs first

(Continued)

Table 5.2

(Continued)

Characteristics		Network Type		
		Mesh	Unruly	Powerlaw
	Power nodes specific to this type of network		#11. Filters and brokers	#12. Hubs #10. Aikido assets
	Other features	• "Wisdom of crowds" • Regression toward the mean	• No wisdom of crowds • Tipping is possible • Thresholds are possible	• No wisdom of crowds • No tipping: multiple hubs • No thresholds • Markets for one are feasible but choices will be per power laws

Figure 5.3

A network in the transition to transparency

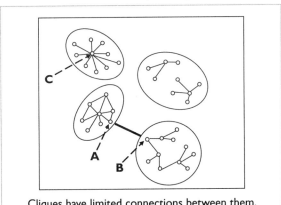

Cliques have limited connections between them.
A, B, and C can function as filters. A and B are brokers.

no preferential attachment, we end up with "an exponential degree distribution, which is similar to a bell curve in that it forbids the hubs" from forming.[28] Finally, if we are not dealing with a very large group, we may get "truncated distributions instead of the long, fat tails of a powerlaw distribution."[29]

In their simulations and empirical analyses, Huberman and his team at Hewlett-Packard found that until information can flow absolutely freely, individual points may wind up in small, partially or fully inaccessible clumps. In the unruly networks that may arise during the transition to transparency, we are likely to see "islands" of information and "cliques" of people who block the distribution of important facts to people outside their own group (see figure 5.3), as described by Watts in *Six Degrees*. In this type of environment filters and brokers have the power to spread information or block it.

Influencing Hearts and Minds

How about sending messages in transparency and about capturing the hearts and minds of consumers? As markets enter transparency, the answers to the question of who gets the message and how will begin to shift. This has important implications for the way businesses can operate effectively in a transitional climate of interdependent decision making. In a fully transparent economy, everyone will know everything instantly. It will not matter who adopts a message first. There is no threshold number of people it needs to get to before it can get everywhere. A message cannot get blocked. The question is, how many votes (or links) will it get?

In an unruly marketplace, however, it *does* matter who gets the message first. It will be spread to others if it reaches the *right group* (i.e., a group in which the message will not be blocked). In the world of transparency, the messages that attract the most votes early on will become hubs. In the interim period of unruliness, however, it will be extremely helpful to make your message visible at points that are hubs (you can try to get your product featured on *Oprah*, say), that have many connections to the right groups to pass the message along, or that are like gatekeepers between your message and your intended audience. These gatekeeper points can be called filters or brokers, and they represent one of the 12 possible power nodes. (See table 5.3 for a comparison of message transmission in unruly and powerlaw networks.)

The critical difference between hubs and filters is that hubs are neutral—they are formed as people *reach out* for information that is instantly available to them and express their votes. In transparency, all people can decide for themselves what message or new product interests them. Filters, on the other hand, tend to screen and make judgments about information before passing it on. In the most basic sense, they are tastemakers. These are the people who, in our transitional world, may still have the power to strongly influence the market. In a world of islands and cliques, they are very powerful. In transparency their power will fade.

Table 5.3

Comparison of message transmission in unruly and powerlaw networks

	Unruly network	Powerlaw network
Starting point	Chances of spreading the message improve if the message starts at a highly connected point (local hub). Even then, a message may not get broad exposure because • the signal may decay, • may get blocked by the local hub acting as a filter or broken, or • may get stuck inside a clique.	It does not matter where in the network the message starts. • Messages do not get blocked. • Messages can be "found" by the entire network.
Influence of filters and brokers (power node # 11)	Filters or brokers may control the exposure of messages.	Filters and brokers are not influential. • The network searches for new messages and "votes" on popularity. • Network members and outsiders cannot influence the path of the message. They should instead learn to read the voting patterns fast and react fast (power node #10). Hubs (highly popular messages) stay ahead (power node #12). Only super-fit new messages may catch up. • Searches will query democratically selected hubs first. It pays to try to influence the content of the messages that will be "found" at the hubs by the searching network.
Information decay	The strength of the message signal will decay as it moves through the network.	The strength of the message signal does not decay.
Thresholds	Thresholds	No thresholds

(Continued)

Table 5.3		
(Continued)		
	Unruly network	Powerlaw network
Tipping	Tipping is possible, an additional reason to expect returns from influencing a filter or broker.	There are multiple hubs; no tipping.

During transitions to transparency, there will be numerous races between networks with *different speeds of information flow.*[30] These kinds of contests occur when two different types of networks, one with less "friction" than the other, come into contact. A surge in appeal may be caused by the "overlay" of a network with even less information friction than the existing one. Huberman studied these when he looked at reputation dynamics. To understand how this works, imagine that there is one network where people slowly develop their firsthand opinion of a company by sampling or buying its product. Overlay that old network with a new network of gossip and secondhand points of view, and enable an exchange of information. Since information spreads much faster and more easily in the gossip network than in the one that requires actual physical encounters with the goods, the secondhand network will reach more people, faster. The secondhand opinions could quickly outrun a reputation built over many years of firsthand experiences. We see this kind of contest when one company announces new products by e-mail while another sends catalogues by postal mail.

Many aggregates and markets will evolve toward the structures and behaviors of powerlaw networks a bit more each day. During this period, companies everywhere should prepare for 80–20 phenomena in markets and among customers. They should be on the lookout for phenomena that do not behave according to the law of large numbers, or regression toward the mean, or any other way of saying "normal distribution," even if market participants or customers are numerous. Most of all, they should be aware that interdependent decision making will turn many interactions into popularity contests. I will talk more about strategies for dealing with powerlaw distributions in chapter 10, which explains how to win in new marketplaces.

PART III

How Transparency Alters the Building Blocks of Profits

Chapter 6

The Four Strategic Decisions in Transparency

In the opening chapters of this book, we have followed the path of our star driver, the vanishing cost of information, to its inevitable consequence: an economy transformed by perfect information. We have focused on the ways in which perfect information and interdependent decision making will undermine our most cherished economic assumptions, sanctify extraordinary profits, and usher in a new era of powerlaw dynamics that will produce dramatic changes in behavior in many marketplaces. In this section, we will translate these macro trends into strategy prescriptions for businesses and investors. Specifically, we will strive to understand how transparency influences four critical decisions each company must make concerning its focus, business model, competition, and marketplace strategy.

The four critical decisions are:

1. What part of the business do we want to own?
2. What is the most profitable way to organize businesses?
3. What competitive threats do we face and how do we win?
4. Which behaviors do we encounter in the marketplace for our products and which strategies will yield the highest returns?

Regarding the first decision, consider that the trend toward perfect information will spur a continuing shift away from vertically integrated companies and toward focused companies. As a number of writers have already pointed out, corporate leaders and investors will enjoy a vast increase in their options for pursuing narrowly focused activities. For these business leaders and investors, the most important issue is strategic: which of these focused companies should I own? Our answer: *to maximize profits, own the businesses with a power node.*

The second decision is about which business model is most conducive to increased returns. In transparency, the ease of monitoring and coordination made possible by perfect information will facilitate many new kinds of arrangements between companies, without the requirement of shared ownership. These new relationships will enable companies to capture many of the same benefits that vertical integration once offered—including protection from such problems as motley crews and hazardous markets—without the accompanying drain on performance and profits. Particularly when they are organized around power nodes, these distributed business arrangements will allow—to varying degrees—the long-term creation of positive sums for all concerned. In transparency, *such a nexus of relationships will replace vertical integration as the prevailing archetype for "the firm."*

This idea is an extension of ongoing thinking about business models. Several authors have said, in effect: Perfect information is here. All companies will be stand-alone companies.[1] In this view, companies have only two options: being focused and going solo in the marketplace or remaining vertically integrated. But in transparency, companies have much greater freedom to compose or arrange themselves. The two options of being focused and stand-alone or being vertical will emerge as extremes. Perfect information will permit so much in the way of oversight and enforcement that the vast majority of companies will be able to structure a wide variety of high-performing and profitable relationships that fall somewhere along the continuum between stand-alone and vertically integrated.

With such a wide assortment of choices, transparency's managers and entrepreneurs will have a great deal to think about as they determine the shape of their companies. It is important to note that the decision about business model is a matter of trade-offs among a long list of factors, not just a few. Indeed, I have identified a list of 14 distinct factors that must be considered when deciding how to organize or shape a business. For the reader's convenience, I have sorted these essential considerations into a checklist of three "buckets" (or three categories) of trade-offs (see table 7.1).

The Three Buckets Checklist is an extremely practical document that will be of tangible assistance in implementing whatever strategies are best for you or your company in transparency. (It should also be used as part of evaluation and action plans for implementing a superior business model, as discussed in chapter 16.) A step-by-step review of the factors in the checklist is something that you can build into your routine each time you look at buying and turning around or reorganizing a company.

The checklist is based on a great deal of preexisting theory and empirical research, as well as on my own findings about the justifications for distributed power relationships. For the most part, the factors included in the three buckets are neither new nor controversial. What is different is our categorization in three buckets and our discussion of how the considerations are influenced by perfect information and therefore how the choice to organize is altered by transparency.

How does transparency alter the evaluation of these trade-offs? With perfect information, Category I arguments that were in favor of vertical integration tend to fade away, and Category II considerations in favor of focus gain more weight. Therefore, in transparency a checklist of Category I and Category II considerations tends to be resolved in favor of focused companies. But Category III issues still remain: assembly of an entire value chain under one roof offers benefits and protections that focused companies operating alone in the marketplace simply cannot reproduce. But thanks to perfect information, focused companies will for the first time enjoy a wide range of options for recouping those benefits—including the development of power relationships that can be used to manage distributed business arrangements.

Regarding the third decision, how does transparency affect competition?

Before transparency, competition was discussed primarily as a fight for market share among the vertically integrated gladiators in industries whose boundaries were clearly defined. Now, with surging numbers of freestanding focused companies at every level of the value chain, we are seeing exponential increases in the number of points of competition among companies providing intermediate goods and services. Once, competition was thought of primarily as a one-dimensional struggle for market share in markets for final goods and services. Now it is becoming *a three-dimensional fight* against horizontal rivals in the same industry, against horizontal rivals outside of the industry and around the globe, and against vertical rivals up and down the value chain. In transparency, *the key determinant of profitability will be the ability to defend or extract returns from vertical competitors.* Those companies that win vertical battles will be the owners of power nodes. The emphasis of competitive strategy needs to be on profitability rather than on market share.

Finally, we turn to the fourth decision about how to successfully navigate the new dynamics in marketplaces. How will transparency change our approach to the marketplaces with a large number of participants, which will include most mass consumer markets for goods and services? Profoundly. As we now know, under conditions of perfect information and interdepedent decision making, *the behaviors of market participants are likely to display the same dynamics found in scale-free networks.* This means two things. First, we will see huge concentrations of choices around the small proportion of points (products, services, people, etc.) that become hubs—and this phenomenon will guarantee that a few select companies will be in the fortunate position of being able to create profits that may be more extraordinary than ever before. Second, in transparency, people will *reach out* for information (or products or services) rather than waiting for it to reach them. Companies in transparency will thrive by anticipating and responding to consumer choices rather than forcing them into being—a new approach that I call "information aikido."

In the following four chapters, we will take a closer look at the impact of transparency on each of the four essential strategic decisions in turn. By the conclusion of this section, readers will have a clear sense of how to frame their answers to the key business questions in transparency. They will be nearly ready to work with the specific strategies for building profit power in transparency that I will outline in the final sections of this book.

Chapter 7

Ownership Focused on Profit Power

You do not need to own the road, only the tollbooth.
    —John Kay, summarizing the view of
        Warren Buffett[1]

What business will bring us the most rewards in transparency?

As we have seen, diminished cost of information not only eliminates the rationale for vertical integration but also greatly boosts the performance advantages of focused companies. The result: an unstoppable impetus for companies to come apart. Even if vertically integrated companies do not break up voluntarily, they will be pushed to do so by investors and the higher performance of focused competitors.

Looked at this way, it is clear what the approach to deciding which business to own should be. The answer is: focus on the parts of the three-dimensional value nexus that offer the highest returns. This means: focus on the power nodes.

In the old economy, industries were clearly defined—they were composed of companies generating similar final outputs. In most industries, the gold standard of corporate organization used to be vertical integration. Vertically integrated companies controlled most, if not all, of the inputs to their final products, including financing, raw materials, components, and intermediary products. They also owned entities that would market and distribute their products and services.

The classic example of vertical integration was the General Motors of the era of Alfred Sloan, which directly produced almost everything that went into its cars, from seats to engines to windshield wipers. Other well-known vertical giants that have since gone through transformations include AT&T, IBM, Dupont, Siemens, and Procter & Gamble. Ownership of all the activities along the value chain at one time seemed the only way for a company to ensure that it could access the inputs it needed, when and where it needed them, at a reasonable and reasonably predictable cost.

As we can now see, this belief reflected the trade-offs of the Three Buckets Checklist that was introduced in chapter 6 (see table 7.1). The choice in favor of vertical integration was on the one hand a response to constraints imposed by the expense and relative scarcity of information (the Category I considerations in the checklist) and on the other an attempt to deal with issues related to positive sums, specifically the problems of market hazards (part of the Category III considerations of our checklist).

As the falling cost of information takes us ever deeper into transparency, there will be fewer and fewer justifications for vertical integration. In the past, it took a vertical stack of one big company owning all the subcompanies to make a finished product; in transparency, a flock of focused companies will be able to produce the same product even more efficiently (see figure 7.1).

Perfect Information Enables Focus

The emergence of perfect information has greatly expanded the number of opportunities for focused companies. Focus, as we have seen, is an alternative to vertical integration. A focused company is one whose leaders have selected exactly which activities they want to perform. Focused companies may produce intermediate goods or services that are sold to other companies in a value chain. They may also produce finished goods and services that are retailed to the final customers. They may be defined as follows:

> FOCUSED COMPANY: One that concentrates on a very narrow set of outputs (goods or services); often these are "intermediary" outputs that will be sold to other companies instead of to final customers.

Ever since the 1970s, we have seen wave upon wave of businesses coming apart. First came the dismantling of conglomerates like Gulf & Western, ITT, and RJR Nabisco, all of which owned many unrelated businesses. They were sliced or unbundled into a set of vertically integrated companies. More recently, in a harbinger of transparency's shift toward highly focused business activities, corporations that seemed to be in only one line of business, such as Marriott, have been further broken up into horizontal slices. In many of these instances, investors have led the charge on the grounds

Table 7.1

The Three Buckets Checklist for shaping business models

Category I: *Cost-of-information considerations for focus versus vertical integration:*

1. Cost of search: cost of finding buyers, sellers, and prices
2. Cost of external coordination relative to internal coordination
3. Cost of external monitoring relative to internal monitoring
4. Cost of internal coordination and monitoring (and its effect on returns to scale)
5. Cost of asymmetry of information
6. Cost of contracts and bounded rationality

Category II: *Performance considerations for focus versus vertical integration:*

1. Economies of scale
2. Design of incentives
3. Allocation of resources
4. Use of resources
5. Organizational flexibility and reslience
6. Attractiveness to investors

Category III: *Positive sum considerations for focus versus distributed business arrangements:*

1. *Benefits of collective action not related to the cost of information:*
   - solving problems of motley crews
   - solving problems of hazardous markets
   - solving problems of lack of complete insurance against any and all contingencies for all possible states of the world
2. *Benefits of association with sources of profit power, that is, power nodes:*
   - capturing and sharing externalities related to brand and reputation
   - access to proprietary ingredients or other products with inelastic supply curves with hold-up potential
   - capturing and sharing regulatory privileges or expertise
   - access to focused financial resources and insurance capability and potential for Pareto-optimal reallocation of risk
   - access to customers locked in by high switching costs and other path dependencies
   - capturing advantages associated with proprietary processes
   - access to powerful distribution gateways
   - capturing or avoiding monopoly treatment associated with dominant position in a layer
   - capturing advantages associated with increasing mutual utility properties
   - capturing information advantages associated with aikido assets
   - capturing advantages of association with filters or brokers
   - capturing advantages of association with hubs

that business units within big companies would operate more efficiently and throw off more profits to shareholders if they were independent. More recently, many corporate leaders have made the same determination proactively for their own firms.

Figure 7.1

Company structures: the trend from vertical integration toward focused companies will continue as transparency progresses

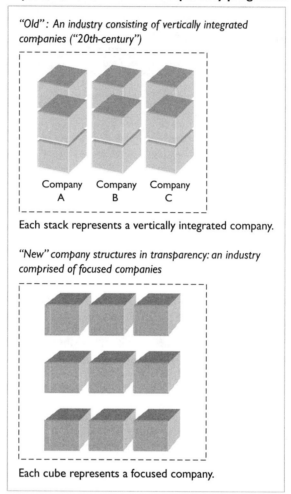

"Old": An industry consisting of vertically integrated companies ("20th-century")

Company A   Company B   Company C

Each stack represents a vertically integrated company.

"New" company structures in transparency: an industry comprised of focused companies

Each cube represents a focused company.

The result has been a steep increase in the number of focused companies over the last 20 to 50 years. This trend will accelerate in transparency. Many of these new focused entities will be founded as stand-alones or successfully spun off or sold from larger enterprises. Among the many examples so far: Lucent, spun off from AT&T; the semiconductor manufacturer Freescale, previously part of Motorola; some Warner Lambert product lines, spun off from Pfizer; many independent Hollywood production companies, some of them controlled by movie stars who were once under the thumb of large studios; Delphi, Visteon, and many other automobile suppliers, which were formerly part of vertically integrated automakers like GM and Ford; Gecis (now Genpact), the Indian outsourcing business, formerly under the wing of GE; FiatAvio (now Avio), once part of Fiat; MTU, spun off from Mercedes; Neenah Paper, once part of Kimberly-Clark.

When we discuss what business to own in this chapter, we are not talking about choosing between industries like petrochemicals or food service. Rather, we are talking about deciding what part or even sliver of the value chain we want to own. If we choose to be focused rather than vertically integrated, do we want to own contract manufacturers like Sanmina-SCI and Flextronics or do we want to own equipment suppliers like Nortel and Cisco Systems? Do we want Esselte or do we want Staples? Whichever slice of the value chain we choose, can participation in a distributed business arrangement allow us to capture some of the positive sum benefits traditionally associated with vertical integration?

The checklist for the most profitable way to organize is shown in table 7.1. With the Three Buckets Checklist, I offer companies a comprehensive worksheet for deciding the composition of their portfolio of activities, the structure of their firm and third-party transactions, and the desirability of a certain business model. The *three buckets* may also be referred to as the *three categories*.

In table 7.1, I provide three buckets of trade-offs that would have to be considered before any business manager or entrepreneur could make this decision. As we ask what business to own, we will focus on Category I cost-of-information considerations and Category II performance considerations. In transparency, both types of considerations will tilt strongly in favor of focused companies. The same Category I and II advantages that are driving the sweeping shift toward focused companies will also enable the most successful focused companies to derive the maximum benefits from power nodes—and these, in transparency, will be the primary source of extraordinary profits.

Category I: Cost-of-Information Considerations for Focus versus Vertical Integration

Cost-of-information considerations play a determining role in whether or not a company is able to stand on its own and be focused, and many economists and other scholars have already discussed them at length. The following is a selection of the most significant of these accepted considerations. Whereas the high cost of information was an impediment to focus, the plunging cost of information is an incentive. Transparency has a beneficial effect on the following.

Cost of Search

Until recently, high search costs and other obstacles to easy information limited the feasibility of markets in general, and for specialized and intermediate goods in particular. This buttressed the argument for vertical enterprises. Often, buyers and sellers simply couldn't find each other—if you were making great car seats in Malaysia, how could you let the automakers know? How could they cost-effectively compare your prices and specifications with those of your competitors? These days, such questions are easily resolved. No matter how obscure your output, the buyers can find you. Looking for financing for that ice-fishing movie? No problem—within a few keystrokes, ice-fishing funders anywhere in the world could be watching your trailer. The disappearance of search and information costs will facilitate markets for intermediate and many other goods.

Cost of External Coordination Relative to Internal Coordination

In the past it was cheaper to do everything related to coordination—the planning and managing of the supply chain, and so on—in-house. These days, it is increasingly affordable to bring together multiple companies (under multiple ownership) to perform all activities necessary to produce a single product, and the costs are falling steadily.

Cost of External Monitoring Relative to Internal Monitoring

Connectivity is so high and the costs of inspecting quality, supervising manufacturing, assuring timely shipments, and managing out-of-stocks from far away are so low that it now matters far less than it used to if the plant or distribution center is in your backyard and owned by you or halfway around the world and owned by a third party.

Cost of Internal Coordination and Monitoring (and Its Effect on Returns to Scale)

The declining cost of information within companies means that a focused company is no longer limited in scale in the way it used to be. Horizontal expansion has historically been constrained by so-called decreasing returns to scale. Decreasing returns were caused by, for instance, the cost of communications, the cost of collecting and managing information, and the cost of negotiating or completing transactions. As those costs tumble downward, companies can grow beyond the limits of those traditional constraints. A focused company can become global and very large before running into decreasing returns to scale. There is no limit to how focused an entity can get, or how thin a sliver of the value chain can be carved out and turned into a global company.

Consider OOCL, a Hong Kong shipping line; it is among a group of fast-growing companies in Hong Kong that handle the warehousing, sorting, and distribution of products made in China for export. The trend among retailers and consumer goods companies in the developed world is increasingly to bypass distribution centers in their final markets. It is far more economical to get goods packed into containers in the right quantity and order to be delivered directly from the port of entry to individual shops.

OOCL is going one step further. It is creating a global focused company specializing in just the sorting aspects. Cited in the *Financial Times*, Erxin Yao, managing director of OOCL for China, "said that his company's logistics arm hoped to attract imports of goods not made in China for sorting at his warehouse to distribute to Japan and Korea."[2]

Cost of Asymmetry of Information

Risks for all parties in transactions are reduced as transparency eliminates asymmetries of information (both before and after the transaction). This results in a decline in the problems of adverse selection, also known as lemons, and moral hazard,[3] both discussed in chapter 3. These were once significant obstacles to dealing with parties outside of direct ownership. Transparency will not eliminate the threat of financial losses caused by willful nonperformance, but it will make it hard for the shirker to keep repeating the offense. Consider, for example, the effects that negative customer ratings are likely to have on dealers listed on eBay or Amazon, or how disparaging posts from dissatisfied guests might affect hotels listed on Travelocity and similar sites.

Cost of Contracts and Bounded Rationality

In a world where information is expensive, the alternatives for structuring options and monitoring conditional contracts are limited. As a result, large, vertically integrated firms—which control producers of inputs through ownership rather than contracts—have traditionally had an advantage. Not so in transparency, which will enable infinite, variable, and changeable contracts that can be enforced at virtually no cost.

Category II: Performance Considerations for Focus versus Vertical Integration

Although cost-of-information considerations provide strong arguments to choose focus over vertical integration, the performance-based arguments for focus may be even more compelling. As it turns out, the actions of many independent, focused companies often produce, collectively, outcomes demonstrably superior to the ones a single, vertically integrated company could have. A company that does not move voluntarily to focus may soon find itself under fierce attack by flocks of focused competitors—and as a result, may eventually be forced to move toward focus whether it wants to or not. Unfortunately, decisions to focus generally have a less positive outcome for companies that have dragged their feet and are forced to make changes from a position of weakness.

Again, there is a large amount of research—based on theory, practical experience, and experimental studies—that demonstrates that focused companies are likely to be more resourceful, efficient, and ultimately profitable. What follows is a sampling of the leading performance-based reasons for focus.

Economies of Scale

While we see companies dismantling, we also see companies growing very large and global in their chosen, narrowly focused layer. Thanks to declining information costs, focused, horizontally organized companies have been able to expand well beyond their previous markets without triggering decreasing returns to scale. Instead of boosting marginal costs, their expanded volume allows them economies of scale and a faster learning curve. As an illustration of economies of scale, consider the First Data Corporation, which was founded in 1969 as a nonprofit bankcard-processing center for a group of Midwest banks. Today, thanks to lower information costs and enhanced connectivity, there seems no limit to the company's geographic reach. First Data has been able to take over processing services for more than 1,900 credit-card issuers in 38 countries across 6 continents.

Customers and clients may often prefer to deal with a narrowly focused stand-alone company rather than with the subsidiary of a vertical competitor, even if both are supplying a similar product or service. A good example of this is Lucent, a telecom equipment manufacturer. Once Lucent became independent from AT&T in 1996, it stopped being shunned by AT&T's telecom rivals,[4] and as a result it grew swiftly until the telecom slump started in 2001. In 2006, focused Lucent took a big step toward global horizontal expansion as it merged with its European competitor Alcatel. A leading motivation for both parties to this merger was a desire to capture economies of scale in research and manufacturing.

Design of Incentives

Focused companies can design, implement, and monitor more effective incentives for their employees and assign areas of responsibility more effectively. Employee motivation is a significant factor in corporate excellence, and focused companies can more easily align incentives with performance of specific activities. Rewards can be tailored to a particular functional skill or group of capabilities. A company of accountants needs a different set of motivators and performance measures than a company of designers of interactive games. The question of what is a proper range of responsibility for any given company is another important issue that is often researched. Focused companies may maintain a more appropriate span of responsibility. Companies close to local markets, for instance, will deal more effectively with local laws, rules, and cultures.

Allocation of Resources

Focused companies are more attuned to market signals (i.e., price signals for inputs and outputs) than their predecessors operating inside vertically integrated stacks. This makes them more efficient at allocating resources than companies that depend on transfer pricing or other artificial pricing schemes among divisions. This is because all activities of a focused company—including purchases of inputs and sales of the goods or services it produces—are subject to market pressures, and prices are visible to all.

Use of Resources

Focused companies are more conscientious in delivering their cash-flow objectives than similar pieces inside a vertical chain, because that's a prerequisite for their survival. The common sense of this is abundantly clear. It jumps at you when you spend time in the bustling factories and warehouses of independent affiliates in Mumbai or Mexico City, where every penny is pinched, and then return to the plush corridors of a headquarters office.

Volumes of research have documented this as well. Managers tend to operate more efficiently when there is no mother ship. They are more likely to reduce waste, to fight for better terms from suppliers and customers, to strive to live up to their commitments to investors—especially if this involves debt obligations—and to take on appropriate levels of risks. All in all, as empirical studies have repeatedly shown, they work harder to increase the competitiveness of their product and the survival chances of their company. It is often remarkable what happens to pieces of companies after they are set free to survive by their own wits. A *BusinessWeek* study discovered that 13 out of 17 companies spun off in 2003 beat the S&P index during the next two years.[5]

In the old, vertically integrated structures, it was often difficult to quantify the performance of individual business units. This will not be the case in an age of focused companies sharing perfect information.

Often companies become focused as a result of being acquired by private companies. In the process they often get burdened by a hefty load of acquisition debt and managers are forced to pay meticulous attention to their cash flow.

Organizational Flexibility and Resilience

A system consisting of many focused companies organized around a power node displays greater adaptability, flexibility, creativity, and robustness than a vertical stack. It can recover more easily when one part is damaged. For example. Coke's Dasani water is produced by independent bottlers. When Dasani water bottled in the United Kingdom was linked to bromate, a potentially carcinogenic chemical, the profitability of the local bottler suffered but its parent Coca-Cola and other Coca-Cola bottlers did not.[6] Should there be any problems with Aquafina attributed to a third-party bottler, PepsiCo would be shielded as well.[7]

As we have seen, flocks of focused companies are often more flexible and innovative than their vertically integrated predecessors.

Although popular accounts of inventions commonly attribute them to a single inventor, in reality the creation of a new, usable technology involves not just hundreds of individuals but dozens of companies and organizations. Many companies acting in concert are able to function far more creatively than a single vertically integrated company can. Some examples of innovation being furthered by a collection of focused companies:

- DWDM (dense wavelength division multiplexing): a technological breakthrough that has contributed to the sharp decrease in the cost of communications. (DWDM lets telecom companies send simultaneous messages in different "colors" through glass cables.) The brains and financing of dozens of companies were required to develop the many pieces of hardware and software required to implement DWDM in high-efficiency, high-reliability fiber-optic networks. In the 1990s, this group of autonomous focused companies did easily outrun the vertically integrated AT&T.

- The creation of a viable aircraft industry, as Peter Senge has noted, required not just a workable airplane but radar, movable wing flaps, and retractable landing gear. All of these were developed by autonomous focused companies. One doubts that one vertically integrated company could have done this alone.[8]

Attractiveness to Investors

Focused companies allow investors more pure plays and better risk diversification. Investors' requirements vary dramatically with regard to returns, time frames, and level of risk. They thus want to invest in companies with risk-versus-reward profiles that match the patterns they are looking for. Vertically integrated or multiproduct companies are really a prepackaged portfolio of cash flow, investment, and risk. The composition of these preassembled packages is entirely under someone else's management. Not surprisingly, investors prefer to assemble their own portfolios: they want the power to mix and match the pieces, and only the pieces that they want. Hence, shareholders have forced a large number of vertical conglomerates to sell or spin off businesses: Motorola, Time Warner, McDonald's, American Express, Cendant, CBS/Viacom, and many others.[9] Hedge funds and private equity firms have led this assault: "In public markets," reported the *Financial Times* in 2005, "big has rarely appeared less beautiful."[10]

In the past, vertical structures often provided capital more cheaply for intermediate product companies than third-party sources of financing. These days, financial markets appear to be increasingly supportive of focused companies in all stages of value chains.

Consequences for Business Models and Industry Structures

In the following chapters we will continue our discussion of the impact of transparency on the competitive environment. Here is the summary of the first-order impact of the vanishing cost of information on the structure of companies:

- End of traditional vertically integrated firms.
- Explosion of focused firms.
- End of traditional industry boundaries.
- End of traditional "characteristic industry profitability." Since industry boundaries are fading, traditional industry definitions are becoming

irrelevant, and concepts of inherent norms of industry profitability no longer apply.

- Focused companies go across traditional boundaries. We will see expanded possibilities for global horizontal competition and expansion for 21st-century companies. Focused companies can get very large and very global before decreasing returns to scale will set in (due to the falling costs of coordination, monitoring, and search).
- Focused companies compete vertically as well as horizontally for returns.
- Returns of winners (those with power nodes) versus losers (those without power nodes) will differ greatly.
- Industry structures and the behavior of market prices will be determined interactively with company decisions on all the above issues.[11]

Focus on the Power Node

As you will remember from chapter 1, power nodes are the source of profit power. Power nodes provide companies with the ability to determine their own profitability, to extract profit from others, and to generate positive sums across a distributed business arrangement. (We will talk more about trade-offs involving positive sums and distributed business arrangements in the next chapter.)

In the transparent economy, therefore, risk-adjusted returns among focused companies will vary greatly. They will no longer be correlated to the average return of a (conceptual) industry. Instead, returns among diverse focused businesses will be related to what kinds and strengths of power nodes—or profit power—they have. There will be striking differences among the returns of the companies that do and do not have power nodes. An assessment of the relative strength of a company's power node will be of decisive importance in determining its worth.

If a company does not have a power node—as for example the scores of companies that make aerospace components, and many of the companies dealing with Wal-Mart and other powerful retailers, do not—it is essential to choose wisely among business arrangement memberships and power relationships. This is the best hope for improving on retaining profits. Non–power node companies can also still offer interesting investment possibilities, as long as investors are aware of the lack of power nodes and pare down their valuations accordingly.

Even non–power node companies may have hidden profit potential. Some companies may actually have power nodes, but have failed to exercise them. Some activities can be turned into power nodes; some cannot. As we shall see, all companies will have to take a hard look at whether it is possible to focus more clearly on profit-power activities. Is it possible just to own the power node? The answer may vary depending on the circumstances—or the perspective of the analyst.

Even so, there may be a temptation to surround a power node with some remnants of a vertically integrated structure. For example, Michael Porter has suggested that it is often useful to integrate upstream or downstream to offset the bargaining power of buyers or sellers.[12] I tend to disagree. In my view, in general, if a company has a power node business, or goes out and acquires one, there is no longer any need to hold on to a weak business in addition to the power node activity. In an age of perfect information, there are fewer and fewer reasons to hold on to lower-performing units that drag down overall returns, and integration therefore is usually counterproductive. It simply dilutes the returns on your power node. Being overintegrated only makes sense in special situations, such as when there is reason to believe that the locus of power will fluctuate.

Owning all parts of a value system does not deliver maximum returns. Owning the parts with the power nodes does!

As we move toward full transparency, companies will need to make decisions about their portfolios and structures based on trade-offs among the three buckets: cost of information, performance, and positive sums. In transparency, as we have just seen, analysis of the first two types of considerations will suggest that focus is preferable to vertical integration. But what forms of business organization can capture vertical integration's positive sums? That is the subject of our next chapter.

Outsourcing and Focused Companies

At first glance, one might wonder whether the focused company model is identical to the outsourcing model in which activities are conducted by contract entities, either within the same country or elsewhere around the world. But it is not. Outsourcing is a more limited phenomenon. It describes the opportunities for flexibility and cost arbitrage gained by openness to outside service providers. Outsiders are already routinely supplying many functions needed to run a company, including customer care, IT work, accounting, and engineering.[13] The provider can be any type of entity: an individual, a vertically integrated company, a stand-alone focused company, or a company belonging to a distributed business arrangement.

Like the breakup of vertical integration, the current outsourcing trend is enabled by the falling cost of information; as noted, this has dramatically reduced the costs of coordination, monitoring, and checking. Outsourcing gives companies a wider range of choices regarding inputs and lets them practice greater cost arbitrage, including wage arbitrage for overseas knowledge workers.

But the trends that make focused companies more effective go beyond this type of arbitrage. The value of becoming focused—as opposed to remaining vertically integrated—will almost certainly continue to increase. There is a performance differential that skews heavily in favor of focused companies.

One may hear that "outsourcing is good for innovation,"[14] but that is a misconception. The benefits to innovation occur because the outsourcing arrangements are usually made to focused companies, whose single-mindedness and structure, as we saw in the previous section, improve their performance for many reasons.

Developing a corporate focus is not primarily a way to reduce costs. It is a strategy for building overall system performance, in two ways. Benefits arise first from performance efficiencies and then from the value proposition of power relationships: if one owns a company with a power node, one can extract profits from the entire distributed business system that surrounds it. In the next chapter, I will discuss the merits of distributed business arrangements in transparency.

Chapter 8

The Shape of the 21st-Century Firm

When we asked what business to own to achieve the highest returns, the answer was: everything else being equal, focus on the business with the power node. Our next decision is: how shall we best organize ourselves to maximize profitability? Can we focus ownership exclusively on the power node? Do we need to work with other companies in order to maximize profit? If so, do we need to own these ancillary pieces, or businesses, or is there a way we can control them to our benefit? How should we shape this collection of loose pieces?

Here we return to our Three Buckets Checklist (table 7.1).

As you may remember, when companies make decisions about their organizations they will have to weigh the trade-offs among three categories of considerations, which are:

I: Cost-of-information considerations for focus versus vertical
   integration
II: Performance considerations for focus versus vertical integration
III: Positive sum considerations for focus versus distributed business
   arrangements

We have already talked in chapter 7 about transparency's effects on the first two buckets. The third bucket will help us understand why a stand-alone company would choose to enter into a business arrangement and how it should shape this arrangement

As Arrow has said, "Organizations are a means of achieving the benefits of collective action in situations in which the price system fails."[1] When economists talked about collective action, they typically meant vertical integration. All Arrow's "situations in which the price system fails" are included in our buckets, either in Bucket I or in Bucket III. In transparency, the price mechanism will obviously be able to work in the Bucket I situations, which are the information-related problems such as moral hazards or lemons. As we have said, in transparency the information-related problems that used to drive stand-alone companies into vertical stacks will largely disappear. The price system can work. Therefore, there will be no need for "collective action" to fix Bucket I situations in transparency.

The same cannot be said, however, of the various types of intercompany issues, such as dealing with motley crews or hazardous markets.

In our checklist, we use the first and second buckets to resolve the question of focus versus vertical integration. In almost every case, the choice will be in favor of focus. By the time we arrive at our Category III considerations, therefore, we are no longer directly concerned with vertical integration, but the Category III considerations still need to be resolved somehow. Historically, these Category III problems have been addressed with vertical integration. In transparency, companies have many more options with regard to organization. So we ask whether a focused company should stand on its own or join in a distributed business arrangement with its partners in the value chain.

The contents of our third bucket include first the positive sum considerations that are the result of collective action and are not related to the cost of information. Take hazardous markets, for instance. These have long led to the prescription of vertical integration. If you owned every business you needed in order to create your finished product, you'd be a lot less likely to get caught short on raw materials or be let down by intermediate-goods suppliers. Your subsidiaries, meanwhile, would reap the benefits of being ensconced in a large company, and thereby sheltered from the market's rough seas. In transparency, these problems will be addressed by power relationships in distributed business arrangements involving a wide array of structures and explicit or implicit contracts. The Aramco partnership is an example of an arrangement that was run by informal, tacit contracts.

Our third bucket also includes a new list of positive sum items, namely those that relate to the benefits of association with sources of profit power. Collective action can realize these potential sums. These positive sum items are the "carrots" of the power relationships in the distributed arrangements.

These carrots are closely related to the sources of profit power, the power nodes. The contents of our third bucket are as follows:

III: *Positive sum considerations for focus versus distributed business arrangements:*
  1. *Benefits of collective action not related to the cost of information, e.g.,*
     - solving problems of motley crews
     - solving problems of hazardous markets (e.g., high variance or, worse, temporary shortages)
     - solving problems of lack of complete insurance against any and all contingencies for all possible states of the world
  2. *Benefits of association with sources of profit power, that is, power nodes:*
     - capturing and sharing externalities related to brand and reputation
     - access to proprietary ingredients or other products with inelastic supply curves with hold-up potential
     - capturing and sharing regulatory privileges or expertise
     - access to focused financial resources and insurance capability and potential for Pareto-optimal reallocation of risk
     - access to customers locked in by high switching costs and other path dependencies
     - capturing advantages associated with proprietary processes
     - access to powerful distribution gateways
     - capturing or avoiding monopoly treatment associated with dominant position in a layer
     - capturing advantages associated with increasing mutual utility properties
     - capturing information advantages associated with aikido assets
     - capturing advantages of association with filters or brokers
     - capturing advantages of association with hubs

We will give examples of these elements further on in this chapter. First, let us look further into the nature of the modern firm.

In most cases, as we have seen, perfect information will break down the barriers that prevented companies from being simultaneously focused, high-performing, and independent. However, transparency will not automatically solve the problems of motley crews, of all hazardous markets, or of matters related to benefits of association with sources of profit power.

For these reasons, we can expect that focused companies in transparency will continue to pursue collective action, and they will devise a great many new and innovative distributed business models to accomplish their goals. Whatever forms these arrangements take, nearly all will be held together by power relationships that create net benefits for all participants.

We will refer to this new archetype for the firm as a distributed business arrangement. Here is a definition:

> **DISTRIBUTED BUSINESS ARRANGEMENT (aka THE 21ST-CENTURY FIRM):** an entity composed of focused companies connected to other companies in an array of possible business structures that are controlled through a nexus of power relationships rather than by ownership. A distributed business arrangement may be global. (Here, the word *distributed* refers to arrangements among entities that are separate, autonomous, but linked).

Distributed business arrangement (or *21st-century firm*) is a broad term for a flexible model, sometimes global, that accommodates a wide variety of business arrangements, any of which will overcome obstacles and capture benefits in both subcategories of positive sum considerations. We will examine these subcategories in more detail later on in this chapter. In distributed business arrangements, long-term power relationships, once possible only within rigid vertically integrated structures or among a very few partners, will be maintained with increasing fluidity and responsiveness across many companies.

In the past, companies were often faced with (or at least many texts claimed they were faced with) a binary choice: they either relied on markets, operating entirely "hands off," or they organized their activities in the straitjacket of a vertically integrated entity (see figure 8.1).

In transparency, companies have more degrees of freedom. They can choose a design anywhere along a continuum between hardwired vertical integration and outright reliance on markets. The middle ground provides a plethora of choices for corporate design.

When we translate it into a graphic (see figure 8.2), this new theory of the firm looks very different from the old one. As we saw in chapter 7, traditional thinking has envisioned only two options for a business model: the solitary focused company operating alone in markets or the vertically integrated company that has acquired other companies in its value chain in order to fend off marketplace uncertainties. In transparency, these two choices will be seen as extremes, and the bulk of the organizational action will take place along the continuum between them. We can envision this continuum as a two-way arrow along which companies create arrangements that bring them the optimum mix of benefits from the focused and vertically integrated options at the poles. Whenever a focused company enters into any of the various distributed business arrangements possible along the continuum, power relationships will assume an essential role in the business relationship.

Figure 8.1

The past alternatives for business models

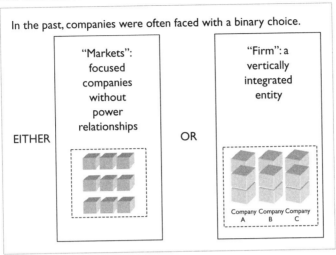

In the past, companies were often faced with a binary choice.

EITHER

"Markets": focused companies without power relationships

OR

"Firm": a vertically integrated entity

Company A Company B Company C

Figure 8.2

The new continuum for business models

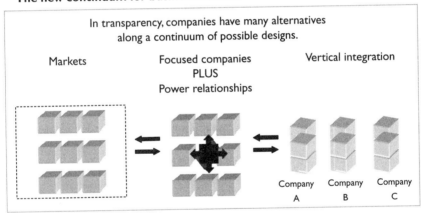

In transparency, companies have many alternatives along a continuum of possible designs.

Markets

Focused companies
PLUS
Power relationships

Vertical integration

Company A Company B Company C

Power is the glue that holds distributed business arrangements together. Profit power companies may use threats of exile from their power node to extract a substantial chunk of the returns from the weaker parties in an arrangement, but they must also offer rewards. As Arrow has pointed out, "the existence of sanctions is not a sufficient condition for obedience to authority."[2] The weak players in transparency's distributed business models will yield to the mighty—but only in exchange for positive sum benefits.

This phenomenon has been observed clearly in industries such as copper, aluminum, oil, electronic components, soft drinks, and Hollywood movie production. This is the essence of power relationships and their durability.

The companies that control power nodes will become the dominant force in multidimensional arrays or nexuses of other companies; in the landscape of transparency, these arrays are likely to replace what we think of as industries or companies today. One way we can conceptualize this new multidimensional business terrain is to envision it as a collection of cubes (figure 8.3).

In figure 8.3, each of the smaller cubes represents a single focused company. Any group of three cubes that form a vertical column in this figure might once have been joined together to make up a vertically integrated company—a "vertical stack." The third dimension that we now add is that of "industry." We can imagine each of the three vertical planes in figure 8.3 as describing a separate industry. In the old days, few business relationships existed in any form outside of the vertical stack, and there was virtually no crossing the boundaries of any given industry.

In transparency, the spatial relationships will be entirely different from the past. In the age of perfect information, any smaller cube—or focused

Figure 8.3

Transparency's three-dimensional business landscape

Each small cube represents a single focused company. One company, shown here in black, can make distributed business arrangements with others, no matter in which industry or level.

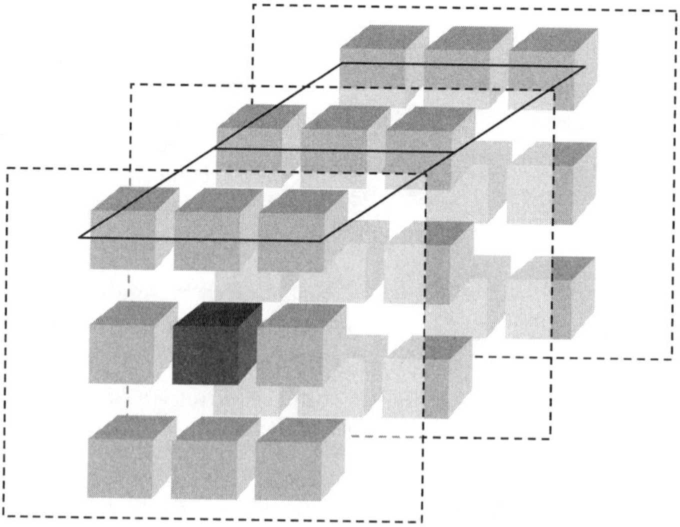

company—may have a relationship with any other. Focused companies newly liberated from old, vertically integrated structures will have to form new relationships with cubes that may once have sat above or below them under the same ownership in a very specific value chain. They may also forge relationships with focused companies that were once part of another comparable vertical stack.

Focused companies may also be able to produce goods that are useful to companies in a variety of industries, as Microsoft does with a number of its products. If so, they can cut across a number of industries (through all the vertical planes of the cube) to occupy an entire horizontal layer. In figure 8.3 this horizontal plane is marked by solid black lines. As you can see, the opportunities for relationships extend in all directions—up, down, across, and even diagonally. This model will be doubly instructive, because in transparency, the universe of potential business allies is the same multidimensional universe as the universe of potential competitors. In transparency, the fortunes of each focused company will depend on its ability to seize its fair share of the returns from competitors in multiple directions and industries. This is a very different picture than we had in the world before perfect information.

In transparency, competition will be an integral part of all business arrangements. One must not harbor rosy notions of a federation of companies in a distributed business model as a "co-opetition" party[3] or a "cooperative constellation."[4] Within a distributed business arrangement, the fight for collectively available returns—even those that have been jointly created—will be vicious.

There are already many noteworthy harbingers of distributed business arrangements. Unbeknownst to consumers, there may in fact be numerous companies involved in producing a single branded end product. For example, as we know, it is not the Pepsi-Cola and Coca-Cola parent companies that put beverages in bottles or deliver soda to grocery stores. Toyota does not own the manufacturers of its engine components or electronics. Nike does not manufacture sneakers. Marriott does not actually own hotels. Nortel does not manufacture much telecommunications equipment, and Sony Ericsson does not make cell phones;[5] in both instances, Flextronics handles the job.[6] Likewise, HP, IBM, and Cisco have passed on much of their manufacturing to Sanmina-SCI.

Though each of these allied companies is constitutionally independent, the working relationships in these cases are far from hands-off. It is sometimes said that a modern airplane is actually a squadron of individual parts—all made by independent companies, but flying in close formation. The same could be said about each of the products or services mentioned here. They are all designed and delivered by companies that work closely together—but when there are sustained and extraordinary profits, there is one company at the core, controlling the power node.

For an example of how creatively transparency's new distributed business arrangements may be structured, let us examine the success of Vizio, a California-based company with a single focus: producing low-priced flat-panel TVs. In the spring of 2008, the company was the subject of a lengthy profile in the *Wall Street Journal*.[7] Vizio was launched in 2002, when its founder, William Wang, realized that many of the components of flat-screen TVs, which were selling for around $10,000, were the same as the components in flat computer screens—and those were components he could buy in bulk, cheaply, from suppliers in Taiwan. Typically, flat-screen TV components had been made in-house by computer-electronics giants in Korea and Japan, but in the computer industry, as the *Journal* explained, those same parts had become "commoditized." As we have said, cheap information enables the creation of markets for intermediate goods. That can give companies like Vizio an opening.

Wang was convinced he could buy components, hire a manufacturer, and deliver flat-screen TVs at half the price that famous manufacturers like Phillips and Sony (which were vertically integrated from R&D to marketing) were charging. Over time, Wang won over powerful U.S. distributors like Costco, BJ's Wholesale Club, and Wal-Mart's Sam's Club. Based on a promise of huge volume, Wang was able to set up a groundbreaking relationship with AmTRAN Technology, a longtime contract manufacturer for companies like Sony and Sharp. The *Journal* labeled the AmTRAN-Vizio arrangement a "new business model" for the TV industry—a distributed business arrangement, as it happens. Wang sold a 23 percent stake in Vizio to AmTRAN, and as a result, Vizio achieved favored status. According to the *Journal*, "AmTran sometimes swallows shipping costs and pushes component suppliers to ensure Vizio's products are high quality and on time. AmTran now gets about 80% of its revenue from Vizio. In turn, Vizio sources as many as 85% of its TVs from AmTran." Wang has since sold another 8 percent of his company to another electronics manufacturer. As you can see, these relationships are all about positive sums.

So far, this is working: in just five years, Vizio has racked up an amazing 12.4 percent share of the flat-screen market in the United States, only a fraction behind Samsung and Sony. Nevertheless, savvy readers may wonder: where is the power node in all this? (If you are one of those, you may be well equipped to make extraordinary profits!) The fact is, for all of its success, Vizio does not appear to have a power node—although its revenues climbed to just under $2 billion in 2007, its margins, by some reports,[8] are only 2 percent, and critics speculate that its extraordinary growth may not be sustainable over the long term. The *Journal* warns: "Vizio may face a shortage of

LCD panels. Neither Vizio nor AmTran produce the flat panels themselves, and the companies that make them may hoard them to sell under their own brands." The article quotes a top Sony executive who argues that Vizio's lack of in-house manufacturing and development resources will hold it back. " 'Vizio doesn't have the kind of resources and money to lock up [flat panel] supply,' he says. 'I think they're in trouble.' "

Sony seems to adhere to the old notion of vertical integration as a defense against the vagaries of the supply chain—but at the same time, Sony, Philips, and Matsushita (Panasonic) were all thrown into disarray as Vizio exploited cost differentials in the value chain. Sony's TV unit is not profitable, as the *Journal* said, and both Phillips and Matsushita had to restructure their U.S. TV businesses. For now, Vizio—launched by a man who mortgaged his house and borrowed from friends to raise the $600,000 startup capital—is winning the battle. Still, Vizio's lack of a power node suggests it has struggles to come, and, in keeping with the new competitive dynamics of transparency, the biggest threats to its returns may come from partners in its own value chain. Vizio hopes that its substantial purchases of large LCD panels will give it the leverage to guarantee an ongoing supply of the more popular midsize panels as well, the *Journal* reports—but at what price?

As you can imagine, getting focused and entering into a distributed arrangement is not in itself a guarantee of making sustained and extraordinary profits. The real trick is developing a power node and using it to deploy focused companies within distributed business arrangements. Managing the power relationships in a distributed business arrangement isn't necessarily easy, either for the companies with power nodes or those without, but it is an essential art. The ability to structure, maintain, and exploit these competitive relationships will be an important focus of business management in the 21st century.[9]

Now, let us look more closely at some of the specific positive sum considerations that the distributed business arrangement is intended to address.

Benefits of Collective Action That Are Not Related to the Cost of Information

Solving Problems of Motley Crews

Companies involved in long-term distributed business arrangements are likely to develop reliable and productive relationships with partners—hence, they also alleviate some of the risks of association with the "motley crew."

In *Creative Industries*, Richard Caves writes at length about the motley crew problem: the difficulties inherent in assembling a team for the first time. Caves has derived many useful lessons from his studies of Hollywood. A modern-day movie producer must bring together an ad hoc assemblage of talent with different skills, techniques, and ways of thinking—and any one of them might turn out to be a weak link that diminishes the whole.[10] It is impossible to know for sure how the participants will function individually, or if they will work together effectively as a group. Needless to say, many filmmakers try to make repeated use of people who work out well—a director may collaborate with the same editor for decades, say, or a star may rely on a favorite makeup person. Consequently, one could think of the overall production function as "multiplicative." Working relationships aren't dictated by long-term contract or ownership, as they were back in Hollywood's heyday, but they can be replicated in ways that recapture some of the efficiencies of the old studio system.

Similarly, the focused remnants of vertically integrated firms will have reason to worry about the performance of important partners, who may fall above or below them on the value chain. Indeed, in some cases, these partners may once have shared the same ownership. A notable case in point involves British Airways, which spun off its Gate Gourmet catering service as a non–power node, low-return business—one that continued to service British Airways flights. In 2005, when the caterer's new owners cut back on staff, the fired workers' former colleagues at British Airways went out on a wildcat sympathy strike that threw the airline's operations into chaos for several days. As we can see, even the seemingly minor parts of a distributed business arrangement can cause a power node company great trouble if they are not properly attended to.

Indeed, in a world of focused companies coming together to produce finished goods, the performance of third parties at every level will have an influence on the quality, pricing, and profitability of almost any product or service. Recently, for example, pharmaceutical companies in Europe and the United States have suffered fallout from unreliable suppliers in China. In early 2008, Baxter International was forced to launch a major recall of its brand of heparin, a blood-thinning medication, which had caused a wave of illness and even death among users in the United States. The problems were traced to a contaminant in the active ingredient, which had been produced at a Chinese factory that was a joint venture of Wisconsin-based Scientific Protein Laboratories and a Chinese partner.

Solving Problems of Hazardous Markets

Distributed business arrangements may provide significant benefits for companies or industries confronted with the problems of hazardous markets. This term refers to the expected distribution of the behavior of the market's prices over time. A market is called hazardous when variances of prices are large, or when distributions are not normal.

Coke and Pepsi and their bottlers provide a simple, proven template for the exploitation of a power node in the context of a distributed business arrangement.

The oil and copper industries illustrate that distributed business arrangements may provide a buffer against hazardous markets, and that power relationships will fall apart if there is no sharing of positive sums, as I have described in "Unraveling of Market Regimes."

Consider the changes in the oil industry between approximately 1972 and 1983. In the 1970s, a viable market for crude oil hardly existed.[11] The spot market, for what it was worth, was very thin. Less than 5 percent of all oil moved at the open-market prices on the spot markets. Most of the crude was sold by oil-producing countries to oil companies on the basis of long-term contracts. The prices in these contracts were called government selling prices (GSPs). Throughout the middle 1970s, the prices of crude were relatively stable, especially for partners in Aramco, which was jointly owned by the Saudi Arabian government and leading oil companies. The largest oil producers contributed to the maintenance of a generally stable price that was lower than the spot market price at its height and higher than the spot market price at its bottom. As a result, oil-producing countries benefited when spot crude prices dropped, and oil companies felt less pain when they rose. This implicit arrangement insulated both sides from the fluctuations of the market. Even if the GSPs resulted in the same weighted average price as a weighted average spot market price over an extended period, the reduction in uncertainty and price volatility created a positive sum for all parties. It was, in effect, a distributed business arrangement. The distributed business arrangement between the oil countries and the oil companies defeated the problems of a hazardous market.

As long as this positive sum was divided in a manner that the parties could live with, and as long as both sides lived up to their end of the deal, all was well. As we will soon see, these types of power relationships will continue as long as all parties feel that they benefit. If not, the arrangements may fall apart, and industries may move toward the extremes of either relying entirely on markets or returning to vertical integration.

In 1978, several non-Saudi OPEC countries broke their side of the bargain when spot market prices ran well ahead of the GSPs with the disturbances in Iran. Several countries cut back on the volume of oil they were willing to sell at GSPs and increased prices on the remainder to the spot market level. Spot prices continued to rise until early 1981, and so did OPEC's GSPs. Starting in 1980, the oil picture changed. Major new reserves in such places as Mexico and the North Sea came into full production. The spot price dropped dramatically. This time, it was the oil companies (except for the Aramco partnership) that broke their end of the bargain, abandoning GSPs to snap up cheaper crude. The buyers had discovered what their long-term relationships with the oil-producing countries were worth. They had observed that nearly all the producers except Saudi Arabia had behaved opportunistically, maximizing their short-term profits at the expense of the buyers. Starting in 1981, the oil companies called for concessions on GSPs, effectively demanding spot market prices. Countries that refused to give price concessions, like Nigeria, saw a big drop in volumes.

In the middle of 1982, I took stock of the state of the oil market. I interviewed oil traders in Rotterdam and London, studied patterns of oil trades, and inquired about terms in supply contracts. As I learned, oil-producing countries had become very creative about getting their oil sold. They extended credit periods and allowed processing and barter deals. They tried to attract buyers while trying to obfuscate about just how low their prices really were. Discounts and spot-market-related formulas became common even on long-term volume deals.

As one company after another started to buy oil from new sources on the spot market or demanded spot market prices from old sources, and as old sources conceded, there was a snowball effect. With more players, the spot market began to work more effectively. It was at this point that I gave my presentation about these developments at Shell Centre, and started the process of convincing the company that oil *was* a commodity.

Over the subsequent year, the wild price swings gave way to lower variance that was reflective of greater volume and a greater number of participants. The spot market was no longer wildly hazardous. This reduced the need for the distributed business arrangements that were already teetering because of the one-sided "cheating" over the past decade. Most of the arrangements were abandoned, and the bulk of the industry moved rapidly toward market pricing.

A similar history played out earlier in the copper industry, as I described in my PhD thesis as well.[12] From 1945 until the late 1970s, copper buyers and sellers maintained a distributed business arrangement. Copper was sold at so-called producer prices. The producer price was less volatile than the spot market price, which in some periods benefited buyers and in others benefited sellers. But this longstanding pricing arrangement, like the ones in the oil industry, would eventually go off the rails when one side behaved opportunistically.

These histories were being replayed in the steel industry in 2008. Rather than risk continuing reliance on open markets for its raw ingredients, ArcelorMittal, the world's largest steelmaker by volume, is entering into long-term relationships with iron ore producers worldwide. The company has long-standing relationships in Indonesia, and it is fostering iron mining in Senegal. In April 2008, as reported by Reuters, it announced a deal with the Brazilian firm Companhia Vale do Rio Doce, which has agreed to supply about 480 tons of iron ore and pellets to ArcelorMittal's plants over the next 10 years. The company said that these contracts were the largest ever signed between a steel company and an iron ore supplier.[13]

As Richard Caves has explained so lucidly in *Creative Industries*,[14] similar dynamics can be observed in the movie industry as well. The arrangements between studios and movie stars have moved from vertical integration (in the heyday of the studio system in the first half of the 20th century) to what amounted to spot market contracts (in the years after World War II) to the current system of long-term relationships that help deal with the motley crew problem. Hollywood also makes sophisticated use of explicit and implicit options contracts that are very versatile in letting the future unfold.

As these examples suggest, the way that companies design their distributed business arrangements will have a dramatic impact on the structure of their industries. In instances such as these, we see how business models and markets coevolve. One company's decision may change the behavior of the product's price. This may make the market appear more or less "hazardous." When companies exit the market in favor of an arrangement with producers, market prices may become more volatile; when more companies participate in the market, the market pricing may become less volatile.[15] This in turn will encourage more companies to rely on market transactions, thereby abandoning their vertically integrated structures or long-standing power relationships.

As we enter transparency, hazardous markets may become increasingly common in a range of marketplaces. Powerlaw distributions—with their 80–20 splits and absence of means—are *inherently* hazardous. Thanks to interdependent decision making, we are likely to see powerlaw distributions in everything from financial markets to consumer choices of product features.

The details of the distributed business arrangements that are put in place to deal with hazardous markets and other Category III considerations will vary greatly. The arrangements between producers and companies in the oil and copper industries were long-standing, but tacit and informal. In the beverage and telecommunications industries there are similar long-term arrangements with explicit contracts, and in the entertainment industry there is a set of long-term relationships guided by a sophisticated array of implicit options and conditional contracts. There are numerous other alternatives to give structure to a power relationship, including franchising, cross-ownership arrangements (à la Vizio), and many types of contracts. All are based on an understanding of positive sum benefits.

As I have noted, perfect information will facilitate contracts that can be extremely detailed and creative in providing for the uncertainties of a project- and arrangement-based future.[16] At the same time, distributed business arrangements may make it possible to be less formal about contract matters, since power relationships can keep partners together (without spelling out all the terms) over extended periods of time and through many eventualities. If parties to the transaction renege on the deal, perfect information makes it much easier to spread the word about bad behavior.

Benefits of Association with Sources of Profit Power, That Is, Power Nodes

Many autonomous, focused companies will choose to enter distributed business arrangements based on ongoing power relationships because the distributed business arrangements generate positive sums. Leading companies not only use power nodes to rule their global business arrangements and maximize returns for themselves, they also improve the prospects for the non-power members of the group. Non–power node companies hope to get a share of the positive sums generated by a company with a power node. This prospect of shared positive sums provides an essential incentive for long-term relationships among companies that might otherwise respond on a deal-by-deal basis to the highest bidder.

This understanding is critical to our forecasts for the structure of 21st-century companies. Generally speaking, companies will *not* form groups or participate in long-term arrangements unless there is a *net positive sum* for the group and unless each member of the group gets at least a fraction of the overall net positive sum. As we have said, power node companies may succeed in laying off risky or capital-intensive aspects of their business and at the same time extracting the lion's share of profits from the non–power node companies. But their arrangement partners will accept such treatment only if at least a morsel of the positive sum gets tossed their way.

In most cases, the positive sums for the non–power node companies in a distributed business arrangement will arise directly from some aspect of the lead company's power node. We will look at all 12 power nodes in detail in chapter 13.

The View from Mars

What might the new topography of companies and industries look like in the transparent age? In 1991, economist Herbert Simon described the then prevailing business scene by asking his readers to imagine "a mythical visitor from Mars" traveling to earth in a spacecraft "equipped with a telescope that reveals social structures." What if another Martian were to fly over in 2020? What would our extraterrestrial see?

Simon's Martian wore goggles that revealed the earth's organizational structures in terms of colors. When vertically integrated firms appeared, they were seen as solid green fields. Market transactions showed up as red lines connecting the green firms. Peering down, Simon's Martian observed similar patterns around the globe. No matter whether Simon's ET was flying over the United States, the then Soviet Union, a far less urban China, or the European community, "the greater part of the space below it would be within the green areas.... Vertically integrated organizations would be the dominant feature of the landscape. A message sent back to Mars describing the scene would speak of 'large green areas interconnected by red lines.'"[17]

A few years from now, the Martian will be offered a new set of goggles. In addition to the old green and red, the ET will now be able to detect power relationships, which will appear as blue, two-way arrows. The ET will note instantly that the huge green swaths are gone; the large integrated firms will have largely disappeared. Instead, the Martian will speak of seeing many smaller, autonomous green dots, many of them still linked by red lines showing market transactions. Above all, the Martian will see oceans of blue arrows depicting power relationships.

The Martian will marvel at the vast numbers of blue, two-way arrows. How the Earthling economy has changed! Companies with strong power nodes have boldly reorganized their activities into global distributed business arrangements that maximize returns and leverage corporate resources. Our ET, of course, will instantly grasp what many humans may be slow to accept: that power nodes and profit power are the legitimate economics concepts that jump out of a field of widespread transparency. In messages beamed home, the ET will observe that focused companies in nexuses of power relationships make this ever-changing world go round.

The Link with Industrial Organization Theory

In this chapter, I have in effect proposed a new theory of the firm. This builds on the research that I started in 1981, first when I studied the copper industry while at Harvard, and then on my work involving the oil industry while I was at Shell, and finally on my dissertation, "Unraveling of Market Regimes." I am not alone in believing that the valuable work on firms by Ronald Coase, Oscar Williamson,[18] and others needed to be updated for a transparent world. Discussions about the "new world" structure of companies include the views expressed in *Blown to Bits* (by Philip Evans and Thomas Wurster), *The Future of Work* (by Thomas Malone), and *The Company of the Future* (by Frances Cairncross). Compared to the discussion in this chapter, these works have focused more narrowly on the implications of information-cost trade-offs per the Coase model—that is, they are focused on our Category I considerations. They predict outcomes based on the trade-off of internal versus external coordination costs. On this basis, they predict the emergence of loose bits, which henceforth deal with each other only in arm's-length, market-based transactions. Several other authors do mention one of the Category II performance-related reasons for creating focused companies, namely the motivational benefits of freeing the pieces. They describe the results as "loose hierarchies" or "cooperating constellations," however, rather than imagining them in a distributed business model. Instead of using one or two criteria to determine corporate design, I believe it wiser to apply the Three Buckets Checklist trade-offs listed in full in chapter 7.

Students of organizational theory will also note that I have de-emphasized the term *hierarchy*. I avoid it because it has been applied with such a wide variety of meanings. In *Hierarchies and Markets* by Oliver Williamson,[19] hierarchy means "vertically integrated firm." For him, "hierarchy" and "firm" are interchangeable with "rigid, hard-wired, vertical structures." In contrast, in *The Future of Work*, Malone uses the phrase "loose hierarchies" in connection with pure reliance on markets—the opposite of what Williamson is talking about when he refers to hierarchies. Malone's end state consists of a jumble of independent, focused activities without any implicit or explicit contracts or relationships between them.[20] Others, such as Gerard Fairtlough in *The Three Ways of Getting Things Done*, invoke "hierarchies" in discussions about internal governance. In that context, hierarchies are tools that make companies' internal operations more effective.

Chapter 9

Three-Dimensional Competition

What competitive threats do we face, and how do we win? And how does profit power relate to this? In transparency, the rise in focused companies will mean that there are many more entities engaged in competitive contact than ever before. Competition will take place in at least three dimensions, and it will transcend all previous geographic and industry divisions. These 3-D battles will pit power node against power node. Rather than fighting for market share, or even simply for income, companies will battle for economic profits—to maximize their risk-adjusted returns over time.

We will talk more about each of transparency's three conceptual dimensions[1] in a moment. But in brief, the dimensions of competition are:

- *Vertical:* Companies in the same value chain compete with each other for the greatest share of returns.
- *Horizontal:* Focused companies battle for market share against other focused companies that do the same thing they do (inside their traditional industry boundaries).
- *Horizontal across traditional industry boundaries.* As industry boundaries fade away, companies that are theoretically in different types of businesses may find themselves facing unexpected rivals for slices of horizontal market share.

This is the multifaceted universe of competition that is described by our cube diagram (figure 9.1).

We have already discussed this cube at length in chapter 8, and as you may remember, one essential point is that in transparency, the worlds of potential allies and potential competitors are one and the same. The scope of competition is therefore very different than it was in the days when the dominant model involved vertical stacks facing off within readily identifiable industries (figure 9.2).

As we can see from the cube diagram in figure 9.1, competition in transparency will take place on an exponentially increasing number of fronts. As we observed in previous chapters, in transparency, focused companies, often in distributed business arrangements, will compete fiercely in new markets for intermediate goods as well as in existing markets for finished goods and services.

As a result, in transparency, competition will be an inherent aspect of virtually every business relationship—and so will questions of power. Indeed, competitions among companies are likely to take place in even more

Figure 9.1

Transparency's three-dimensional competitive landscape

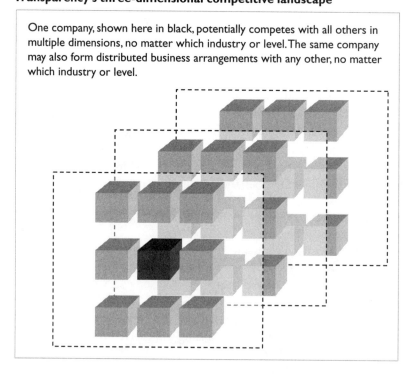

One company, shown here in black, potentially competes with all others in multiple dimensions, no matter which industry or level. The same company may also form distributed business arrangements with any other, no matter which industry or level.

Figure 9.2

"Old" competitive battles: Similar vertically integrated companies fought for market share within well-defined industries

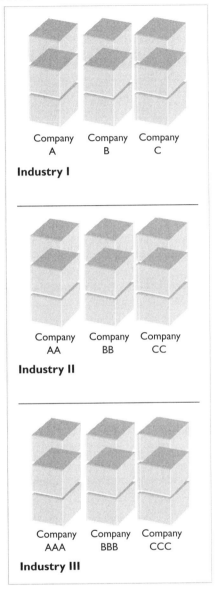

Company   Company   Company
A   B   C

Industry I

Company   Company   Company
AA   BB   CC

Industry II

Company   Company   Company
AAA   BBB   CCC

Industry III

dimensions than the three that we have outlined above, but for the sake of simplicity, we will limit our discussion to three dimensions in this chapter.

This 3-D competitive perspective is a distinct departure from competitive analyses that are oriented toward the single dimension of horizontal competition for market share within a well-defined industry, as illustrated in figure 9.2. This 3-D perspective does build on Porter's five-forces framework for industry analysis and strategy development in *Competitive Advantage*. Porter's framework also moves beyond purely horizontal considerations. Porter recognizes vertical competition, if only implicitly, in that he says that one must assess pressures from suppliers and buyers in order to evaluate a company's overall strength.

This book's 3-D competitive approach takes on board the lessons of the five-forces framework and advances it by presenting a new view of competitive battles that is appropriate for our era: first, by noting that in transparency, with the competitive environment consisting of focused companies, we can expect that these vertical pressures will be the key determinants of competitive success; second, by defining competitive success in terms of superior risk-adjusted returns rather than in terms of market share; and third, by focusing on the sources of profitability, the power nodes, as the determinants of such success.

My prescription for dealing with vertical competition differs from Porter's because of my emphasis on maximizing returns. I believe that a firm should not integrate forward or backward if market power is present among its customers or suppliers, as Porter would suggest, because the integration of weaker (i.e., lower returns) pieces into stronger (i.e., higher returns) pieces tends to drag down the average returns of the strong pieces. If you are the leader of a company that lacks strong profit power, and your company is at the mercy of a vertical competitor with a strong source of profit power, do not merely seek to merge with this stronger firm. It is all right to seize a strong power node competitor. But do not continue to own the non-power pieces if your aim is to maximize returns. (Boise Cascade, you will remember, *sold* its low-power paper products and forest businesses when it bought OfficeMax.) You may choose to orchestrate and control non-power pieces as part of your global business model—but only if this adds to your own returns.

In transparency, every company will have to design a 3-D competitive strategy. Similarly, when we make investment decisions, we will have to evaluate how well companies are performing—or could perform—in transparency's 3-D competition. As part of the template for winning in 3-D competition that we will apply in chapter 17, I have devised a grid that companies can use to plot their competitive position—or relative power node strength (RPS)—in each of the three dimensions. Vertical positions are evaluated based on the relative strength of power nodes, while RPS in the horizontal dimensions is measured as relative market share.

Let us now look in more detail at each of the three competitive dimensions.

Vertical Competition

Vertical competition will rise to a position of paramount importance in transparency. Vertical battles are fought among companies that might once have been part of comparable vertically integrated structures. Each company in a sequence of intermediate products or services is fighting to cut out the largest possible piece of the profits at every stage of the multidimensional process from inspiration to finished product. You encounter "buyer" opponents in the markets of your product, and "seller" opponents in the markets for your inputs.

In transparency, returns will far more often be determined by interactions with vertical competitors than by any dealings with customers or look-alike horizontal adversaries. The relationships of Pepsi, Coca-Cola, and their bottlers (see chapter 1) are a great example of vertical competition. As we learned from that, in vertical competition, power nodes will be the decisive determinants of profitability and risk. The company that controls a power node can hold on to its own returns and capture returns from both upstream and downstream opponents. (We will look at power nodes in detail starting in chapter 12.) Even within distributed business arrangements, vertical competition for collectively available returns will be brutal.

Parker Hannifin provides another powerful example of how one can use profit power to increase returns in vertical competition. Parker Hannifin is a maker of industrial parts such as valve and jet engine seals. A number of its parts are key ingredients to other companies making components for airplane engines and other products—and for some of them, there are no competing manufacturers. For many years, Parker Hannifin priced its products with no regard for how essential they were to the companies that bought them. Eventually its management reviewed this pricing strategy and increased its markups on those products for which it was a key supplier. These products represented a special-ingredient power node (power node #2). Between 2002 and 2007, the company raised prices on these products an average of 5 percent with no backlash—clear evidence that Parker Hannifin had profit power over its customers in the value chain. The result? In 2007, the *Wall Street Journal* reported that "the company says its new pricing approach boosted operating income by $200 million since 2002. That helped Parker's net income soar to $673 million last year from $130 million in 2002. Now, the company's return on invested capital has risen from 7% in 2002 to 21% in 2006."[2]

When Parker Hannifin raised its prices, it extracted profits from other companies or customers down the line. In other words, it was able to exercise its profit power to win in vertical competition. As we will see when we explore the individual power nodes in chapter 13, there are a multitude of ways that companies can use power node to win in vertical competitive battles.

Horizontal Competition (inside Traditional Industries)

This is the kind of competition many textbooks describe: a straightforward fight among companies producing similar finished products for a larger slice of horizontal market share. We will continue to see this kind of competition in transparency—but now the fights will be global, as perfect information allows increasing numbers of narrowly focused companies to expand their reach around the world. In another shift, some of the fiercest horizontal competition will take place among companies making intermediate goods.

Although vertical power positions will often be the most important factor in transparency's 3-D competitions for returns, horizontal relative market share is both more familiar and more readily measured than a vertical power position. Business leaders may be tempted to focus their competitive strategy primarily on horizontal market share—just as investors may be tempted to give it special credence as they evaluate company prospects—but this would be shortsighted.

In the past, large relative horizontal market share was seen as a clear indicator of a consumer product's profitability. This is no longer necessarily so. In recent years, leading retailers—Wal-Mart, Costco, Home Depot, and so forth—have used their distribution clout (power node #7) to diminish the profit margins of many consumer-product suppliers, even those with extremely popular brands (power node #1). In order to assess how a contemporary consumer business can actually perform in terms of returns, it is often more important to know the terms of its relationship with major vertical competitors than it is to have exact figures on horizontal market share.

This is not to say, however, that large horizontal market share will not be useful. In some cases, it is a significant factor in helping to create three-dimensional power to gain and hold profits. This has been true for Microsoft and Intel, one a maker of operating systems and the other a supplier of computer chips. Both companies have a power node in increasing mutual utility (power node #9): the greater the number of customers that use their products, the greater the value those products have. In Microsoft's case, the snowball effect has been so huge that something like 90 percent of desktop computers now run on Microsoft's software. Any PC that lacks compatibility with either Microsoft or Intel is now at a near-fatal disadvantage. Consequently, it is the computer manufacturers that are at the weak end of the multilayer vertical battle among power nodes. Numerous desktop makers have gone out of business over the years, and even the returns for IBM's former PC business were not rosy, but both Microsoft and Intel have maintained comfortable profit margins throughout. This is an example of the distribution players not having enough clout—that is, not having strong enough power nodes—to hollow out the profits of the intermediate players in the value chain, in this case Intel and Microsoft.

Although for the most part competition for horizontal market share may look like familiar territory, we can expect to see some significant new wrinkles in those markets with many participants that meet the four conditions for powerlaw dynamics. These dynamics will have significant implications both for competitive strategy and for returns. In transparency, the preferential attachment dynamics associated with hubs will be an extremely potent weapon in developing horizontal market share. Moreover, products that achieve broad market share as a result of hub dynamics may be largely immune to traditional forms of competition involving price. Preferential attachment phenomena may allow companies the luxury of maintaining higher profit margins for their hub products, and as a result those products may have a distinct advantage in vertical competitions for returns. We will describe all these dynamics in much greater detail in our next chapter, in which we cover the wide range of changes we can expect to see in marketplaces that have been transformed by transparency.

Horizontal Competition across Industry Boundaries

When industry boundaries fade away, the competitive universe expands to include previously unthinkable rivals. Apple is moving to supply entertainment programming for its whole range of electronic devices—which means everyone from TV networks to Netflix will now have to contend with Apple as a rival. And Microsoft, in addition to supplying operating systems for PCs, has branched into selling software for television systems, game boxes, mobile phones, and Internet search—all businesses that, theoretically, are well outside the bounds of the traditional PC computer industry. In 2000, AT&T was dismayed to learn that Microsoft wanted to be in charge of the software on mobile phones. Today, BlackBerry should keep an eye on iPod. The list will go on. We can expect many more battles like this.

Power Node Battles and Relative Power Node Strength (RPS)

In transparency, every three-dimensional competitive battle is a conflict between power nodes. The outcome will be determined by the relative strength of the competing power nodes. Just as we looked at underlying drivers in order to understand present and future economic conditions, anyone hoping to predict the victors in power node battles will need to consider the trends in the landscape of 3-D competition in which the company operates. You can predict the outcome of the power node battle—i.e., who will get the largest share of the profits—if you map out the relative power nodes strength (RPS) of the competitors.

What follows are a few illuminating examples of power node battles.

Estée Lauder

According to the *Wall Street Journal*, longtime CEO Leonard Lauder built the cosmetics firm's success by forging "deals that secured prime real estate in every major U.S. department store at a time when the big retailers controlled the high-end beauty business." Meanwhile, Lauder built the company's brands (power node #1) into such powerhouses that Lauder was actually able to control the stores' display spaces and dictate the timing of promotions. That strategy worked for decades, but Estée Lauder's Relative Power Node Strength (RPS) began to pale as Federated Department Stores (now Macy's, Inc.) began to snap up chains, including Macy's, Bloomingdale's, Marshall Field, and Filene's. Macy's, Inc. now has dominant position in a layer (power node #8), which allows it to exert considerable profit power over suppliers. As the *Journal* writes, "The new Goliath shuttered dozens of outlets and began squeezing suppliers like Estée Lauder for better terms."[3] As a result, Estée Lauder's earnings and stock price fell. The company has been exploring new niches where the strength of its brand will still hold sway, among them one-brand stores, Internet activities, and international expansion.

Seadrill

Oil companies have often seemed almighty. Using a power node analysis, however, the profit potential of independent oil companies seems dubious. These companies own a relatively small percentage of their own oil reserves, which means they are often at the mercy of spot markets for pricing and dependent on deals with sovereign suppliers for volume. When they do have fields that are their own and want to extract more oil from these fields, most of the large oil companies rely on outsiders. The outsiders have a power node capability (power node #6, proprietary process or modus operandi) that the oil majors might have invested in more consistently. To develop oil that is more challenging to get at, the majors wind up working with an array of specialized firms that look for oil, build rigs, install them, staff them, run tankers out to them, and even run the satellite systems that help to position lines of pipe in the sea. Modern information systems are what make the coordination among all these autonomous operations possible.

Tapping into increasingly remote reserves of oil now not only requires well-organized processes, but also expensive and specialized equipment. Some of this equipment is so rare (power node #2, special ingredient) that several oil giants have been forced to bow to companies like Seadrill, a Norwegian company that has invested heavily in deepwater rigs and in 2008 charged oil companies up to $600,000 a day to use one. Such enormous pricing power over oil majors is an indication that Seadrill has a power node. In decades past, the drilling capability of the sort that Seadrill owns might have been the property of a vertically integrated oil company. But now that rigs are available for rent on the open market, even a smaller oil company can arrange for tools to make a big financial bet on drilling. In its article on Seadrill's owner, John Fredriksen, a welder's son who is now worth $7 billion, the *Wall Street Journal* notes that "his success is part of a broader power shift from Big Oil—the Shells, Exxons and BPs of the world—to the oil-field-services sector."[4]

The Disney-Pixar Battle

The Disney-Pixar battle is another example of how power node strength can shift over time. At the start of their relationship, Pixar, whose largest shareholder was Apple founder Steve Jobs, was shifting its primary focus from selling computers to producing animation. Disney was a movie company with a powerful distribution arm (power node #7). Disney held the strongest power node. It had the greatest RPS. In 1991, the two companies made a multiyear, three-picture deal for $26 million. Its first product was 1995's *Toy Story*, a hit so explosive that it fueled a $1 billion IPO for Pixar later that same year—as well as a renegotiation of the Disney deal. In 1997, the two companies agreed to a new five-picture deal, under which the two companies would split development costs and profits—though Disney would retain all story and sequel rights and collect a distribution fee. Pixar's first five features (*Toy Story, A Bug's Life, Toy Story 2, Monsters, Inc.,* and *Finding Nemo*) grossed a combined $2.5 billion.

By the time that second contract was up for renegotiation in 2004, Pixar's creative special ingredient (power node #2) had become the stronger of the two power nodes. Pixar contributed about half of Disney's operating income from films,[5] and Disney's other options for animation blockbusters were limited. As a result, it was clear that Disney would have to forsake a substantial share of profits if it wanted to maintain Pixar as a creative partner. Negotiations were heated and led to a damaging stalemate that didn't break until after Disney's senior management changed. In 2006, rather than lose access to Pixar's uniquely creative movie ideas, Disney acquired Pixar for approximately $7.4 billion. "It's as if Nemo swallowed the whale," *Fortune* declared.[6]

The story of Pixar and Disney is an excellent example to show that the vertical profit battle can be the dimension that matters most to a company's profitability.

It is also an excellent example of how 3-D competition involving power nodes can work. We see how a smaller company with a strong power node (Pixar) can hold on to its profits even in the face of bitter competition from a much bigger company in the same distributed business arrangement (Disney). Indeed, 13 years into their partnership, once-tiny Pixar was in a position to hollow out Disney's profits. As a result, Disney wound up paying dearly to purchase Pixar—or, in effect, to acquire Pixar's power node. Whether this kind of vertical integration was the ideal strategy for Disney is debatable. That Steve Jobs did the right thing by investing in and then developing and using Pixar's power node is not.

The Microsoft-Intel Relationship

A respectful standoff is what you get when two powerful players in different horizontal layers accept that their power nodes are of similar heft, that each needs the other, and that they can create positive sums between them. The Intel versus Microsoft relationship is a good example. Players of balanced power will cajole for returns; they will try everything they can think of to break the power position of the other. But they will be careful not to spoil the positive sum game for the two of them relative to third parties. By dovetailing their introductions of new operating systems or powerful chip enhancements, the software company and the chipmaker have reduced their respective risks and enhanced their respective profits.

Chapter 10

Strategies for Powerlaw Marketplaces

You cannot succeed if you play soccer on a cricket field.
—Napier Collyns[1]

Now we turn to the fourth and last of the strategic decisions: how to win in new marketplaces that are being transformed by transparency.

In transparency, consumer choices and many other economic phenomena will tend to reflect 80–20 powerlaw distributions. In other words, anything can become a "fashion": cars, universities, computers, trading strategies, industrial equipment, political candidates, diet plans. Getting customers to buy your products will feel like a popularity contest. Customers are likely to move in herds, shaping their preferences in response to what others do. The companies, products, services, and people that are the beneficiaries of these kinds of dynamics are the equivalents of hubs.

By now we have a handle on the impact of transparency on group decision making and on dynamics in marketplaces. In chapter 5, we charted the dominant characteristics of marketplaces in transparency (see tables 5.1, 5.2, and 5.3). One of the most significant findings was that we can anticipate the distribution of the outcomes in circumstances where the four requirements for powerlaw networks are fulfilled—typically, in large groups where information travels freely and there is interdependence of decision making.

In this chapter, we will explore the implications for strategies for companies in these marketplaces.

Before we go further, it is worth taking a moment to consider how explosive the impact of powerlaw dynamics can be. When we look closely, we discover that some of the most stunning successes in recent business history can in fact be traced to the early emergence of power laws. These dynamics can be given much credit for the extraordinary success of Google (founded in 1998; S&P 500 in 2006), Oprah Winfrey (the United States' wealthiest self-made woman), and *Harry Potter* (J. K. Rowling is the world's first billionaire author[2]), and even for the resurgence of Apple (thanks largely to powerlaw benefits arising with the iPods and related products).

The following are the principles that should guide strategies for powerlaw marketplaces:

1. Flip your perspective
2. Follow the principles of hub dynamics:
   - Hubs grow through preferential attachment
   - Hubs that get ahead tend to stay ahead
3. Own, control, buy, or be a hub
4. Exploit the advantages of hubs
5. Take advantage of powerlaw (80–20) distributions
6. Practice information aikido

Flip Your Perspective

For many of us, understanding marketplaces in transparency will require a shift in understanding. Most of us instinctively think of messages (links) traveling to people (points), but to succeed in the 21st-century economy you will have to turn that idea around. Information doesn't reach out to people; people reach out for information. Therefore, we (our choices, our votes) are the links; the messages we gravitate toward (whether they are embodied in products, services, Web sites, or candidates) are the points. Looking at a diagram of a network, we may imagine that links are emanating from the points, like rays from the sun, but the reverse is true: the links are converging on the points. To thrive in transparency, companies and investors will need to pick up on the energy of the links—to see where the choices are going. This is the basis of information aikido.

Follow the Principles of Hub Dynamics

In transparency, the effect of perfect information and interdependent decision making will be to greatly amplify the frequency of appearance of hub dynamics. In any given powerlaw network, one hub will be a clear front-runner, but we will also see several lesser hubs that can readily be listed in descending order of importance. As we saw in chapter 5, the rule of thumb that is often used to describe such a powerlaw distribution is: in powerlaw networks, 20 percent of the points get 80 percent of the choices. As you will remember, this is the pattern we observed in the distributions of hits among search engines, with Google far ahead, Yahoo!, Baidu, and Microsoft trailing, and everyone else in the dust. Those front-runner hubs, the greatest beneficiaries of power laws, will have profit potential that far exceeds anything in the old economy. There were always bestsellers; now there will be megasellers—and the megasellers are hubs.

Hubs Grow through Preferential Attachment

How does a humble point flower into a hugely connected hub? At its moment of origin, every point that becomes a hub is endowed with some kind of allure. In general, the source of any given hub's initial appeal will fall under one of three headings: either it was there *first*, or has an innate *power of attraction* (we will talk about Oprah Winfrey as an example), or it serves as a *focal point of search* (we will talk about Google). This kind of categorization is useful because eventually it will provide us with guidance about how best to take advantage of a given hub.

As we mentioned in chapter 9, powerlaw dynamics in a market for a consumer product can translate into a large horizontal market share. For an example of how quickly and powerfully hub dynamics can build market share, we can look at the rapid escalation in the size of the initial U.S. print runs for the first three books in the *Harry Potter* series, which parlayed its inherent power of attraction into a juggernaut of preferential attachment. The series is published in the United States by Scholastic. The initial print run for *Harry Potter and the Sorcerer's Stone*, which was published in September 1998, was 50,000 copies. For *Harry Potter and the Chamber of Secrets*, published in June 1999, the figure was 250,000 copies. And for *Harry Potter and the Prisoner of Azkaban*, published only three months later in September 1999, the figure was 500,000 copies. As we can see, the anticipated size of the audience had jumped tenfold in just a year. (As of early 2008, the seven books in the series had sold 375 million copies worldwide.)

Hubs That Get Ahead Tend to Stay Ahead

The dynamics of preferential attachment are responsible for our second hub-related principle. As you may remember from chapter 5, if two points (ideas, products) have equivalent appeal or merit, the point that already has a greater following (or number of links) will stay ahead (in terms of proportional following or number of links). This principle accounts for the stability of leading hubs. It also provides them with a competitive advantage, since only a far superior offering can catch up. As we have mentioned, we can see one leading example of this dynamic when we look at the relative positions of Google and Microsoft in the search-engine rankings. Microsoft is a much larger company than Google, but no matter how many resources it expends, Microsoft cannot manipulate the dynamics of preferential attachment to benefit MSN.com.

Whether we recognize it or not, we have already encountered countless examples of the principle that hubs that get ahead tend to stay ahead. In fact, we have probably helped to generate a few hubs ourselves. The fact that newspaper lists of most-read articles generate more readers for those articles is one example of this phenomenon. Similarly, many search-based sites, such as Amazon and Netflix, collect reader ratings and reviews. There have been reports that some authors have organized their friends and contacts to write positive reviews or to buy books in batches to elevate a title's position in a given week's sales ranking. As always, the idea is that if a book appears to have sold more, it will sell more.

Digg, which is generally described as a community-based news-popularity Web site, is actually built around this principle. As the *Economist* explained,

> any registered user can submit a story he has found on the internet. The new submission then appears on an "Upcoming" stories web page. Other users can vote for the story by clicking on a "digg it" icon. If the submission collects enough diggs fast enough, it is promoted to the first page in its category—say science or business. If it does really well, it also makes it on to the digg.com home-page, the equivalent of a newspaper's front page. However, when its popularity fades and the digg rate decreases, it is relegated to a more obscure part of the site and replaced by a new, upwardly mobile piece.[3]

This is an excellent example of how commonplace decisions about sorting and prioritizing lead straight to powerlaw distributions. The stories that get ahead stay ahead.

Hubs will play multiple roles in our discussions of transparency. As the four conditions for powerlaw networks are met with increasing frequency in every aspect of society, we can expect that hubs and hub dynamics will become a commonplace feature of every economic and social landscape around the globe. At the same time, in a corporate context, hubs will function very specifically as power nodes. Because hub dynamics can manifest themselves in so many distinct situations, the ways that hubs will translate their enormous popularity into extraordinary profits will vary widely. In chapter 13, when we address the use of hubs as power node #12, we will talk about the specific means by which companies can use hubs and hub dynamics to build profit power. In this chapter, we will examine transformative effects that hubs, along with powerlaw distributions, will have on marketplaces generally.

Be or Control a Hub

Throughout our discussion of transparency, we have talked about the power relationships among companies—about the struggle to create and retain one's own profits, and the attempt to leverage profits by exploiting the hard work and investment of others. As we shall see, these same factors are constantly at play when we talk about hubs. The world of hubs divides into two camps: some people or companies or products are services *are* hubs; others seek to *control* hubs. In this sense, "control" is shorthand for "seek profit by association with." Hubs attract an incredible volume of traffic. If you can position your "message" to be seen—and be seen being seen—as those choices arrive at the hub, you will increase the odds that your message will become a magnet for choices as well. We will talk more about such "control" aspects later, both in this chapter and in our discussion of hubs as a power node.

For now, let us provide two examples of leading entities that are hubs, and have therefore been the constant object of constant bids for "control." The first, Google, is a *focal-point-of-search hub;* the second, Oprah Winfrey, is a *power-of-attraction hub.* Although preferential attachment is the source of power for all hubs, the tactics for capturing the benefits of preferential attachment will vary depending on the underlying nature of the hub.

Google: Focal-Point-of-Search Hub

Google is consistently innovative, technologically speaking, but its status as a focal point of search and beneficiary of ongoing preferential attachment dynamics is the key element of its sustained success in attracting customers. As we have seen, this is what has allowed Google to stay so far ahead of even the mighty Microsoft in attracting customers to its search product— and even more important, it is also the basis for Google's strong profitability. Google has used the *profit power* of its status as a *hub.* Searches have always been free to users, but starting in 2000, Google began selling space for small advertisements targeted to individual search queries, charging fees only if users actually clicked on the promotional links. As *The Economist* explains, "As the largest search engine, Google attracts more advertisers and can serve up more relevant advertisements. This in turn attracts more users and advertisers, and so on."[4]

Advertisers, of course, pay for access to Google's vast pool of users. But there are other parties who try to take advantage of its hub dynamics for free. Google, for instance, uses algorithms to decide which possible solutions to a search inquiry have been most useful to other readers, and lists those first. Some people attempt to work the system so that Google is certain to list their site near the top whenever certain search criteria are used. This is an example of trying to "use" or "control" a hub. Since a site that appears at the head of a Google page is far more likely to be clicked than a link further down, the ranking is self-perpetuating. Sites that receive volumes of traffic steered by Google have an improved chance of inspiring hub dynamics of their own.

Oprah Winfrey: Power-of-Attraction Hub

Oprah Winfrey has built her internationally syndicated daytime talk show into an empire. Through the power of her personality, she attracted an avid following of viewers who have come to trust her and welcome her advice. "No one should underestimate the connection that Winfrey has with her audience," wrote *Forbes*. "Her fans—viewers of her television show, readers of her magazine—are not sheep, but they tend to respect her opinions and believe that what she says speaks directly to them."[5]

Oprah has translated her hub status into extraordinary profits: her TV show is syndicated worldwide, and she has parlayed her renown into a successful magazine, a radio show, movie and theater productions, and a Web site. In 2007, *Forbes* estimated her net worth at $2.5 billion.

For many of the people and companies around her, however, Oprah has also been the source of positive sums. Her on-air book club, for example, has generated lavish revenues for the publishers and authors who have had the good fortune of being selected. Oprah is not a filter in the strict sense of the concept we introduced in chapter 5, which is a type of power node (#11). She apparently does not block information, and her job is not to endorse products on the basis of her expertise. Her fans eagerly come to her because they want to catch what she has to say. When she tells them she has read something exciting, millions of them are willing to pick up that book as well. Titles that are picked for Oprah's Book Club evidence power laws; they are now responsible for a disproportionate share of book sales. In 2003, the *Economist* reported that, "of her 46 picks to date, 16 hit the top of the *New York Times* bestseller list within weeks of her benediction.... [T]hree Oprah picks alone meant a gain of $60m in sales for Penguin, according to *Publishers Weekly*."[6] When Oprah put her book club on hiatus, authors petitioned her to bring it back, arguing that overall fiction sales had dropped.[7]

In recent years, Oprah has also aired periodic episodes in which she celebrates products she describes as her "favorite things." Hundreds of companies submit products hoping to win her favor. Her own Web site gets 4 million hits a day when those shows air, and some smaller companies, particularly cosmetics companies, have catapulted to national status on the strength of her endorsement. To complete the cycle, Oprah has begun cashing in on her own profit power by selling her favorite things at the Oprah Store.

The visibility of being associated with a hub like Oprah has been enough to launch several of her regular guests as minor hubs in their own right. Dr. Phil, for example, started as a guest of Oprah Winfrey. Audiences liked him and sought out his advice; he's gone on to have shows and magazines in his own name. That point wasn't lost on then Senator Barack Obama, who enlisted Oprah to mobilize voters during his 2008 presidential campaign.

Exploit the Advantages of Hubs

In transparency, it will be important to apply as much creativity and resourcefulness as possible to the question of how to best exploit the advantages of hubs. As we can see from the examples of Google and Oprah, the goal is to position your product or service so that it can benefit from the patterns of interdependent decision making that might lead to the boon of preferential attraction. This is the source of the hub's profit power and your positive sums. If you want to boost sales of your timepieces, you might persuade Tiger Woods to wear your watch. If you want people to notice your sports car, you might arrange for Matt Damon to drive it in his next action thriller.

We see a continuous stream of product placements in "controlling the hub" and "benefiting from association" strategies. Corporate leaders and marketing chiefs need to take a hard look at whether such placements are worth the product placement dollars. Are the products placed near real hubs and in programs that do have the power-of-attraction dynamic, or are they near minor players who are not hubs?

If you're seeking to promote a product, you might look for hubs in novel places or in new guises. Vodka makers, for example, are willing to sponsor birthday parties and other events for popular young "scenesters"—as long as they can "make the case that they can generate buzz for their products and that they will invite the right kind of crowd that hits their ideal demo," one 28-year-old partyer told the *New York Post*.[8] Approaches similar to these have been highly touted by marketing gurus in recent years, in books with titles like *Buzz Marketing*[9] and *Groundswell*.[10] Some writers talk in terms of "pulling" rather than "pushing" consumers.[11] This is a step in the right direction, although it does not go far enough. In transparency, consumers are neither pushed nor pulled—they look for themselves.

Once a product becomes a hub, it enjoys numerous advantages. Given the rules of powerlaw networks, only newcomers with extreme fitness can catch up to existing hubs. As a result, in transparency, it is harder to use price differentials to dislodge market leaders. A new product is unlikely to cut into an older hub's market share by offering prices that are only slightly lower. Instead, an equivalent new product is likely to require a significant difference in quality or price to develop a following that can approach the first position. The Vizio flat-screen TV, which we discussed in chapter 8, is an example of such a product. It came onto the market with prices that were as much as thousands of dollars lower than the competition's. Another example of a new hub product is the Flip, a tiny video camera made by Pure Digital Technologies that retails for the very low price of just over $100. By 2008, within roughly a year of the Flip line's introduction, the company had seized 13 percent of the camcorder market.

In general, where preferential attachment is involved, competing on price is not as straightforward as it used to be. Until recently, price and quality were thought to count for a great deal, and companies devoted a lot of energy to persuading customers that their products were the best made or offered the greatest value. In an age of interdependent decision making, however, price is only one element of the fitness of a new point (or product). Intangibles involving social or cultural appeal may become equally important. These are often the forces that explain the power of attraction of items or people or ideas that become the object of preferential attachment.

As a result, companies that are the beneficiaries of hub dynamics will often be able to increase horizontal market share and use this stronger horizontal position as a tool (power node # 8: dominant position in a layer) in vertical competitions to enhance their margins of profit. Hub dynamics will give them a distinct edge in transparency's 3-D competitions. In transparency, hub power nodes and their preferential attachment dynamics will be a source of profit power and may weaken the historically reliable weapons of price and quality.

This can work in two ways. First, products that begin to benefit from hub dynamics may be able to grab a large share of the market even if they are sold at prices that are above the norms in their industries. This is true for many types of goods at all price levels, but it is particularly evident in the market for luxury goods, where the attribute that confers status may actually be the item's extreme cost. As Radha Chadha and Paul Husband write in *The Cult of the Luxury Brand,* particularly in emerging luxury markets like China, "The use of luxury brands is not linked to the sophistication level of the consumer—it answers only to the need to show wealth."

Consider the phenomenon of high-end designer handbags. Thanks to perfect information, which in this instance is enabling the instant transmission of alluring cultural imagery to markets around the world, the lust for high-priced accessories has become a worldwide phenomenon. Japanese women have been known to take out loans to pay for Vuitton, and at stores like Bottega Veneta, customers beg and plead for a top place on the wait list for a season's hot new design. This is herd behavior at its best—or worst. Extraordinary profits are certainly the result: some reports suggest designer bags sell for more than a dozen times as much as they cost to make. Luxury bag makers are able to sell more while also charging more because of the hub power node of preferential attachment, which is also driving their horizontal market share.

Second, hub products that sweep to the lead in horizontal market share will also have an edge in maintaining it. A company selling a product with hub status is likely to retain its vertical price advantage even in the face of competition from lower-priced competitors. As we have discussed, Apple has found it quite easy to maintain the market share and price levels for its iPods, even in the face of competition from less expensive products that are also of superior quality.

Even more remarkable, these price advantages may extend to companies or products that are only indirectly associated with hubs. One recent example of a successful bid to "control" a hub—in this instance, by making a deal that leverages a celebrity hub's power of attraction—involves Clear, an antidandruff shampoo made by Unilever. In 2007, the consumer-products giant launched Clear in several markets in Asia. The company hired a hugely popular Korean star named Rain to star in a Clear commercial, then shrewdly posted the spot on YouTube—a site that is a magnet for video searches. According to *BusinessWeek,* nearly 25,000 Rain fans have sought out and downloaded that ad, and Clear has seen rapid surges in market share in China and the Philippines. That is one of the reasons that Unilever has been able to sustain its markups on Clear—the shampoo is priced 10 percent higher than its chief competitor, Head & Shoulders, which was previously the most expensive popular shampoo in these emerging markets.[12]

Take Advantage of Powerlaw (80–20) Distributions

Whenever you observe 80–20 patterns, or best sellers, or blockbusters, or other indications that the bulk of choices are going to a few hub points, you are likely to be in the presence of a powerlaw distribution. You should be on the lookout for products, people, services, etc., that are hubs or that have hub potential. This is where you will find *profit power*.

Obviously, early recognition of impending powerlaw distributions may have ramifications for the way companies conduct their business. The companies that are most likely to be profitable are those that own and that know how to capitalize on the hubs. Marketing and manufacturing programs can be revised to make the most of the profit power of the products that have hub potential. The vast majority of the products or SKUs that do not have hub potential should be phased out and replaced with new experiments, or at a minimum should be managed with great cost discipline. One company that effectively already uses such an approach is Frito-Lay, which continually tests new snacks and ramps up production on the ones that catch on with consumers. This is a powerlaw-era strategy that might benefit those consumer products companies that persist in shouldering all the labor and expense of manufacturing and distributing a full product line, especially if only one or two products generate the bulk of sales. In transparency, business leaders may rightly ask: if it is clear that a product is failing to catch on in a marketplace that tends to have obvious hubs and powerlaw dynamics, would it be wise to pursue further investment?

Among other things, powerlaw distributions will have ramifications for "one-to-one marketing," a much-touted strategy that is enabled by low information cost. The concept of "markets for one" is based on the idea that in the future all products can be personalized—options on cars, snack flavors, the design and color of jeans—and marketed and distributed to the targeted individuals at low cost. For instance, in *The Long Tail: Why the Future of Business Is Selling Less of More*, Chris Anderson posits that the assortment of products available to customers can grow greatly because of lower distribution and search costs enabled by online technologies. He also proposes that consumers put more value on personally targeted products than on products with mass appeal.

Indeed, as we have said, thanks to the falling cost of information, it will become increasingly feasible for companies to offer choices to individuals in a targeted fashion and for individuals to find out about products far and wide. Undoubtedly, the growth of online retailing and other developments that are enabled by the falling cost of information have greatly increased consumers' access to a wide range of products available globally.

However, this wide range of options will not necessarily result in an equally broad range of actual consumer selections. In fact, based on the understanding of the economics of perfect information that we developed in chapters 2–5, we would predict the contrary. We would predict that people's personal choices will, more than likely, end up being distributed in a concentrated fashion, with 80 percent (or more) of the purchases or choices getting focused on the 20 percent (or less) of products that are enormously popular compared to the rest. One-to-one marketing in transparency (when the four conditions for powerlaw distributions are achieved) is unlikely to produce "flat" distributions or normal distributions among the actual customer choices. It is apparent, for instance, that auto buyers, even when presented with countless options for their cars, will tend to choose predominantly for the same few features.

Empirical evidence confirming our predictions based on the economics of perfect information about the concentrations of customer choices is abundantly available, as reported, for instance, by Anita Elberse in her article "Should You Invest in the Long Tail?" in the *Harvard Business Review*. She investigated the actual sales patterns in the music and home-video industries. Her analysis revealed a high degree of concentration among the customer choices when "selection is vast and search is easy." Using the terminology of this book, we would paraphrase this as: when the conditions for powerlaw distributions are satisfied. For instance, she found that the top 10 percent of titles on Rhapsody, an online music service that allows its 60,000 subscribers to choose from a huge database of songs (more than 1 million tracks), accounted for 78 percent of all plays. Elberse and a colleague, Felix Oberholzer-Gee, also looked into the weekly sales of home videos, as reported by Nielsen VideoScan. Their research showed that the number of titles that only sold a few copies almost doubled in a given week from early 2000 to the middle of 2005, while the assortment increased and online access functionality was improved.

On the surface this would appear to support the thesis about the flattening of the distribution. However, upon closer inspection they found that the concentration of customer choices actually increased. For instance, over the same period in 2000–2005, the number of titles with no sales at all in a given week quadrupled. Moreover, they found an increase in the concentration of winners: from 2000 to 2005, the number of titles in the top 10 percent of weekly sales dropped by more than 50 percent. In the same article, Elberse reports that, according to Nielsen SoundScan, of the 3.9 million digital tracks sold in 2007, 91 percent sold fewer than 100 copies. Finally, in another study analyzing recorded-music sales for 2005–2007 based on Nielsen SoundScan data, Elberse found that "the concentration in digital track sales is significantly stronger than in physical-album sales." This finding supports our thesis that reducing the cost of information until search costs approach zero (one of the four conditions) tends to increases the likelihood of powerlaw distributions. Search costs are much closer to zero for digital track sales than they are for physical retail distribution.

Practice Information Aikido

The dynamics of transparency require an entirely new philosophical approach—one in which responsiveness and adaptability are the chief means of attack. This may seem counterintuitive, but in fact transparency demands a new kind of combat. When envisioning contests in the marketplace, we should not think in terms of overrunning a battlefield with new products and taking over shelves by superior force. Things will no longer be so simple. In transparency, business leaders must learn to practice what I call *information aikido*—which is a reference to the Japanese martial art that teaches combatants to win by redirecting their opponents' energies in ways that benefit the person doing the redirecting.

In aikido, the route to victory lies in perceiving the energy of economic choices as soon as it begins to flow. The earlier you can pick up on the collective patterns that will lead to preferential attachment, hubs, and powerlaw distributions, the better your chance of steering that energy for your own ends. Business leaders and investors in transparency will have to become skilled at sensing or seeing the movements of the marketplace, and responding to those movements more quickly and effectively than anyone else does. For companies that learn to practice information aikido, the technologies of perfect information will be a great asset. Power node #10 is "aikido assets"—equipment or processes that equip companies to respond to the movements of the consumer herds with lightning speed.

In transparency, whenever we are dealing with marketplaces with many participants (such as consumer markets), it is likely that success will derive not from taking up a fixed position, but instead from going with the flow of shifting dynamics. A company can no longer thrive if it functions like one of those kings who sat in a castle and directed armies at the populace. Instead, it might be better off acting more like a modern politician—one who takes frequent opinion polls, experiments with messages until one catches on, and crafts legislation to suit the expressed desires of the voters. For almost any approach to ruling, there is a time and a place. The *time* for the aikido master approach is transparency; the *place* is marketplaces with many participants. For those masters with the greatest skills and the strongest power nodes, extraordinary profits will be the result.

PART IV

The Four Rules for Maximizing Profits in Transparency

Chapter 11

From the Four Strategic Decisions to the Four Rules

As we have seen, economies in transparency will bear little resemblance to earlier economies characterized by expensive, scarce information. By now, we should be feeling far more confident in our understanding of the startling changes taking place in the economic world around us.

Where some others have seen only turbulence, we have identified an orderly sequence of events that will inevitably lead us beyond old and failing models and into transparency. We have examined the roles of perfect information and interdependent decision making in creating ongoing imperfections in markets. We have applied a new paradigm we call power-law economics. For business leaders and investors the question that logically follows is this: what is the optimal route to extraordinary returns in this new world of transparency?

In the preceding section, we considered the effects of transparency on four essential strategic business decisions: What shall we own? How do we organize? How do we compete? How can we win in the marketplace?

The answers are as follows.

Answer to question 1, about companies and about what to own: In transparency, companies will be able to generate extraordinary and sustainable returns, and power will have a greatly expanded role in the achievement of profit. Companies that focus their ownership on business segments with a strong power node are likely to have higher returns.

Answer to question 2, about business models: The businesses with the highest potential valuation in transparency will be superior in taking advantage of the many degrees of freedom granted by transparency to shape their company at will, as well as in deploying their power nodes within their chosen distributed business arrangement. Transparency enables a greatly expanded range of options for business structures, including ownership, cross-shareholding, contracts, and noncontractual relationships or understandings among companies. At the extremes are vertical integration on the one hand and a total reliance on arm's-length interactions with other companies in the marketplace on the other. In transparency, the general case will be somewhere in between: most companies will choose to enter into some form of distributed business arrangement. The most enduring of these arrangements will create *positive sums* for the weaker parties in the relationship as well as the power node owner. The power node owner has the greatest influence over how the distributed enterprise will fare and what financial and ancillary benefits will accrue to whom.

Answer to question 3, about competition: The outcomes of the competitive battles will be determined by the relative strengths of power nodes in three-dimensional competitive battles and by the comparative robustness of the combatants' distributed-business-arrangement designs. We can expect intense competition over the extraction of profit and the allocation of risk among companies in the 3-D environment, including those in distributed business arrangements. In vertical competitions, interactions with other players will be full-out battles for returns, not cooperative skirmishes.

Answer to question 4, about powerlaw marketplaces: The most effective responses to these new marketplaces include strategies that foster the conditions for preferential attachment, exploit the benefits of controlling existing hubs, and perform information aikido. In markets increasingly characterized by transparency, and therefore satisfying the four conditions for powerlaw networks, companies will encounter market phenomena and customer behavior that will reflect powerlaw dynamics, including 80–20 distributions and hubs. Companies that can exploit these dynamics will have profit power. Therefore, hubs and aikido assets will rise to the fore as new power nodes for transparency. Powerlaw dynamics will bring new muscle to some older power nodes as well.

These answers lead us directly to the Four Rules for Maximizing Profits in Transparency.

The Four Rules for Maximizing Profits are:

1. Focus on profit power and own businesses with power nodes.
2. Organize as a focused company that orchestrates power relationships and capitalizes on the positive sums of distributed business arrangements.
3. Use power nodes to win in 3-D competitions and gain extraordinary economic profits.
4. Follow strategies designed to succeed among the marketplace dynamics of the transparent economy (power laws and hubs).

The Four Rules are your strategies for building extraordinary profits in transparency. In part VI we will see how to implement each of these strategies.

As you can see, power nodes are at the core of each of the Four Rules to Maximize Profits in Transparency. We now will give power nodes our full attention: they are the subject of Part V, coming up next.

Power Nodes: Transparency's Sources of Profits and Competitive Weapons

Chapter 12

The 12 Power Nodes

In this chapter we will discuss each of these 12 power nodes in depth:

1. Brand
2. Secret, special, or proprietary ingredients
3. Regulatory protection
4. Focused financial resources
5. Customer base with switching costs
6. Proprietary processes or modus operandi
7. Distribution gateways
8. Dominant position in a layer
9. Increasing mutual utility
10. Aikido assets
11. Filters and brokers
12. Hubs

Power Node 1: Brand

McDonald's is a power node brand.[1] Big Macs, Golden Arches, and Ronald McDonald are recognized in more than 100 countries around the world. The brand attracts customers—billions have been served—and its success and reputation and profitability allow the company to extract favorable terms from franchise operators and suppliers. The company itself has boasted that its brand drives global opportunities, provides access to new markets and attractive financing, attracts high-level employees, and can attract other top names for marketing arrangements.

Other power brands include Louis Vuitton, Cartier, Gillette, and Nike. Obviously, a power node brand is not just what the dictionary tells us a brand is: "a type of product manufactured by a company under a particular name" or a "brand name."[2] It is a set of images, including reputation, of a product, a service, or an entire company in the minds of consumers, competitors, and investors.

Companies may have hundreds or thousands of brands, like Anheuser-Busch InBev or Unilever or Nestlé; a few brands, like PepsiCo, Coca-Cola, and Philip Morris; or only one brand name for all the company's products, such as Chanel, Dell, Intel, Philips, Tata, Toto, or Virgin.

Not all brands are power nodes. Only brands that can deliver superior returns are power nodes—and those are the subjects here. It is very costly to build and maintain a brand, especially a global brand, and there is no point in building a brand for its own sake. Do not pour money into a brand unless you expect to see a return on your investment.

Many consumer brands command significantly higher retail prices than store brands, but their owners carry a heavy burden of advertising and marketing costs to maintain broad visibility. If all a product has is name recognition, it is not a power node brand.

How can you tell a brand with power node potential apart from one which does not have it before you make the investment? Look for brands that, under their umbrella, can marshal enormous forces in their support outside their company—forces that can enhance their profitability, improve their risk, or reduce their investment. For decades, as I mentioned in chapter 9, the Estée Lauder cosmetics brands were so powerful that department stores agreed to let Lauder control its display spaces and dictate the timing of promotions.

We have noted that Coke and Pepsi are power node brands, for reasons that we examined at length in chapter 1. They provide an excellent model of the way that a brand power node can be used to extract profitability from other players in a distributed business model.

Philip Morris, the owner of Marlboro, by far the world's most powerful global cigarette brand, has been able to use its brand power node in a different way—as leverage against the world's most powerful regulatory regime, the Chinese government (power node #3, regulatory protection). Like many other cigarette makers, Philip Morris has long sought broader entry into China, but the Chinese government refused to allow access unless the company agreed to share various profits. Philip Morris had never before shared control over Marlboro's manufacture, sale, or distribution, including the right to collect excise taxes, but ultimately it agreed to a manufacturing and licensing deal with two Chinese state-owned tobacco companies. The outcome of this power node battle is a draw. It takes a truly spectacular power node to hold one's own vis-à-vis the Chinese government. Thanks to its Marlboro brand, Philip Morris has become the first U.S. cigarette maker to gain wide exposure in the huge Chinese market.

In the course of this book we have discussed many power node battles involving brand. With consolidation in the U.S. retail layer (merged department store chains, big box stores), many brands have had trouble maintaining their leverage against the distribution gateways (power node #7) that they once had. In recent years, some brand theorists have begun to talk about a shift in power from "product-centered" to "customer-centered" brands.[3] These brands[4] market themselves not as excellent products per se, but as goods or services that have been created in response to what consumers have said they need. Readers of this book may view this customer-centered brand strategy as a step toward applying the information aikido approach to the marketplace that we described in chapter 10.

In his blog, Johnnie Moore, coauthor of *Beyond Branding*, writes that it is helpful to think of brands as things "that emerge as a result of all the encounters between people who belong, with varying degrees of enthusiasm or loathing, to the community around a brand."[5] In transparency, the success of brands as power nodes will be heavily influenced by this process of interdependent decision making. Brands that are successful in triggering preferential attachment can become hubs. In transparency, those brands that can become hubs will be even stronger as power nodes. As I will discuss further in the entry for hubs (power node #12), among the brands that have so far benefited from hub dynamics are Apple and Harley-Davidson.[6]

Power Node 2: Secret, Special, or Proprietary Ingredients

A secret, special, or proprietary ingredient is a scarce resource that a company owns or controls to a significant extent and that cannot be easily duplicated or substituted. This ingredient must be crucial to the finished product or service of this company or to other companies. One can find proprietary ingredients in every industry. Examples include medical compounds, intellectual capital, creative ability, specialized skills (of, e.g., a surgeon or a master craftsman), products, and designs—and even raw materials.

Gold is a quintessential example of a special ingredient. (According to the American Museum of Natural History, it has been estimated that, worldwide, the total amount of gold ever mined is 152,000 metric tons, only enough to fill 60 tractor trailers.[7]) So are truly precious stones; the Anglo American and DeBeers companies built empires out of their control of a proprietary ingredient called diamonds.

Monsanto has famously boosted sales and customer dependency with the proprietary "one-year" seeds it developed through genetic engineering. Discussions of "peak oil" suggest that crude oil may be or become a special ingredient.

Some companies create a power node by combining special ingredients. For instance, the jeweler Van Cleef & Arpels combines the special ingredient of the rare raw materials (gold and precious stones) with the special ingredient of superlative craftsmanship to produce its priciest one-off pieces.

We can spotlight the importance of the special ingredient power node by providing an illustration of what happens when you don't have one. Let's consider the makers of antifreeze for cars—the owners of brands like Prestone and Zerex, which have no obvious power nodes. What is antifreeze? It is essentially ethylene glycol with a few additives. Ethylene glycol is the special ingredient for antifreeze makers. Ethylene glycol is made from a humdrum petrochemical product called ethylene. Ethylene is used in the manufacturing of many other products, including an extensive alphabet of plastics. The volume of ethylene glycol that is produced each year is small compared to the output of ethylene. The spot market for ethylene glycol was so thin it did not deserve to be called a market.

In 1986, the private equity group of First Boston bought Prestone (and a number of other consumer products) from Union Carbide. The new owners of Prestone had the foresight to obtain a multiyear contract to purchase ethylene glycol from Union Carbide at an advantageous confidential pricing formula. Not long after the deal was completed, several events took place—including refinery accidents and increases in feedstock price—that cut the available supplies of ethylene glycol. Suddenly this chemical was not just ferociously expensive, but also in short supply. Many of Prestone's competitors who did not have a secure source had trouble obtaining it at any price. Retail prices for antifreeze skyrocketed. For Prestone, which thanks to its Union Carbide contract had access to adequate supplies of ethylene glycol at below-market costs, profit margins exploded. As a result of its forward thinking, the company was not at the mercy of the special-ingredient power node. The company experienced windfall profits in 1989–1990. Many years after this episode, investors remain wary of investing in an independent antifreeze business unless it has a secure long-term contract or other arrangement that offsets its dependence on someone else's special-ingredient power node.

Proprietary-ingredient power nodes are particularly easy to spot in the pharmaceutical industry. Teva is a large global generic drug manufacturer. It also produces raw materials, which it sells to competitors. According to an article in the *Wall Street Journal*,[8] during the 2004 race to market a generic version of Neurontin, an epilepsy and pain drug that was bringing in billions for Pfizer each year, Teva obtained patents on its own formulation of Neurontin's active ingredient and its manufacturing process for this active ingredient. In so doing, it created a bind for Alpharma, a small company that had been the first to produce generic Neurontin and had thus been granted a potentially lucrative six-month exclusivity period from the Food and Drug Administration. In order to get its product to market in a timely fashion, Alpharma was forced to buy the active ingredient from Teva—at very high prices. A Teva executive estimated that the deal extracted 20–50 percent of Alpharma's potential profits during that six-month period and transferred these to Teva, the *Journal* reported.

Many of the wealthiest creative artists in the music industry have built their fortune on this power node. Their source of power is control over their proprietary ingredient, which in this case is creative output and intellectual property. Because they have managed to keep a large degree of control over their own content, they can extract returns from the music industry at large—not just through fees from concerts and album releases, but from royalties on songs and arrangements.

An article in *The Times* of London reported that, of the Rolling Stones, Mick Jagger reportedly was worth around £180 million in 2005 and Keith Richards about £165 million.[9] Paul McCartney is said to be worth about £800 million, Andrew Lloyd Webber £700 million, Madonna £235 million, David Bowie £120 million, and Sting £185 million.[10] Other musicians who are also global brand names, but did not maintain control over their creations, did not do as well. The profits flowed to the entity that controlled the rights to the music.

In some cases, it may be possible to acquire or invent a secret ingredient power node if you don't have one. Companies can exercise a high degree of creative control over secret ingredients; indeed, they are often the outcome of a company's resourcefulness in upgrading or redeploying its existing products or processes.

Sometimes, there is a secret-ingredient power node hidden in plain sight. As you may remember from chapter 9, Parker Hannifin reviewed its product line and discovered that a number of its parts were absolutely essential to its customers but had few alternative manufacturers. Parker Hannifin was able to raise its prices for these products and extract higher economic profits as a result. Companies should look carefully to see whether they too own any proprietary ingredients that they have failed to exploit.

There are many ways to find or devise a "special ingredient" power node that can be used to pull returns out of the system. An example is Pepsi's creation of Aquafina drinking water, which I will discuss in chapter 13. In recent years, numerous companies have used proprietary ingredients in ways that boost margins, enhance competitive advantage, or even facilitate global expansion. Here are some additional examples:

Procter & Gamble is by most accounts a truly outstanding company. Unfortunately, it traditionally has not had any obvious power nodes that would let it reorganize into a global distributed business arrangement. This is a drag on returns and is making global expansion very resource-intensive. In the past few years, however, P&G has taken steps to reinvent its processes so that it might develop a special-ingredient power node and use it as a linchpin of a distributed business arrangement.

The company has begun relationships with third-party manufacturers in China that are very similar to Coke and Pepsi's relationships with bottlers, but for detergents. An article at Economist.com describes a "low-cost manufacturing method" in which "P&G provides secret, high-value 'performance chemicals' to Chinese partners, who add basic ingredients and packaging before distributing the products." For P&G, the secret chemicals become a power node. They make it possible for P&G to turn manufacturing and other downstream functions over to Chinese partners. Production costs are lower for the Chinese than they would be for P&G, and they are closer to the local market. P&G avoids tying up its capital and reduces its exposure to risk. This is an excellent model for expansion into fast-growing, far-flung markets.

Dubai proves that a special ingredient can be many things—even waterfront property. Because it has the smallest oil holdings of any of the seven Arab emirates, Dubai has chosen to diversify into tourism and trading. The most valuable residential real estate in the world is often on waterfront property, so Dubai is adding more than seven miles of beachfront, much of it on landfills shaped like palms, on which it will build as many as 200 hotels as well as housing for a city with a population of hundreds of thousands. Dubai hopes its special ingredient, which has already attracted worldwide media attention, will be worth billions in property sales and revenues from tourists.[11] In addition to offering this special ingredient, Dubai has offered incentives to companies, hospitals, universities, and other institutions that together may create a Silicon Valley–type atmosphere. The emirate is hoping to foster the preferential attachment dynamics that may eventually allow Dubai's popularity in both corporate and recreational markets to become self-perpetuating.

Power Node 3: Regulatory Protection

Power nodes may be derived from regulatory protection. This protection can take many forms. It includes privileges granted by a regulatory regime, such as the right (often captured in licenses) to run businesses such as hospitals, nuclear power plants, banks and other financial institutions, or phone companies. It includes rights to use scarce national resources, like air frequencies (for radio, television, or wireless phone services) or offshore drilling rights for oil. Regulatory protection extends also to certifications of professions, such as medical doctors, electricians, lawyers, Wall Street brokers, and real estate brokers. It also includes permits, like import permits for agricultural products (note the cases of imports of Argentine beef into the United States and of U.S. beef into South Korea), building permits and zoning restrictions, and fishing permits.

Regulatory protection often creates restrictions that transfer wealth *to* the beneficiary (of the regulation) *from* potential competitors. This we saw in the example where the Chinese government would not allow Philip Morris access unless it agreed to share the Marlboro profits—which are likely to be juicy, thanks to its being the first foreign brand in the fast-growing Chinese market.

In many other instances, regulatory protection creates restrictions that transfer wealth to the beneficiary of the regulation and transfer the cost to consumers and the overall economy. For instance, despite shortages of physicians in many areas in the United States, barriers to foreign professionals appear to have increased in recent years. "In 1997, after the American Medical Association complained that the inflow of foreign doctors was depressing wages for doctors already in the country, a new set of restrictions on foreign medical residents was put in place," says Dean Baker of the Center for Economic and Policy Research.[12] According to one estimate, reports Baker's colleague Eric Freeman, "the potential economic impact of freer trade in professional services is at least an order of magnitude higher than most of the items that currently dominate the trade agenda."[13]

In the United States, a famous example of regulatory protection historically has involved phone companies. The so-called regional Bell operating companies (RBOCs), like SBC, Bell South (both currently AT&T), and Verizon, were handed regulatory protection for their local phone services when the original AT&T was broken up. History has shown us how strong this power node can be. As we have seen, in the battle for local customers between RBOCs like SBC and Verizon on one side and AT&T on the other side, SBC and Verizon have won, and AT&T has faltered.

The stronghold of these companies still persists; as evidence, consider the still relatively limited competition for local wire-line services and apparent oddities in charges for voice versus data traffic. Since voice traffic is treated differently by regulation than data traffic, consumers can speak for hours to friends far away and spend close to nothing if they use their computer to transmit such communication as data. But if they used wire-line phones to talk, they might run up a sizable bill.

Another example of regulatory protection is patents. In the case of IBM, we can see a clear example of the dollar value. The company has made greater use of its patents by selling the intellectual property contained within them. Writing in the *Harvard Business Review*, Kevin Rivette and David Kline noted that this preeminent computer company "boosted annual patent-licensing royalties a phenomenal 3,300%—from $30 million in 1990 to nearly $1 billion [in 2000]. This $1 billion per year, it should be noted, is largely free cash flow—a recurring net revenue stream that represents one-ninth of IBM's annual pretax profits. . . . To match that sort of net revenue stream, IBM would have to sell roughly $20 billion worth of additional products each year, or an amount equal to one-fourth its worldwide sales."[14]

Power Node 4: Focused Financial Resources

Access to financial capital is the lifeblood of any company. A competitor with a strong capital base has a huge advantage over less well-capitalized competitors. I call this power node "focused" financial resources because even better than plain access is capital that provides a company—or its distributed business arrangement—with the wherewithal to accomplish things it could otherwise not accomplish (with another source of capital). Often, this means developing innovative forms of access to capital that other enterprises cannot duplicate, and then deploying that access to exert control in ways that other financial sources do not.

When capital markets are well developed, all companies in theory can turn to them to borrow or to issue equity. In theory, capital markets should be of help to companies in getting through their ups and downs in earnings and financing needs. In practice, as was borne out by the crisis of 2009, this may not be true. Many creditworthy companies cannot get access to capital markets at reasonable costs when they have extraordinary needs for capital, which might occur when companies start up from scratch, start new product lines, enter new markets, or encounter a recession. This creates opportunities—and power nodes—for other, better-financed companies. Companies with deep capital resources can improve access to capital markets or develop innovative capital sources for other companies and use this leverage as a power node. These capital resources may smooth out cash flow for the weaker partner, moderate its ups and downs in earnings, or reduce fluctuations in capital needs. These benefits may even enable the needy company to survive.

Toyota is a well-known example of a company that has used its capital strength as a power node within its network of hundreds of suppliers. "In both the North American and Japanese automobile industries, the manufacturers buy many parts and systems from outside suppliers, while making others themselves," report Milgrom and Roberts. Toyota often demands the manufacture of components that the third-party manufacturers are asked to design themselves. The components, as Milgrom and Roberts continue, "are quite specific to Toyota's models. The relationships between Toyota and its subcontractors are close, complex, and long term. They are marked by extensive sharing of information and costs and by Toyota's active involvement in advising its subcontractors, although Toyota often has no ownership interest in these firms."[15]

Toyota helps its suppliers of automotive component parts to smooth out their capital equipment investment cycles and by giving them sales and production targets over multiple years. The focused-capital function allowed Toyota and other Japanese auto companies to "select suppliers before the parts specifications were made final" so that they could "exploit the suppliers' expertise in design engineering" and "design parts to fit the capabilities of the suppliers' existing equipment."[16]

This example demonstrates the use of a power node by the most powerful company in an arrangement to finely orchestrate the activities in its distributed business model without burdening its own investment capital and returns with ownership.

Another example of how focused financial resources can work is the so-called creditwallah found in Indian rural villages. A creditwallah is a small company or individual that performs a dual function. The first function is to provide loans for working capital to many little shops so that they can build their inventory of staple goods and basic brands. The second is that often the creditwallah is also acting as the central account collective for larger consumer companies. As a result, a corner store owner must honor his payables for the bulk of his products to one source—the creditwallah. If the shop owner does not pay for, say, the shampoo inventory, the creditwallah may block credit for other products, and the little store will be out of business. A creditwallah has more leverage over small stores than a multinational (that sells a narrow line of products) might have in collecting for its individual product lines from thousands of corner stores. The creditwallah, therefore, has a power node relative to the little shops as well as relative to the packaged goods companies.

Our final example is the microcredit concept that has been put forth by Mohammad Yunus of Grameen Bank, who won the Nobel

Peace Prize in 2006. Microcredit is an adaptation of the focused financial resources power node. Villagers who may be in remote parts of Bangladesh, and who have little or no financial resources, get small loans from Grameen Bank to finance their startups or working capital. Microcredit organizations such as Grameen Bank generally aim to promote a wider dispersal of financial resources by lending to villagers who would not receive loans from traditional banks. This gives many rural people an opportunity to earn a livelihood that they would otherwise not have. Microcredit institutions such as Grameen Bank are for-profit operations that charge commercial credit terms to their customers. Clearly these banks have a great deal of leverage over villagers who could not get credit elsewhere regarding the terms of the loan. They have a power node. Grameen Bank and similar institutions, however, choose to exercise restraint in the use of their power node rather than exploit the customers. By breaking down a barrier to capital they create positive sums, of which they pass the bulk to their customers. In contrast, other microfinance institutions do use, or abuse, their power node to the fullest. For instance, Banco Compartamentos, a Mexican lender to the poor, is accused, as reported by the *Economist* in 2008, of charging "interest rates of 100% a year, little different from what illegal loan sharks demand."[17]

Power Node 5: Customer Base with Switching Costs

A customer base that is loyal is a valuable power node—especially if its loyalty is maintained through the high cost of switching to another vendor. In contrast, a customer base with high turnover, or so-called "churn," does *not* provide much power node power.

A switching cost for customers is inherent when switching suppliers requires a major investment in time, money, or attention. The effort involved in changing ingrained routines or habits may also represent a high switching cost. For years, many people have refused to switch from Microsoft-based PCs to Apple computers (and vice versa) because the difference in the operating systems, or even what is labeled "the look and the feel," seemed hard to adjust to.

Increasing switching costs makes customers more loyal. That is why airlines aim to increase the switching costs of their most valuable customers through frequent-flyer plans, which bestow such privileges as faster luggage retrieval and access to airport lounges on premium members who rack up miles year after year after year.

A large installed base of customers with high switching costs can be a source of enormous profitability. Customers with a big investment in capital equipment are an example of a group with high switching costs. The remarkable profitability of air-conditioning businesses owned by American Standard and others is the result of highly stable and predictable service revenues from a large installed base of air conditioners. GE's customers for its power station turbine business are similarly locked in. GE capitalizes on this locked-in customer base by means of service contracts. These contracts provide a consistent source of profitability for GE.[18]

Especially when business systems are installed companywide, as they often are in the case of telecommunications or corporate-management software, the turmoil associated in installing new systems becomes an argument against switching. This type of switching cost has been a boon to the German software company SAP, which has one of the world's largest captive customer bases. As the *Financial Times* reported, "In enterprise software…the high cost of switching suppliers makes change unlikely. 'Most people who have been through [a big software] implementation don't want to do it again—it's like giving birth to a hippo,' says Mr. Richardson, an industry analyst."[19]

Even when WorldCom's accounting practices led it to disgrace and bankruptcy over a period from 2003 to 2005, its blue-chip corporate clients largely did not abandon the company. The reason: WorldCom held a power node in a customer base with high switching inertia similar to the power node of its closest competitor AT&T. As it turned out, over one-third of the largest U.S. companies were WorldCom customers. WorldCom was supplying these big industrial and financial firms with more than just plain old phone services: it was providing communications functions that were critical to running their plants, trading floors, customer service operations, supply lines, and computers. Many of these WorldCom clients were effectively locked in.

To be sure, as the telecom industry experienced turbulence from oversupply and price competition, large corporate customers did demand price concessions from WorldCom, which added to the company's financial woes. But they could not afford to terminate their relationship with WorldCom and risk the potential upheaval of transition to another provider—even if they could find a competitor with a similar package of services. A large share of major corporations chose to maintain WorldCom as their number one or backup provider.

The same advantage, of course, applied to the few other providers of corporate communication services in the United States. The value of the power node could be gauged by the large discounts needed to get customers to switch between telecom providers. In one instance reported by the *Wall Street Journal*, WorldCom in 2004 tried to woo about 500 of AT&T's corporate customers. It could only attract them by guaranteeing "price cuts of between 25% and 40% from their existing rates."[20]

It was the awareness of WorldCom's power node that gave a group of financiers the insight to acquire control of WorldCom as it was heading for Chapter 11.[21] After WorldCom had emerged from bankruptcy, the new owners sold WorldCom to one of the large RBOCs, Verizon. In this acquisition, Verizon obtained an extremely valuable power node, the customer base with high switching costs, that it had not been able to build itself.

Power Node 6: Proprietary Processes or Modus Operandi

A proprietary process or a modus operandi can be a power node.

A proprietary process is like a secret ingredient, except that it is embedded in a method. A modus operandi is "a way of operating or doing something"[22]—or, if you strictly follow the meaning of the Latin term, it is the way in which something or somebody is *supposed* to operate. In this context, we are referring to the methods and procedures that guide the people, equipment, or systems in a company.

The effectiveness and the proprietary nature of a process (and therefore its value as a power node) depend on "the existence of shared principles and practices that span" all participants and "to which the members subscribe in a deep way. Such a set of guiding principles and practices—a doctrine—can enable them to be 'all of one mind' even though they are dispersed and devoted to different tasks. It can provide a central ideational, strategic, and operational coherence that allows for tactical decentralization."[23] This quote comes from a book about terrorist operations, but it applies just as well to a focused business that has gained its coherence from a common set of proprietary processes.

Here are a few examples.

Pharmaceutical companies have developed proprietary processes to move drugs through the approval processes of the U.S. Food and Drug Administration. Many of these pharmaceutical companies are also eager for new products to replace revenues from their older drugs whose patents are expiring. They have been able to use their expertise with regulatory procedures as a power node to capture returns from R&D companies that know how to develop drugs but not how to deal with the FDA. In recent years, for example, Eli Lilly and Company and Amylin Pharmaceuticals, a small biotechnology company, have teamed up to bring a diabetes drug called exenatide to the regulatory finish line.[24]

In the very different arena of snack foods, a modus operandi involving distribution helps to explain much of Frito-Lay's success. As evidence of how ingrained and consistently applied the company's processes are, consider this: I once came upon a perfectly set up display of Frito-Lay snacks in a little shack I'd reached only after a boat trip and a horseback trek down a dusty road in the Dominican Republic.

Sometimes the process is a big secret. Chemical companies or pharmaceuticals often choose not to patent their products—because patents eventually expire and become public—but instead keep the process hidden from emulators. Procter & Gamble, for example, has gone to great lengths to preserve the mystery surrounding its proprietary process for manufacturing diapers. P&G has recently developed a lower-cost manufacturing system that includes 150 suppliers in China, Brazil, India, and Vietnam. The members of this group manufacture various parts of the machines that produce P&G diapers, but the final assembly takes place under wraps at what the *Financial Times* described as a "secret plant" in Shanghai.[25]

Sometimes a proprietary process is public knowledge but very hard to duplicate. The process may have become ingrained as part of company culture or may be actively perpetuated through rigorous training. FedEx is profitable because of its well-publicized process, which gets your package where you want it to go, all the time, on time. To achieve such uniformity, as *BusinessWeek* noted, "FedEx plows 3% of total expenses into training, six times the proportion at most [comparable] companies,"[26] in addition to investing in the hardware side of the business.

Sometimes, the importance of a modus operandi may be overlooked. For an oil company whose greatest source of profits is its in-house sources of crude oil, the ability to manage oil exploration and extraction projects would be a power node. At one time, Royal Dutch Shell did have highly disciplined teams overseeing these operations. According to the *Financial Times*, "Shell once ran one of the industry's most tightly controlled project management operations, but analysts said it lost that capability after laying off technical staff in the 1980s and 1990s, when oil prices were low."[27] In subsequent years, Shell farmed out too much of its project management work, and its costs rose dramatically compared with those of its peers. "Shell's dependence on contractors may help explain why it has lost control over costs at some of its largest projects," the *Financial Times* article reported in 2005. "This summer, the company said the price tag of Sakhalin-2, a giant natural gas project in eastern Russia, had *doubled* to $20bn" (emphasis added). After conducting its own internal review, Shell concluded that its overreliance on outsiders may have been the problem. Therefore, Shell hired 1,000 technical staffers in an attempt to remedy the situation. " 'We want a strong cadre of in-house project professionals, which will give us the option of looking to take in-house some of the work currently done by contractors,' the company said."[28]

This situation is not specific to Shell, but applies to most oil majors. It is so-called oil service companies, like Schlumberger, that have honed their processes for oil exploration and production over the last few decades, not the oil majors. This means that oil-rich national governments and national oil companies can go around the majors, relying on the expertise of oil service companies instead to develop lucrative new fields. An executive at one big European oil company has reportedly said that Schlumberger had forced oil majors to "question what it is we bring to the table."[29] In other words, having given up or lost their modus operandi power node, the oil majors have lost a great deal of profit power vis-à-vis the oil-rich nations and potential partners.

Superior modus operandi has long been a source of profit power, as we can see from another Dutch example. This positive example, however, comes from the second half of the 16th century. The manufacture and export of cloth was one of the main industries of England at that time. As historian Charles Wilson recounts in his book *Profit and Power*, the exported commodity "was white cloth, which was dyed and finished in the Netherlands to form in turn an important article of further sale and re-export."[30] In other words, the Dutch bought undyed cloth cheaply from the English, finished it, and then sold it back to the English at greater cost. Much to the chagrin of the English, the Dutch used their superior proprietary processes to add value to "a semi-manufactured product of English origin, squeezing out of it for themselves a major part of the potential profit."[31] The English did not have the proprietary-process power node. The Dutch did.

In 1613, the British developed a scheme to recapture these profits from the Dutch. They intended to revitalize the practice of dyeing cloth in England and exporting finished goods. Their plan included blocking trade and dishing out government incentives for British firms to finish the cloth. To make a long story short, the scheme was a "disastrous failure."[32] British cloth exports fell dramatically. Customers did not like the English version of the finished goods as well as the Dutch one. The English at that time could not find a way to duplicate or better the Dutch modus operandi.

Power Node 7: Distribution Gateways

Distribution power in general derives from distribution channels, a distribution force, or a distribution approach that gets a company close to its customers without intermediaries. In fact, a distribution gateway more often than not is the intermediary that other companies must go through in order to reach their final customers.

For Wal-Mart, the world's biggest retailer, the leverage available from its 4,000 stores in the United States and 2,900 stores elsewhere is immense. Kraft and Kellogg get 14 percent of their sales from Wal-Mart; General Mills gets 16 percent.[33] Even companies with renowned brand names have little profit power relative to Wal-Mart. Wal-Mart maintains customer loyalty by passing along, in the form of lower prices, many of the benefits it gains by exercising its power—at the expense of consumer goods companies' profitability.

For most suppliers, the more you sell to Wal-Mart, the less you make. In a recent study by consultant Bain & Company of 38 companies doing 10 percent or more of their volume through Wal-Mart, only 24 percent sustained above-average profitability and shareholder returns. Procter & Gamble, which sells 18 percent of its goods through Wal-Mart, was one. But the study noted that even P&G could only manage to maintain such profitability "by shifting business away from basic products such as paper towels, which can easily be knocked off by a private label, to higher-margin products such as health and beauty care."[34] Among other things, P&G has innovated by developing toothpaste with whitening stripes and positioned its upscale Olay creams as an alternative to Botox.

As we can see, the tug-of-war between Wal-Mart and its suppliers is a contest of power nodes along a vertical value chain. Brand power nodes are struggling to maintain their profit margins in the face of intense pressure from distribution power nodes. In the case of well-known consumer products that depend on giant retail outlets for mass-market volume, distribution clout is often winning.

The Industrial and Commercial Bank of China (ICBC) also has a distributed network. When traveling through China, it is hard to miss that the bank has an amazing network of local branches. This gives it a great power node. "With 18,000 branches nationwide and 150 million individual customers,"[35] ICBC can reach an enormous segment of the population. These retail customers are a source of cheap deposits as well as a source of revenues from new financial products. The capital markets' recognition of this power node has contributed to the ICBC's whopping valuation. Its initial public offering in October 2006 was the world's largest IPO to date at the time.

Meanwhile, Hindustan Lever Ltd., Unilever's Indian affiliate, provides an example of creating a distribution power node in order to reach previously untapped markets. In 2005, the *Wall Street Journal* reported, most Indian companies were focused on urban areas, where margins were thin, and overlooking the rural villages where the majority of the population actually lived. Hindustan Lever recruited a female distribution force to "sell more goods to tens of millions of low-income rural consumers it couldn't reach before. Today, about 130,000 poor women are selling Unilever's products in 50,000 villages in India's 12 states and account for about 15% of the company's rural sales in those states. In total, rural markets account for about 30% of Hindustan Lever's revenue."[36]

Power Node 8: Dominant Position in a Layer

A "layer" is a conceptual horizontal slice of the vertical value chain. Control over a layer in a value chain gives companies a strong power node relative to companies in other layers, either before them or after them in the value chain.

There are a variety of ways to acquire control of a layer. Obviously, having a superior product and gaining market share is one route. In some industries, government regulation is another—as, for example, was true in the long-distance transport layer of the telecommunications industry, not only in the United States but also in countries around the world, up until the 1990s. The long-distance transport layer business is technologically based—it corresponds to one of the standard technical "layers" that telecommunications engineers have defined in building communications services. But many other types of layers are conceptual, and, indeed, they may not achieve wide recognition as layers until some company comes along to fill them. An example of such a company is First Data, which began by occupying what was once viewed as little more than a back-office niche and which has since expanded to provide services in that layer for companies around the globe.

Both investors and business leaders would be wise to analyze the power node situation in all the layers surrounding a company's activities. If there is even one layer that is dominated by a few players with the power to extract profits, there may be few returns left for companies in the less cohesive layers. If there are dominant companies in several layers, the situation for weaker companies and their shareholders is likely to be even worse. In the case of the desktop computer industry, one might have anticipated that Compaq would suffer while Intel or Microsoft would prosper.

Layer-based power nodes exist in numerous industries, even agricultural ones. Consider the layers of loose tea leaves and of packaged tea. There are only a few global buyers and packagers of tea, such as Lipton and Tetley. They dominate the layer of packaged and branded tea. Tea leaves, in contrast, are produced by thousands of small to medium-sized tea plantations. It should not be a surprise that the plantations' returns are generally slim.

If you are at the mercy of a larger power node and if the opportunity presents itself, it is worth considering buying into the power node layer and getting out of your tough spot. In the tea industry, Tata Tea Ltd. did just that. Tata Tea, which, as the owner of tea plantations, was at the receiving end of Lipton's power node, opted in 2000 to buy Tetley Group,[37] "Britain's number one maker of tea bags" and the world's second-largest branded tea company. As if following our prescriptions for focusing on power node businesses, Tata Tea has been selling off its plantations ever since.[38]

Many food companies have opted for single-category leadership over broad diversification. A dominant position in a category gives a company better bargaining power with retailers and promotes numerous economies along the supply chain. In 2004, Kraft Foods sold off its candy businesses, including Altoids and Life Savers, to Wm. Wrigley Jr.[39] For Wrigley the purchase was intended to bolster its standing at the candy racks. In 2008, in a $23 billion deal financed by Warren Buffett, Wrigley was in turn bought by Mars. "The transaction would create a confectionery behemoth," the *New York Times* wrote. "The scale and scope of a Mars-Wm. Wrigley Jr. combination...would bring together a big stable of brands with worldwide distribution."[40]

Power Node 9: Increasing Mutual Utility

Sometimes, additional tangible benefits accrue to all existing users of a product whenever that product attracts an additional user. Even better, the larger the base of users grows, the more attractive the product is to potential future users. This is called increasing mutual utility. Products with increasing mutual utility are well positioned to get ahead and stay ahead—and therefore to reap extraordinary profits.

The dynamics of increasing mutual utility are like the preferential attachment dynamics that are responsible for the creation of hubs, but they are embedded in tangible functionality. As you can imagine, the mutual utility power node will become even more potent in transparency. Those products that become hubs will attract a disproportionate percentage of horizontal market share. For those hub products whose value increases with each new user, preferential attachment and mutual utility will feed on each other, making the product harder and harder to beat.[41]

The telephone, of course, is a classic example of a product whose value increased with each additional customer. What good was a phone if there was no one to call? For this reason, AT&T's earliest mandate was to deliver near-universal phone service in the United States.

More recent examples abound. The value (or utility) of craigslist to a user posting a classified ad increases if more people search the site, and vice versa. Microsoft parlayed the increasing mutual utility properties of its PC operating system into another sort of power node, dominant position in a layer. As the number of iPods on the market grew, so did the incentive of music publishers to license songs to iTunes. The more songs were available through iTunes, the greater the incentive to get an iPod. And so on. The more users these systems have, the more value there is to everyone.

In chapter 10, I introduced the idea of "information aikido." Aikido is a Japanese martial art whose techniques involve using the energy of the opposing force. Using minimum effort, the aikido master employs the attacker's momentum to his or her advantage. In transparency, the skills and assets that allow companies to apply aikido techniques in dynamic marketplaces will become a leading power node.

An aikido-master approach will come in handy in any marketplace in transparency that displays power laws—in other words, in most markets with large numbers of participants. As we have said, in a world of instant information, it will no longer be useful to plan advertising and marketing campaigns aimed at winning the "hearts and minds" of consumers. Like those parents jumping ahead of the phone tree, customers will have already reached out for the information they need on their own. If they find a source that they like, other customers will find out about it, and they in turn will tell others.

The key to information aikido is being able to perceive and move with the momentum of the network. It isn't possible to tell the network what to do; as you'll remember, information in powerlaw marketplaces cannot be directed. But you can find ways to tap into the flow. Companies using the aikido approach must do three things:

- *Sow seeds*: Make your messages (products, services, etc.) available at zero cost for the aggregate of customers in a powerlaw network to find. Companies should develop the means to toss out many ideas or products and see which ones germinate. Frito-Lay, as we have mentioned, is constantly putting new flavors and packaging in the marketplace.
- *Conduct surveillance*: Look to see which messages are catching on (attracting the votes of the aggregate); pay as much attention to the success or failure of everyone else's messages as you do to your own. This is about perceiving the momentum. Companies must have the resources and skills to listen for messages from the network, to observe patterns of information (which ideas are getting support and about to take off), and to spot emerging hubs and ride the wave of their success. Numerous low-cost information technologies will facilitate this process. In early 2009, Procter & Gamble's pioneering Pampers. com Web site averaged over 13,000 hits a day. [42] In addition to offering advice, it solicits feedback, which has led to the creation of at least one new product line.
- *Practice aikido*: React quickly to the network's responses to your messages as well as to what you learn from the network. This is all

about "using the energy." Companies that correctly observe movement in the network must be ready to go with the flow and capitalize early on preferences. This may require a rapid retooling of sourcing, manufacturing, and distribution. If a new Frito-Lay snack shows promise, production and distribution get ramped up fast. If a product does not take off, it is discontinued. As you can see, this does not bode well for indecisive companies, or for companies whose culture makes it difficult to give up a project.

These are the aikido assets that make up this power node. Companies that rely on aikido assets often are skilled in all three of these activities, since they fit together into a single resilient advantage. Some companies that employ the aikido approach will need specific capabilities and infrastructure to execute the three actions above. Others, such as Wal-Mart, which we will discuss in a moment, perform one of the three actions and deliver value to associated companies that can execute the rest of the aikido moves.

In addition to Frito-Lay, companies that are already making excellent use of aikido assets include Intel (semiconductors) and Zara (clothing). A *BusinessWeek* article quoted Intel's chief financial officer, who said, "New forecasting software will let the company react more quickly to changes in demand, reducing the time it takes to shift chip production lines from a month to as little as two days. Just one such nimble maneuver can save Intel $1 billion."[43]

Let us look closely at Zara, the world's second-largest clothing retailer by revenues. Zara has built its success on information aikido, and its rivals have rushed to catch up. Zara has already acquired a reputation for up-to-the-minute fashion and for honing a discipline of continually improving its processes. Now Zara is streamlining even further, shaving minutes and hours of wasted time. Store clerks collect anecdotal information about what customers ask for and try. The *Wall Street Journal* reports that store managers "use new hand-held computers that show how garments rank by sales, so clerks can re-order best sellers in less than an hour—a process that previously took about three hours." Such new orders arrive in stores within two days. At Zara headquarters, the *Journal* explains, sales managers sit at computers and monitor sales around the globe. "When a garment sells well—or flops—they quickly tell designers sitting nearby to whip up fresh designs."[44] These sales managers also monitor store-by-store sales. According to *strategy + business*, this capability is so well developed and comprehensive that Zara "can sell some 80 percent of its products at full price—about twice the industry average."[45] While keeping all this capacity for speed and responsiveness in-house requires huge capital expenditures, the margins gained by avoiding markdowns more than make up for the investment. Zara's ability to execute an aikido approach is a tremendous source of power in the apparel industry.

In the case of Zara, having a vertically integrated manufacturing capacity greatly boosts its agility in the marketplace—and therefore its profitability. If aikido assets are to be successfully employed across a distributed business arrangement, there will have to be a great deal of cooperation among the members of the arrangement. If not, there may be difficulties. If one party in an arrangement conducts surveillance, but no one else will act on it, how useful is the information?

Here again, we must stress the importance of power relationships. As one might expect, Wal-Mart is adept at information aikido's second action, conducting surveillance, and gets its suppliers to perform action number three, which is the rapid response. Wal-Mart uses an array of technologies, including RFID chips and other increasingly low-cost information-gathering devices, to develop up-to-the-minute data on customer preferences. If the company has reason to believe there's an item that customers might want, it has the clout to demand that its suppliers produce such an item.

For example, when Wal-Mart noted that shoppers were buying the artificial sweetener Splenda over older, aspartame-based varieties, it insisted that Coca-Cola rush into production with a Splenda-sweetened Diet Coke—thus forcing the beverage giant to delay rollout of an aspartame-based soda it had already planned. In this case, Wal-Mart used the immense leverage of its distribution power node to force Coca-Cola to do its bidding. One power node may be used to enhance the performance of another. As always in power relationships, there is the potential for positive sums: swift responsiveness to consumer trends is likely to benefit all parties in the distributed business arrangement.

Power Node 11: Filters and Brokers

The terms *filter* and *broker* are often used interchangeably, although the two are not identical. Strictly speaking, the definitions are:

- **FILTER**: a network point that is effectively the *only* connection between two cliques. Information in unruly networks travels freely within cliques (which may also be referred to as groups), but it rarely traverses their boundaries, at least not without help. A filter is theoretically the only point through which information can be passed from one clique to another. A filter is often a person whose recommendation or influence can influence others easily.

- **BROKER**: a network point (a person, service, etc.) that is one of the *few* points to be connected to several isolated cliques (of people, products, etc.) and is therefore able to spot opportunities for interaction. A broker can bring members of isolated cliques together for deals and exchange of information.

We discuss brokers and filters together because they play similar roles, either spreading or blocking the spread of information to other points in a network, and because they are both endangered by the same set of dynamics that will be brought about by transparency. Filters and brokers often have influence in situations where objective information is hard to obtain, where people do not have confidence in their own judgment, or where a surrounding group that can readily see the broker or filter's choices does not have the time or resources to process relevant data on its own.

Since brokers and filters render opinions and judgments and exert influence on consumers, they can potentially be either very dangerous or very useful to companies. Not surprisingly, they often get paid handsomely for their services. Readers of chapter 5 will recall, no doubt, that the roles of many brokers or filters will soon be diminished because transparency will undo the blocking aspect of their function and permit information to flow freely around them. Nevertheless, expertise will remain a valuable commodity. A handful of brokers and filters working in highly specialized fields are likely to retain their profit power, even into transparency.

For the most part, brokers are easy to identify—bringing people and services or companies or products together is part of their job description. Examples include travel agents, stockbrokers, and literary and film agents, among many others. These sorts of brokers provide benefits by helping to put forth information that facilitates opportunities for transactions.

The positions that have powerful potential for brokerage may not always be obvious. For instance, fashion stylists, who might once have seemed to occupy a rather low position on the totem pole, can be powerful brokers. "Beyond their own good taste," reported the *Wall Street Journal*, "many star stylists, with their ties to photographers, starlets, socialites and journalists, are big-time networkers. Much as lobbyists wield influence in Washington, stylists can curry favor with the magazines they work for and the fashion crowd they run with." To prove the point, the *Journal* quoted a designer complaining that a stylist "came in one morning and wanted to rip the sleeves out of my amazingly beautiful dress."[46]

Filters come in many guises. They may be family doctors, deejays, or public relations agents; the famous ones tend to be charismatic personalities or connoisseurs. Filters can have remarkable power. A prime example is wine maven Robert Parker, whose graded recommendations have determined the fate and financial success of many a vintner. He has even been called "a palate with power."[47]

"Wine dealers tell the story of a guy who bought a case of wine, didn't like it, and returned the remaining 11 bottles," writes Elin McCoy.[48] "A couple of weeks later, he came back and bought the wine again. The price had doubled, but he had to have the wine anyway. Robert Parker had just given it 95 points."

"Parker has cast such a spell over wine drinkers that a glowing review often doubles or triples the price of the wine," McCoy explains. "A negative review can make a label almost impossible to sell. Mr. Parker's judgments can even affect the sales of wines that have reputations earned over the course of a century or more—like Cheval Blanc, considered one of the dozen or so greatest French wines."[49]

According to some critics, Parker has acquired so much power that winemakers actually alter their products to meet his likes and dislikes. Wine writer Alice Feiring charges that wineries pander to Parker's palate, using "technology and additives to rack up Parker points," and wind up making soulless, "standardized wine."[50]

Magazines can also be powerful filters. The *New Yorker,* for instance, has been a filter for literary writing. Similarly, editorial pages reflect the curatorial view of fashion magazines. "Appearing in an editorial section of a magazine, rather than an ad, suggests to consumers that the publication is endorsing the designer,"[51] writes the *Wall Street Journal*. If products are featured in the editorial section of a magazine, they have been granted the approval of a powerful filter.

In the past, very few members of the public would ever have seen couture fashions if publications hadn't found room for photographs of runway shows on their pages. Still, it seems quite likely that filters like fashion writers and editors will continue to provide a useful function. An expert eye is something it may take years of study and observation to acquire, while many buyers may not trust their own tastes. And when it comes to actually spending money, they may want some reassurance that the couture in question is not merely outlandish but also chic. Moreover, they may want to be sure that everyone around them knows it, too.

Thus, even when it comes to reassuring customers on subjective matters of taste, filters will still play a role—especially at the high end. A publication selling book reviews will have to compete against the thousands of write-ups available for free on sites like Amazon, Barnes & Noble, or Google. A collector of expensive art, on the other hand, may feel the need for a connoisseur: someone who can inspect the product, judge its quality, and project its worth as an investment. The assurance by this sort of expertise cannot be easily supplanted.

Guillaume Gauthereau of Lalique, a French luxury brand of crystal and glass, believes that high-end customers prefer products or a selection of products that have been "curated" by a filter. Art dealers and museums often act as filters. These days, luxury goods retailers may be able to obtain an imprimatur of quality for their products by getting the blessing of reputable museums. Giorgio Armani, the fashion designer, for instance, sponsored a show tracing the evolution of his work that made the rounds of some of the world's leading art institutions. The jewelry firm that I have helped to start, Mehr-un-Nissa, uses the finest high-karat inputs and irreplaceable craftsmanship, and it has an inalienable pedigree. Yet it was very helpful that Mehr-un-Nissa designs were selected by New York's American Museum of Natural History and by Tokyo's Mori Art Center Gallery. For a newcomer like Mehr-un-Nissa, there are great benefits to receiving confirmation from leading museums that it is truly creating museum-quality pieces.

In transparency, as I have mentioned, the mechanistic role of the filter, that of being the physical conduit between one "island" group and another, will be undermined. In many instances, the taste-making functions of filters will be assumed by preferential attachment or the efficiency-of-search aspect of hubs—whether the hub is a bookselling site posting reader reviews or a celebrity agreeing (for a fee) to use a new product while the paparazzi are on hand. Hubs that perform de facto filtering functions are likely to have exponentially greater influence on consumers than early generations of filters ever did.

We can already point to numerous industries in which an expanded flow of information has begun to loosen the hold of brokers. Wall Street brokerage firms have been undermined by electronic trading, travel agents by sites that allow consumers to book their own tickets, and real estate brokers by online postings. Those brokers who do the best in the future will be those who bring some level of skill or discernment or provide some kind of screening function that remains too labor-intensive for clients to do themselves. Literary and film agents will still have to cull promising projects, for instance.

Filters are also likely to see their blocking function undone by transparency—as many of them are well aware. In the *New York Times,* fashion writer Cathy Horyn had this comment after being banned from a runway show by designer Giorgio Armani: "The wonder to me is not why a designer like Mr. Armani bans a journalist. Rather it is why he doesn't use the power of digital technology to take his message directly to the public, effectively knocking out journalists who complain that his clothes are out of touch."[52]

Unlike Armani, pharmaceutical companies are working actively to get past filters. Several companies have started to offer an abundance of medical information direct to the public, including advertising pitches for their drugs. Physicians, historically, have acted as filters between pharmaceutical companies and patients who may need medicine. If a doctor doesn't prescribe a drug, the patient isn't likely to know it exists. Pharmaceuticals have therefore have spent hefty sums on marketing efforts courting the filter-doctors and trying to convince them to prescribe their products. As is often the case with filters, the doctors' power is a double-edged sword for the drug companies. They found that in some instances, the filter-doctors acted as blocks of resistance to introducing new drugs! Now, ironically, some pharmaceutical companies are trying to go around the blocking filter-doctors.

In recent years, drug companies have tried a new strategy of disbursing information directly to patients. We have seen many examples of pharmaceutical companies launching advertising campaigns aimed directly at the buying public. In 2000, for example, Bayer Corporation went straight to the airwaves with claims that its aspirin could prevent heart attack and stroke.[53] And in 2007, Pfizer came under attack for using Dr. Robert Jarvik, an inventor of the artificial heart, in ads for a cholesterol drug.[54] By providing free information and reducing search costs for buyers, pharmaceuticals are trying to dismantle the stronghold power of physicians—in other words, they are moving away from an "islands" model and trying to create a powerlaw network topology.

So how will this battle for prescriptions play out in transparency? In the case of pharmaceutical companies, doctors, and patients, we will see a number of new relationships. Pharmaceutical companies need to walk a fine line between deferring to their filters' expertise ("ask your doctor") on the one hand and going around those same filters to market new medications on the other. Even in transparency, doctors can be expected to remain as filters—not just because they legally are the ones who are allowed to write prescriptions, but also because medical practice requires specialized knowledge and the ability to make judgments based on experience that patients mostly lack.

Similarly, filters and brokers may continue to survive in situations where people, rightly or wrongly, do not trust their own judgment in making decisions or their own ability to process the available information.

We should expect, however, that the power of the majority of filters and brokers will be undermined by transparency. This is because filters and brokers are fundamentally products of environments in which information does not flow freely. Hubs, on the other hand, are natural products of perfect information. Next, we will turn to hubs.

Power Node 12: Hubs

A hub is one of the most effective power nodes imaginable in the transparent economy. Along with aikido assets, hubs are one of two new power nodes to emerge in transparency. We talked about the impact of hubs on transparency's new marketplaces in chapter 10; now we will take a closer look at the ways business leaders and investors can capitalize on this emerging source of profit power by creating or controlling a hub. Not every hub will automatically be a power node. Companies—or anybody aiming to use the power of hubs—will have to find their unique mechanisms to translate the hubs' immense energy and popularity into profit power.

Hubs are products, services, people, ideas, cities, etc., that are the beneficiaries of a virtuous self-reinforcing popularity pattern. Hubs naturally emerge in transparent environments among large groups—in other words, in powerlaw networks. They are a consequence of powerlaw dynamics. A hub in such a network is an entity that has attracted a disproportionate number of choices. "Disproportionate," in this context, simply means more choices than a statistician would predict from a random distribution. In fact, as we have described in chapter 5, if the right conditions are present—as they often will be in transparency—choices will be distributed according to a powerlaw distribution. As you may remember, when people see a powerlaw distribution in action, they often casually refer to it as an 80–20 distribution, as in "20 percent of the books attract 80 percent of sales revenues." As you appreciate, as a general statement this is at best only approximately correct. At least the 80–20 picture conveys the concept.

If we think about the 80–20 dynamics in terms of market share in any large consumer aggregate in transparency, we will begin to understand what a souped-up engine of economic profits hubs can be. Companies whose primary source of power lies in their appeal to members of large-scale consumer aggregates will have the greatest opportunity to receive a high-octane jolt from powerlaw dynamics.

The most important characteristic of hubs is that they don't try to push information out to other points; instead, other points reach out to hubs for information. Whatever the nature of its initial appeal, a hub grows as a result of preferential attachment. When consumers in transparency reach out for information and successfully locate it, others will see what they are doing and follow them to the same location. As a result, in transparent networks we are likely to see vast concentrations of interest in just a few places. Being a hub is not the same as being a filter or broker (power node #11). A hub is a result of network dynamics when information can flow freely. Filters and brokers thrive in climates of limited information, and they exercise control over the flow of information.

A hub attracts votes and choices because, as a result of interdependent decision making, agents in the network are attracted to the products, candidates, and so on that they see attracting the greatest numbers of votes and choices, or because they go to search for information in the places where they see the largest number of other people looking.

The points that become beneficiaries of preferential attachment and emerge as hubs therefore fall into one of three categories. Either they were there first or they are *focal points of search* or they have an inherent *power of attraction.*

Focal-Point-of-Search Hubs

As we discussed in chapter 10, Google is an example of a focal-point-of-search hub. The "go-to" person in your office is an example of a focal point of search. Similarly, the most efficient way to find information in a power-law network is to look to the sources of information that other people look to. Useful sources of information may—again thanks to the dynamics of preferential attachment—become hubs. Search-based hub Web sites include bookselling sites, movie databases, consumer-products ratings sites, dating sites, and even many news sites.

Power-of-Attraction Hubs

As we discussed in chapter 10, Oprah Winfrey is a power-of-attraction hub. Some people or products attract viewers, assignments, clients, buyers, or users either because they were there first or because of their inherent superior fitness, which could lie in their quality, talent, beauty, design, or any number of other attributes. Top models and movie stars, stellar architects, and iPods and iPhones are such hubs. When a point gets to take an early lead because of power of attraction, it can stay ahead because of the subsequent processes of preferential attachment. *Harry Potter and the Philosopher's Stone,* the first book in the adventure series, took off rapidly because friends recommended it to friends. The book itself then became a hub, as others wanted to know what was attracting so many people to read it.

In chapter 10, we made the distinction between "being" and "controlling" a hub. We will maintain that distinction here, but we will frame the discussion in slightly different terms. Since we are interested in the question of how to obtain a power node, we will talk specifically about the possible methods of *creating a hub.* Next we will discuss the option of taking control of a hub by *acquiring the hub* company or hiring hub employees. Last, we will talk about *controlling a hub* without actually owning it, either by influencing the hub or by benefiting from direct or indirect association with it.

Creating a Hub

No entity can ever be certain of triggering hub dynamics—it is the agents in the network, those continually arriving points of network theory, who decide what they need or like. Nevertheless, entities that act strategically, whether these are Web sites, companies, cities, or even candidates, can orchestrate conditions that may have an elevated *potential* to inspire preferential attachment. This is true for both the focal-point-of-search and the power-of-attraction types of hubs.

One of the clearest examples of creating a hub that is a focal point of search and using it to derive great competitive advantage is of course Google. Google was first able to trigger preferential attachment because it had designed a search engine that worked better than existing search engines, and users began to switch. Later generations of computer users, of course, simply followed their predecessors. Google was also ahead of its competitors in figuring out how to translate hub traffic into profits, as we have also explained.

Consumer Reports is another focal point of search that has profit power. The magazine was always a focal point of search, but when it went online it was able to offer many more of its expert product reviews to consumers, and in a much more up-to-date manner. Moreover, unlike most online publications, it was able to convince readers to pay for its services. At the end of 2007, consumerreports.org passed the 3 million mark in paid subscribers. Only about 600,000 of those subscribers overlapped with the 4.5 million readers the print edition already had.

The key to winning the focal-point-of-search battle is meeting the need of economic actors in transparency to "know everything"—fast—and then seeking a business model that will make that pay.

In transparency, many companies may find methods to heighten the allure of their products in ways that may help them to to trigger preferential attachment and emerge as power-of-attraction hubs. Often this will mean trying to create a culture or sense of community around a product. The more intimate a sense of connection people have with the product, the more they will want to spread the word to friends. The more friends you have on your side, the closer you get to preferential attachment.

In transparency, the products most likely to be the beneficiaries of 80–20 powerlaw distributions are those that come to be associated with some aspect of interdependent decision making. For instance, anyone who believes that status or any other individual or social virtues can be acquired or expressed through use of a product is automatically involved in interdependent decision making. Many luxury goods, notably designer handbags, have already benefited from hub dynamics. As Dana Thomas, author of *Deluxe: How Luxury Lost its Luster,* told the *Wall Street Journal,* "Luxury has always conferred status, but [in the past status was usually] associated with superior quality. [These days] we don't buy luxury branded items for what they are but for what they represent."[55]

Herd behavior reflecting interdependent decision making isn't limited to fashion. When people speak about the "culting" of brands, they are speaking of brands' hub potential. A famous example of a company that was able to build preferential attachment by encouraging interdependent decision making is Harley-Davidson. In 1983, its management founded the Harley Owners Group (HOG), a "brand community" that now numbers a million members. HOGs are sponsored by the company, but the members organize all the events, which emphasize the joys of being a Harley-Davidson owner. Participants buy and wear plenty of Harley accoutrements, thus effectively extending the company's advertising reach (for free!). As we can see, this sort of preferential attachment is self-perpetuating—and enduring profit power may be the result. These days, Harley management is concerned about the aging of this core customer base, but during the decades that preferential attachment was fueling the growth of the HOG network, Harley sales grew at an average of 37 percent a year.

Apple is a company for which power of attraction has triggered the boon of preferential attachment across much of its product line. It produces superior products that combine functionality with aesthetic pleasures and has parlayed that into a growing base of devoted fans. Despite this strong brand identity, it can be argued that Apple did not reap the benefits of powerlaw dynamics and achieve hub status until after 2001, when it introduced a sleek portable digital music player called the iPod. Apple had sold 150 million iPods by September 2007, gained a 70 percent share of the digital music player market, and watched its stock price soar.[56] Interdependent decision making played a role. If we consider a 2005 Piper Jaffray & Co. survey of digital music device use among American teens, of whom 56 percent owned an iPod, 14 percent a Sony, and 7 percent an iRiver, and so on, we can observe a pattern that very much resembles a powerlaw distribution.[57] (By the fall of 2008, the number of students with iPods was up to 84 percent.)[58]

The business of selling iPods itself is quite profitable, but Apple has also used its hub power node to build related power nodes that increase its leverage over business arrangement partners. From 2001 to 2007, there were over 3 billion music downloads to those iPods through iTunes[59]—and as a result, Apple developed a distribution power node that won competitive battles over pricing with the music industry's far weaker special-ingredient power node. As a result of the iPod's popularity, Apple may be able to build market share at relatively low cost for new Apple products that are in or beyond the original PC business.

Cities and institutions have also been able to cultivate their power of attraction in hopes of inspiring preferential attachment dynamics. An example is Dubai, with its enormous waterfront developments aimed at attracting businesses and tourism. Another is Washington, D.C., which is beginning to enjoy preferential attachment as a high-tech center.[60] And finally there is Singapore, which has already achieved hub status and is aggressively pursuing efforts to maintain the hub's "fitness." Singapore attracts superb talents in the financial, medical, and technical fields. As the *New York Times* reported in 2004, "Singapore is also benefiting from incentives offered by the government to attract investment by pharmaceutical companies including GlaxoSmithKline, reducing reliance on production of disk drives and other electronics."[61]

Something similar is afoot at academic institutions that hire great teachers and provide scholarships to strong students. Leading universities are hubs, places where very smart kids want to study because they recognize where the market has gone. Places where very smart kids want to work are hubs for brains: Renaissance Capital, Infosys, McKinsey, Goldman Sachs, Bain, Google. These institutions understand preferential attachment very well. Each year they bid aggressively for the top youngsters.

As we mentioned in chapter 10, and will mention again when we talk about "controlling" a hub below, one way to create a hub may be simply by associating with an existing hub. In effect, the spin-offs of popular TV shows are examples of how the exposure afforded by association with front-runner hubs may trigger enough preferential attachment to produce at least a minor hub.

Acquiring a Hub

It is a possible to buy a company or even in effect acquire a person who is a hub, just as you might choose to buy any other power node. Indeed, given the difficulties of catching up to leading hubs, this is likely to be a frequent phenomenon in transparency. As we have said, Microsoft's attempt in 2008 to buy Google was a leading example. But there are many others. Almost any Web site that begins to attract huge volumes of traffic, particularly from a desirable demographic, is likely to be an object of great interest. The key is to figure out if the hub has profit power. It is quite possible to overpay for a pseudo hub without profit power—as we have learned from the notorious example of AOL and Time Warner.

It is possible to buy hub companies, of course, but it also possible to employ hub individuals. Superstar employees who draw flocks of clients are hubs, for example. These people may be big generators of profits for your company. Since they are power nodes in their own right, they have a lot of clout over their employers. They have the wherewithal to siphon profits from the companies they work for. If their employers tried to resist their demands, employee hubs might go elsewhere. When that happens, these employers will likely lose a big chunk of revenue, and their competitors will gain a new source of profit power.

Mergers and acquisitions stars Bruce Wasserstein and Joe Perella are examples of bankers who managed to develop into hubs while they were still employees early in their careers. Clients flocked to them. Since they have become hubs, they have relocated their services several times. Together or apart, the two men have spent their lucrative careers cycling back and forth between operating boutique firms and occupying increasingly powerful positions at investment banks.

For this reason, many companies try hard to limit the development of hubs within their own ranks—from Goldman Sachs to Elizabeth Arden Spas. If you, the owner, can build your organization as a mesh in which star power among employees is evenly distributed, the organization is likely to be stable, even if a number of partners get lured elsewhere. If you allow hubs to form, on the other hand, your organization is not stable. Goldman Sachs is an example of an organization that for many years was structured like the kind of mesh network that we described in chapter 5. In contrast, First Boston in the late 1980s was an example of an organization with hubs: a few bankers were a lot more famous than most of the others. As might be predicted based on this understanding of network structures, the mesh organization was less vulnerable to departures of senior bankers than the hub organization. The departure of Wasserstein and Perella in 1987 significantly damaged this firm's mergers and acquisitions efforts.

When North Castle Partners bought Elizabeth Arden Spas, it tried to limit the development of hubs in its ranks by instituting tough measures to gain control over the potential hub employees. "One change that was particularly annoying: Stylists were prevented from communicating directly with customers to make appointments," the *Wall Street Journal* wrote. "One goal was to encourage [customer] loyalty to the spa itself, rather than individual employees. The company reckoned that if employees left, an endemic problem in the business, they would be less likely to take clients with them"[62] as a result of this measure.

Controlling a Hub without Ownership

Just as billboard space can be bought along a busy highway, so opportunities for visibility may be purchased from hubs. Celebrities are hubs whose appeal clearly lies in the power of attraction, and they often cash in on their resulting profit potential by selling endorsements that boost sales—hence the popularity of supermodel perfumes and sports-star sneakers.

Promotion may be even more effective if it's not explicitly couched as advertising. Product placement, therefore, is another useful method for controlling a hub. In terms of benefiting from a hub based on power of attraction, few examples are as clear as the rewards of having your product—jewelry, clothing, hip gloves—on a nominee who walks the red carpet on Oscar night. "Fashion houses won't place a price tag on the publicity they gain from dressing a star" for the Oscars, "but they agree it drives retail sales. And with color ads in some magazines costing more than $110,000 apiece, designers say a high-profile appearance is worth hundreds of thousands, if not millions. 'It's like winning the lottery,' says Caroline Herrera," whose designs have been worn to the Oscar ceremony by the likes of Renee Zellweger and Salma Hayek.[63]

Taking a similar approach in a different milieu, Nike has begun employing people it calls "influencers" to reach segments of the market to which it doesn't have easy access using traditional means. One of these influencers is Mr. Cartoon, a young graphic artist whose aesthetic choices, the *Wall Street Journal* writes, are closely monitored by "a certain crowd that is young, Latino and hip-hop."[64] Mr. Cartoon is a hub, and to his followers he is a tastemaker. Nike is controlling a localized hub in hopes of enhancing its image with a desired demographic.

Products can also benefit from the power of attraction of other hub products. Indeed, as we have mentioned, it is sometimes possible that an association with one hub will lead to the creation of another. Here is an example of how one entrepreneur was able to exploit the power of attraction of celebrity hubs to create a hub source of profit power all her own. The *Wall Street Journal* told the story of Danielle Friedland, who launched a Web site on which she published photographs of stars and their babies, identified the specific make of the items they were wearing or using, and provided links to the relevant store. As of May 2008, celebrity-babies.com was getting about 10 million page-views a month. A mention there can spark a run on an item. In 2007, the site drew $500,000 in advertising revenues from companies eager to reach its audience of mothers.

A number of hub phenomena are at work in the story of the South Beach Diet, which began life as a book and got a huge boost when President Bill Clinton—another hub—mentioned that it was helping him to lose weight. An online publishing company, Waterfront Media, bought the rights to the diet, launching a Web site that not only promoted the regimen but also created an online community of dieters. Just as the Harley-Davidson owners' groups did, these communities generated preferential attachment. Finally, Kraft Foods, a company eager to buffer its earnings against concerns about obesity, signed a deal that would, the *Wall Street Journal* recounted, "allow Kraft to put the 'South Beach Diet' moniker on some of its products, such as cheeses and desserts. It is the first time Kraft has aligned itself with a specific diet, and the first time 'South Beach' has licensed its name to food products."[65] Kraft is hoping to change its image, inspire preferential attachment, and boost revenues via association with a dieting hub.

As we have seen, there are various ways to control hubs that are focal points of search as well, whether by trying to manipulate a search result or by placing an ad. In their professional community, certain doctors are focal points of search for their colleagues. These doctors may be famous for their research or may speak frequently at conferences, about advances in treatment, for example. They are essentially the go-to people for medical information. In a transparent world, we can expect the reputations of such specialists to be distributed via power law—that is, a few doctors will get the overwhelming number of citations. As a result, a recommendation by a doctor with a leading reputation will carry a lot of weight with other doctors because he or she already is their focal point of search.

Power Nodes and Hub Potential

Finally, let us look at what happens when power nodes and hub dynamics are combined.

This is not a trivial subject because we are speaking here of the impact of transparency on the strength of the power nodes themselves.

There are a number of power nodes that become stronger in the context of powerlaw dynamics. The hub potential of older power nodes is summarized in table 12.1). The four power nodes with the greatest hub potential are: brand (#1), secret or proprietary ingredients, particularly those of the creative variety (#2), customer base with switching costs (#5), dominant position in a layer (#8), and increasing mutual utility (#9).

Hub dynamics have the potential to greatly increase the profit potential of any of these power nodes. First, hub dynamics may have a tremendous impact on market share. As we discussed in chapter 9, large horizontal

Table 12.1		
Hub potential of power nodes in transparency		
	High	Low
Power node (and number)	1. Brand	3. Regulatory protection
	2. Secret, special, or proprietary ingredient	4. Focused financial resources
	5. Customer base with switching costs	6. Proprietary processes or modus operandi
	8. Dominant position in a layer	7. Distribution gateways
	9. Increasing mutual utility	

market share can often become a potent force in vertical competition for returns. Second, if a company has obtained profit power thanks to a power node, hub dynamics will tend to strengthen the winner's position.

For example, a brand that sparks preferential attachment dynamics among customers is likely to be a power node brand—strong enough, perhaps, to trump even the strongest distribution power node. Increasing mutual utility joined with hub dynamics will propel a product's customer base into a swift upward spiral that can lead to dominant position in a layer. If hub dynamics kick in to greatly expand a customer base that also has switching costs, the long-term profit outlook for the company that serves these customers will certainly be enhanced. Hub dynamics have the potential to provide an express lane to profit power.

The companies that can cultivate their power of attraction will probably find it relatively easier to inspire hub dynamics. Even if a company's power node isn't based on brand, building a strong brand identity may be one way to trigger the kind of interest that will spark preferential attachment. As we have seen, Apple has created a hip image for its brand and encourages all sorts of interactions among its users, whether in retail stores or through sharing technologies.

Chapter 13

Managing the Power Nodes

To the victor belong the spoils.
—William Learned Marcy[1]

Power nodes are this era's sources of profit as well as your weapons in transparency's competitive battle. They are at the core of the Four Rules for Maximizing Profits method. If you want to maximize returns in transparency, you need to know your power nodes and know how to use them.

In this chapter, you will learn how to do just that. Our discussion of power nodes is practical stuff. Most of what we discuss is based on my hands-on experience. I have helped companies create or acquire power nodes and even helped develop power nodes they may not even have known they had.

We discussed each of them at length in chapter 12. In this chapter, we will provide an overview of how to develop and wield these power nodes, a managerial skill that will be increasingly essential for business leaders as transparency takes hold.

Although power nodes as a source of profit power have existed in some varieties for centuries, in transparency they will play a more prominent role than ever before. Over the course of this book, we have made four central points about power nodes in this regard:

- In the aftermath of vertical integration, extraordinary profits will increasingly go to focused companies with power nodes. Power nodes are the *key to returns*—power node companies use them to extract profits from, and lay off risks and capital expenditures to, other companies they deal with in their business arrangements. Looking for power nodes will help us identify the most lucrative part of the value chain.

- Power nodes are the *glue* that holds together distributed business arrangements consisting of focused companies. Power node companies have high returns because they own only high-return activities; the power node allows them to control the rest of the distributed business model without owning it.

- There will be many more competitive interfaces in transparency (see the cube depicting 3-D competition in figure 9.1), and therefore there will be many more occasions when power nodes are needed to extract or defend profits. In the past, the companies fighting for horizontal market share were often very much alike—similar structures, similar products, similar skills. The various units along the value chain never had to compete either horizontally or vertically; they were safely locked up inside vertical behemoths that ultimately did battle only in markets for finished goods. In transparency, every big and little piece of those old value chains will be out in the world and flexing its particular muscles to fend for itself. The new vertical competitive battles are about returns, and not over market share or other secondary objectives. The new *competitive weapons* are power nodes, because they are the means of maximizing returns.

- Transparency will create new power nodes such as hubs. Hub dynamics will have tremendous potential to magnify the profit power of older power nodes. Those older power nodes with the greatest potential to benefit from hub dynamics are the ones whose profit power derives from having a strong following among large numbers of individual customers, namely, brand, special ingredient, customer base with switching costs, a dominant position in a layer, and increasing mutual utility (see table 12.1). We talked about the hubbing potential of older power nodes in chapter 12's entry for hubs (power node #12). When we add hub dynamics to the power node picture, the odds that there can be extraordinary profits become much higher.

Transparency's competitive battles will pit power node against power node: distribution versus brand, for example, or special ingredient versus distribution, or brand versus regulatory protection. As you delve into the 12 power nodes, you cannot think of any of them in isolation—you have to imagine how each might fare in combat with any of the other power nodes. The outcome of competitive battles is determined by the relative power node strengths.

In a sense, then, transparency's competitive battles are like a corporate version of the well-known hand game of rock, paper, scissors. In the game, rock beats scissors beats paper beats rock. In the business world, outcomes involving power nodes are predictable if you pay attention to the relative power node strengths (RPSs) of the competitors. This is why one has to compute and map relative power-node strength (RPS) on a company versus company basis, as shown in chapter 17. We can see examples of "distribution beats brand"—that would be Wal-Mart—but we can also find many cases where strong brands triumph over distributors. In table 13.1 I have summarized a number of the power node battles that are discussed in this book. We have discussed one or more examples of a power node battle for each of the 12 power nodes. In this table, we see the power node leaders, the winners of the power node competition, juxtaposed with the other players in their distributed business arrangement.

Moreover, though certain power nodes may hold sway for decades, or even longer, no power node is immune to changing economic conditions or new competitive pressures. Business shifts involving power nodes can pose enormous strategic and managerial challenges, particularly if a company's greatness has been built around a power node that is now under siege. We have already seen how wrenching it was for AT&T, around 2000, to come to terms with the loss of its power node in long-haul network capacity. Partially as a result, the company was slow to take advantage of its remaining power node, a customer base with switching costs.

A more recent example involves Microsoft, which became one of the world's biggest companies because it was so successful in exploiting the power node potential of its business in supplying operating systems for PCs. Nevertheless, the company is now facing challenges. As the *New York Times* put it, "the center of gravity in computing continues to move away from the personal computer, Microsoft's stronghold, and to the Internet."[2] To update its power node or to develop a power node that will prevail in this developing environment, of course, will require all of Microsoft management's considerable resourcefulness.

We can learn from several examples of companies that resolved their power node predicaments with audacious moves. Boise Cascade, as we know, reversed its fortunes when it undertook the radical step of getting out of the woods and into the store—in the form of OfficeMax and its distribution power node. Another company that responded to trying circumstances with a bold makeover is De Beers, the South African diamond giant, which embarked upon a new strategy when its domination of the world's

Table 13.1

Using Power Nodes in 3-D Competitive Battles: Power Node Leaders versus Participants in Distributed Arrangements

Power node	Power node leaders	Participants in distributed arrangements
1. Brand	Pepsi-Cola and Coca-Cola	Bottlers, such as Pepsi Bottling Group (PBG) or Coca-Cola Enterprises (CCE)
2. Secret, special, or proprietary ingredients	Owner of chemical inputs to drugs, for example, Teva	Drug manufacturers, such as Alpharma
	Aquafina/Pepsi-Cola	Bottlers
	The Rolling Stones	Music companies
	Proctor & Gamble: owner of proprietary technology of Pampers machines	150 component suppliers in Brazil, China, Vietnam, and India
	Producers of ethylene glycol, such as Union Carbide, Mobil	Antifreeze companies, such as Prestone
3. Regulatory protection	Owners (licensees) of wireless spectrum, such as Sprint, AT&T Wireless	Wireless affiliates
	RBOCs, such as Verizon, SBC, and Bell South	Local customers
	U.S. medical doctors	Foreign-trained doctors; U.S. patients
4. Focused financial resources	Toyota	Automotive parts manufacturers
	Creditwallahs	Shopkeepers and large consumer food companies, such as Unilever and Pepsi
5. Customer base with switching costs	AT&T Business Services; MCI-WorldCom Business Services	Long-haul network providers
	Walgreen CVS	Local customers
6. Proprietary processes or modus operandi	Pharmaceutical companies managing FDA process, for example, Eli Lilly	Biotech and R&D companies that are seeking FDA approval, for example, Amylin
	Hotel management companies like Hyatt, Marriott	Hotel real estate owners
7. Distribution gateways	Wal-Mart	Suppliers, including branded companies such as Procter & Gamble

(Continued)

Table 13.1

(*Continued*)

Power node	Power node leaders	Participants in distributed arrangements
	Lipton Tea (Unilever)	Tea growers
	Staples, OfficeMax	Office products manufacturers, such as Esselte
8. Dominant position in a layer	Category leaders such as Unilever (ice cream), Cadbury (candy), Mars	Stores
	Intel	Computer manufacturers
	Microsoft operating system	Computer manufacturers
9. Increasing mutual utility	eBay	Competing auction houses
	craigslist	Headhunters, temporary-work agencies
10. Aikido assets (sow, surveillance, aikido)	*Sow*	
	P&G (pampers.com)	Competing toiletries companies
	Surveillance	
	Wal-Mart	Packaged goods companies
	Zara	Competing clothing companies
	Aikido	
	Zara	Competing clothing companies
	Frito-Lay	Competing snack products
	Intel, AMD	Computer manufacturers
11. Filters and brokers	*Filters*	
	Family doctors/drugs prescribed	Pharmaceutical companies, nonprescribed drugs, patients
	Robert Parker/ recommended winemakers	Winemakers not recommended
	Brokers	
	Fashion stylists	Out-of-favor designers
	Financial advisors/favored products	Financial-product creators with less favored products, customers
12. Hubs	*Hubs displaying the power of attraction*	
	Harry Potter books	Other publishers, book vendors
	iPods	Other music distributors, record labels and movie studios, Netflix and Blockbuster
	Capital markets operations at top-tier investment	Issuers of equity and debt, investors

(*Continued*)

Table 13.1

(Continued)

Power node	Power node leaders	Participants in Distributed Arrangements
	banks, such as Morgan Stanley, Goldman Sachs	
	Star bankers/employers	Other investment banks (employers)
	Star places to work	Competitors
	Star students	Other universities
	Oprah Winfrey, book publishers	Competing authors, publishers
	Hubs as focal points of search	
	Google	Advertisers

raw-diamond supply (a special-ingredient power node) had started to wane. De Beers's grand plan provides us with a useful illustration of how a company can retool its existing assets to establish a new power node when its old power node is dwindling.

As the *Wall Street Journal* reported, De Beers Group "still controls about 60% of the world's raw diamonds. [But] in 2001, realizing that uncut diamonds were becoming a commodity, the company decided to shift its strategy: It would relinquish its reliance on a fading and controversial monopoly and focus instead on the more profitable branded-goods business, developing its own finished products and retail stores."

De Beers set up a $500 million joint venture with LVMH Moët Hennessy Louis Vuitton, the eminent producer of luxury goods. As the *Wall Street Journal* put it, De Beers "shocked the staid world of high-end jewelry in 2001 when it unveiled plans to create a luxury retail chain, putting the De Beers brand into direct competition with the group's own high-end retailer-customers, such as Tiffany, Cartier and Harry Winston." Eventually, the chain may comprise as many as 100 high-end boutiques selling De Beers-branded diamond jewelry. " 'It is our strategy to build one of the largest [jewelry] companies in the world in 10 years,' Bernard Arnault, chairman of LVMH, said at the time."[3]

De Beers's original power node, diamonds as a proprietary ingredient, disappeared with the growth of diamond supplies that are outside of its control. De Beers is countering the loss of one power node with an attempt to create two new ones: a luxury brand and a chain of luxury retail stores. Rather than risk letting the profits from its potential new brand power node end up in the hands of established jewelry chains with potentially stronger distribution power nodes, De Beers and LVMH have attempted to develop their own high-end distribution system.

In table 13.2 I have summarized the examples of successful power node creation or acquisition that we discuss in this book.

Of course, you should not wait until your company is under threat before you look for avenues to bolster its power nodes. In fact, you must always be ahead of events. The Four Rules for Maximizing Profits method's four sets of evaluation and action templates, the material of section VI, will be of great use in helping companies to anticipate possible competitive threats. There are numerous ways to create and maximize the potential of power nodes which involve a solid overhaul but not a complete U-turn or the tearing apart of a company's activities. Although some power nodes will rise or fall because of economic change, many others will come about only as a result of smart strategic thinking, exceptional understanding of the unique aspects of a company's sources of excellence, or managerial ingenuity. Power nodes are tools that reward entrepreneurial savvy and management skillfulness with increased returns and shareholder value.

I can cite one example from my days at Pepsi-Cola International (PCI), when we were building the international drinks business. In the mid-1990s, we at PCI learned that, contrary to PCI's wishes, many of our international bottlers were producing their own brands of water. Pepsi-Cola at that time did not have a water brand. We wanted our bottlers to focus exclusively on Pepsi brands, which were both our power node and the center of our distributed business arrangement-to-be. But it was difficult to curtail activity outside of Pepsi brands without being able to offer the bottlers an alternative water product. Pepsi couldn't very well ask the bottlers to give up water altogether, since both the bottlers and Pepsi were aware that water was a fast-growing business opportunity.

What could we at PCI do? It was not easy to plug the product hole with a large acquisition. Brands such as Evian and Badoit are bottled "at the source" only, as the water comes out of the ground. These brands require systems that move bottles full of liquid around the world. That was a problem. In the Pepsi system, the only thing that traveled across borders was our secret ingredient—the concentrate syrup. The water in soft drinks is added locally, by the bottlers. The only filled bottles in the Pepsi system are those departing from the bottlers' plants. Furthermore, many consumers in developing countries did not want source water. They distrusted water coming from a well—and you would distrust it, too, if you lived in a country where drinking water from tube wells came laden with arsenic.

Table 13.2

Illustrations of successful power node acquirers and creators

Power node	Power node creators and acquirers
1. Brand	De Beers: shifted emphasis from selling wholesale diamonds, a power-losing enterprise, toward building the De Beers brand and building a distribution gateway with a chain of luxury retail stores in a joint venture with LVMH.
	Tata Tea Ltd. moved from selling loose tea from its Indian tea plantations toward developing a branded tea business. In 2000, Tata Tea bought Tetley, the world's second-largest tea brand. In 2005, Tata Tea sold off the majority of its equity holdings in 17 tea plantations.
2. Secret, special, or proprietary ingredients	Teva is able to extract profits by selling hard-to-duplicate chemical formulations, which are essential ingredients in certain patented and FDA-approved drugs.
	Pepsi, needing a bottled-water product to keep its bottlers loyal, invented Aquafina, incorporating a proprietary ingredient of salts that add a distinctive taste. Pepsi charges its bottlers a premium price for the "secret ingredient" of these salts.
	The city of Dubai had limited waterfront property, the most valuable real estate in its region. So it expanded that property vastly by creating landfill peninsulas in the shape of palm trees, with many "leaves" that maximize the amount of shoreline.
3. Regulatory protection	Verizon Wireless, Sprint Wireless, and AT&T Wireless, among others, have acquired regulatory protection in the form of rights to use part of the U.S. wireless spectrum.
	IBM has earned billions of dollars in revenues by selling patented intellectual property.
4. Focused financial resources	Toyota uses capital access as a power node to effectively provide insurance and security to its network of a few hundred automotive-component suppliers. In return it extracts quite a share of the increase in combined shareholder value.
5. Customer base with switching costs	Booz Allen has developed a consulting practice with long-running contracts with U.S. government entities. This business was sold to Carlyle for $2 billion in 2008.
	Service contracts with effective, locked-in customers, whether for industrial air conditioners (American Standard), steam turbines (GE), or jet engines, are an ongoing and stable source of revenue.

(Continued)

Table 13.2	
(Continued)	
Power node	**Power node creators and acquirers**
6. Proprietary processes or modus operandi	FedEx employees know how to get a package delivered on time; the company's investment in training is one of the keys to its success.
	Procter & Gamble has developed a proprietary assembly process that allows it to make use of low-cost components manufactured across a distributed business arrangement of Asian companies without surrendering secrets about the proprietary manufacturing process that is embedded in its machinery.
7. Distribution gateway	Boise Cascade gave up on forest products and instead acquired OfficeMax, a distribution gateway for paper and other business supplies.
	The Industrial and Commercial Bank of China (ICBC) has opened 18,000 branches that give it access to 150 million people, a huge base of customers for the bank's financial products.
8. Dominant position in a layer	Microsoft had its first success with a PC operating system in 1981 and went on to establish such a dominating position in that layer that it was able to protect its returns against all sorts of hardware manufacturers.
	Food companies that were previously diversified are focusing on single-category leadership: Cadbury-Schweppes in chocolates and candy, Kraft in cheese, Mars in chewy candy.
9. Increasing mutual utility	eBay started from scratch about a decade ago. Its growth was fueled by the fact that its value to buyers and sellers increases every time another buyer or seller comes online. The success of craigslist is based on the same principle.
	The more people buy Apple's iPods, the more incentive there is to make music and programming available to iTunes. The more programming is available for iPods, the more valuable they are. And so on.
10. Aikido assets (sow, surveillance, aikido)	Zara (clothing): *Sow*—put new clothing lines into the marketplace and watch closely; *Surveillance*—implement up-to-the-minute monitoring of sales data, plus systematic collection of anecdotal reports of customer response; *Aikido*—based on this surveillance, designers constantly revise fashions, and stores receive new styles twice a week.
	Wal-Mart does extensive monitoring of inventory (surveillance) and may ask suppliers to create new products in response to

(Continued)

| Table 13.2 | |

(Continued)	
Power node	**Power node creators and acquirers**
	consumer trends (aikido in the context of a distributed business arrangement).
11. Filters and brokers	Filters: Wine-rating czar Robert Parker, high-end art curators, and fashion writers have created profitable businesses out of their filter status.
	Brokers: fashion stylists, literary and film agents, real-estate brokers.
12. Hubs	Hub Web sites are created when enough visitors come, initially for efficiency of search, to spark preferential attachment. Sites like Google and Amazon have already demonstrated huge profit power.
	Apple created conditions that fostered preferential attachment and turned products like iPods and iPhones into hub brands. Motorcycle maker Harley-Davidson revived its brand by encouraging HOGs (Harley Owners Groups) that created preferential attachment dynamics for the bikes.
	City-states like Singapore and Dubai have deliberately turned themselves into hubs. They have fostered attractiveness to investors, businesses, scientists, and other important and influential people. Once they come, others will follow. Elite schools and businesses try to build hub status in a similar manner.
	Oprah Winfrey is a hub. Convincing Oprah to recommend your book or cosmetic, or even your candidacy for president, is a great way to capitalize on her attractiveness and immense visibility as a hub. Trends can be born and huge individual sales can be made as a result of an association with a hub.

The breakthrough in our thinking emerged as we participated in various water taste-test sessions. We realized that what gave source waters their distinctive taste were salts and minerals—and we could provide those! All Pepsi had to do was create a "secret ingredient" that bottlers could add to purified water anywhere. The result was Aquafina, which is what you get when bottlers add a package of Pepsi salts to purified tap water and alter its flavor. Pepsi charges its bottlers for this secret ingredient, just as it charges for cola concentrate. With that, Pepsi had created a powerful new power node. Aquafina has become a tremendous success. In the U.S., it is now the top-selling water in the fast-growing wholesale bottled-water category. In 2006, it had an 11.3 percent share in the U.S. market.[4]

As we consider these aspects of power nodes, it is evident that they should be a major focus of 21st-century business management. In the final sections of this book, I will offer templates that will enable business leaders to conduct a rigorous evaluation of their companies' power nodes—and then, of course, to develop an action plan. Implementing such an action plan may require a great deal of effort and resolve, since radical changes within corporations will often not come easy.

Any major decisions involving power nodes are important ones, and they will invariably demand careful consideration of numerous trade-offs involving returns, costs, taxes, and so forth, as well as skill in communicating with shareholders. Moreover, as I have mentioned, it is not unusual for corporate fiefdoms to develop around long-standing power nodes, and individuals with power bases may be reluctant to surrender them, no matter what the best interests of the shareholders may be. As a general rule of thumb, while companies should nourish the power nodes that will best serve them in 3-D competition and in the marketplace, they should avoid the development of associated fiefdoms.

Many focused companies with power nodes will participate in distributed business arrangements. The successful orchestration of these arrangements is a necessary skill for corporate managers in transparency. As we saw in our discussion of the motley crew, picking the right partners is critical, and knowing when to apply the carrots and sticks to members of a distributed business arrangement is an essential art.

A company controlling the power node around which a distributed business arrangement is organized must continually balance the allocation of system economics to ensure the viability of all parties.

The companies most successful at orchestrating distributed business arrangements have done a number of things well. They have adjusted to suit their own strategies, adapted to changes in competitive environments and local circumstances, and tended to the health of their partners. Coca-Cola and Pepsi-Cola, for instance, have made temporary changes to their business models to facilitate global expansion or to reorganize or right-size their bottlers. As we have seen, companies in the oil and pharmaceutical industries have also adapted their business models over time. This requires focus, skill, and resources.

In the early chapters of this book, I took pains to argue that in transparency extraordinary profits are a legitimate economic concept. Perfect information will create its own kinds of market imperfections, causing many markets to be permanently out of equilibrium. Understanding this is an act of liberation, because it frees investors and business leaders to exercise their considerable resourcefulness to generate, preserve, and multiply those hefty returns. Any company that is serious about maximizing economic profits and creating maximum value for shareholders will turn to its arsenal of power nodes. Wield them well!

PART VI

The Four Rules Method for Maximizing Profits

Chapter 14

The Four Rules Templates and How to Use Them

This book's mission is to enable companies and investors to generate extraordinary returns in the age of global transparency that is rapidly dawning all around us. We began our effort by mapping out the ramifications of the declining costs of information for standard economic theories. We then applied our insights about the economics of perfect information, examining the ways in which perfect information and interdependent decision making will alter the foundations for achieving extraordinary profitability in transparency. Specifically, we investigated how transparency affects four critical strategic decisions concerning optimal company focus, business models, competition, and marketplace strategy. We used our answers to derive the Four Rules for Maximizing Profits in Transparency. In this chapter we get down to the nuts and bolts, and put all this knowledge to work in producing optimal returns.

We will use the four rules as the basis for a comprehensive and practical approach to strategy and investing in transparency. This is the Four Rules for Maximizing Profits in Transparency method.

If applied with discipline, the Four Rules for Maximizing Profits in Transparency method will provide a complete toolkit for producing extraordinary profits as marketplaces evolve.

Using the four rules templates that I will present in this chapter, anyone seriously interested in valuing or maximizing the value of a business can accurately assess its condition by undertaking a step-by-step review of its actual or potential power nodes, business model, competitive circumstances, and market options.

Over the next four chapters, I will present the Four Rules for Maximizing Profits in Transparency method in a series of templates outlining evaluations and action plans. Corporate leaders can implement the Four Rules method to achieve the highest possible profits for their shareholders. The four rules apply equally for investors, but investors have expanded degrees of freedom and even more uses for the four rules templates than corporate management teams.

To address some of these additional applications, I have devoted chapter 19 to considering the Four Rules method from the investor's point of view.

It is important to remember that the Four Rules method and its templates spring directly from the imperatives of the transparent economy. They are real-world instructions for using profit power to maximize returns.

The Four Rules for Maximizing Profits in Transparency:

1. Focus on profit power and own businesses with power nodes.
2. Organize as a focused company that orchestrates power relationships and capitalizes on the positive sums of distributed business arrangements.
3. Use power nodes to win in 3-D competitions and gain extraordinary economic profits.
4. Follow strategies designed to succeed among the marketplace dynamics of the transparent economy (power laws and hubs).

The Four Rules are summarized in the master template shown in figure 14.1. This template will be the basis for our discussions in the remainder of the book. As you can see, this template consists of four boxes, each referring to one of the four rules.

Now we are ready to put this book's teachings about how to use profit power to maximize returns into practice. This master template for the Four Rules for Maximizing Profits "folds out" into a series of templates outlining evaluations and action plans for each of the four rules. Here we go!

The Four Rules for Maximizing Profits Evaluation

Companies start by evaluating their businesses, strategies, and actions through a series of tests. The answers to these tests will clearly indicate how well a company is positioned to earn extraordinary returns and what areas

Figure 14.1

The master template for the Four Rules for Maximizing Profits

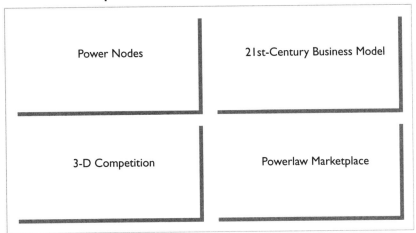

| Power Nodes | 21st-Century Business Model |
| 3-D Competition | Powerlaw Marketplace |

the company will need to focus on in order to follow the Four Rules. To help companies and investors apply the method in a disciplined, efficient, and repeatable manner, I have summarized these tests in the Four Rules for Maximizing Profits Evaluation template (see figure 14.2). This template is broken into four components:

1. Power Node Evaluation
2. 21st-Century Business Model Evaluation
3. 3-D Competitive Strength Evaluation
4. Marketplace Evaluation

As you can see from this evaluation template, each of the tests consists of a number of key questions. The tests help to identify outright winners, spot unrealized potential for extraordinary returns, highlight any current shortcomings, and flag future problems. Business leaders and investors should follow the Four Rules for Maximizing Profits Evaluation templates to be systematic about testing a company's fitness and prospects, and to formulate the Four Rules for Maximizing Profits action plans.

The Four Rules for Maximizing Profits Action Plan

Depending on the outcome of the tests, companies and investors can determine or implement action plans to target each of the four areas. Managers can articulate and implement their corporate strategy. Investors can use the

Figure 14.2

The Four Rules for Maximizing Profits Evaluation: four templates

POWER NODES

1. Is there a power node? In which activity?
   a. If yes: What about the future?
   b. If no: Answer questions 2 and 3
2. Can you create or acquire a power node?
3. Are there ways to maximize returns if you can't obtain a power node?

21ST-CENTURY BUSINESS MODEL

Are you set up to use your power node?
1. Do you own (only) the right pieces?
2. Do you have an optimal business model?
3. Third bucket: are you orchestrating your power relationships well?

3-D COMPETITIVE STRENGTH

1. Determine your RPS: 12 × 12 matrix
2. Assess 3-D performance: RPS vs. risk-adjusted ROIC
3. Determine gap: strength vs. performance

Dimension	RPS (>1, =1, <1)	ROIC
Vertical: up and down		
Horizontal in industry		
Horizontal across industries		

MARKETPLACE

1. Diagnosis of aggregates and marketplace
2. Are you using the right strategies?
3. Are you prepared to make the most of your power nodes in transparency?

Figure 14.3

The Four Rules for Maximizing Profits Action Plan: four templates

POWER NODES

1. Maximize the use of existing power nodes
2. Create or acquire a power node
3. Maximize returns from businesses without power nodes

21ST-CENTURY BUSINESS MODEL

Optimize business model structure and management to make the most of your power node

1. Focus on ownership of the right pieces
2. Implement the optimal business model
3. Third bucket: manage your power relationships

3-D COMPETITION

1. Use power nodes to win in 3-D competition
2. Increase returns to match your RPS
3. Manage distributed arrangement

Dimension	RPS (>1, 1, <1)
Vertical: up and down	___
Horizontal in industry	___
Horizontal across industries	___

MARKETPLACE

1. Prepare to win with speed
2. Use hubs: three variations
3. Practice information aikido; use aikido assets

Four Rules to formulate their investment or financing plan of action, as well as to monitor the implementation of the action plan by the company's management. For this, they can use the Four Rules for Maximizing Profits Action Plan template (see figure 14.3) to assist companies in implementing new strategies. This template has four components:

1. Power Node Action Plan
2. Business Model Action Plan
3. 3-D Competition Action Plan
4. Marketplace Action Plan

Over the next four chapters, we will review each pair of evaluation and action plans in turn, fleshing out the bare bones of the templates with examples and strategic advice, as well as short lists of key mistakes to avoid. In chapter 19, we will consider the templates again, this time from the perspective of the investor.

Chapter 15

Rule #1

Power Node Evaluation
and Action Plan Templates

In this chapter we will go through the steps to implement the first rule for maximizing profits: focus on power nodes. The first step is to choose exactly what business you are to be in. Choose your focus based on its power node potential; the key to the success (i.e., returns) of your chosen activity will be to own and exploit a power node. You need to map out your value network to make sure you can control it with your power node. If you are an investor, seek companies that have control of a power node, everything else being equal.

The Power Node Evaluation and Power Node Action Plan templates are shown in figure 15.1. The tests for this evaluation are as follows.

Power Node Evaluation

1. **Is there a power node?**
   a. *If yes, assess:*
      - How future-proof is it? Are there any foreseeable threats involving competition, changing markets, or a disappearing network?
      - Is the ownership of the company properly focused on the power node?

- Does the company use the power node to extract maximum economic returns? Does the company extend, defend, and build the power node dynamically over time?

    b. *If no, answer questions 2 and 3.*

2. **Can you create or acquire a power node?**

    What potential power nodes exist for this enterprise? Can the company obtain a power node, whether through acquisition, innovation, or organic growth?

3. **Are there ways to maximize returns if you can't obtain a power node?**

    Is it possible to join in a distributed business arrangement that will allow the company to share in the positive sums generated by another company with a power node?

    To answer this, the company needs to identify:

- Which is the strong power node in your value chain? Who owns it?
- What is the nature of the distributed business arrangement that the company is part of? Does the power node company in this arrangement generate net positive sums? If so, how are they shared?
- Is there a better, stronger, fairer competitive network?

Assessment

A power node assessment requires a rigorous and tough-minded approach. Some companies that look to the future may make the unwelcome discovery that their power node is going to disappear. Others may be surprised to discover they lack any true power nodes.

A number of prominent packaged good companies, for instance, have lots of brand names but few many meaningful power nodes. One example

---

Figure 15.1

Rule #1: power node evaluation and action plan templates

POWER NODE EVALUATION	POWER NODE ACTION PLAN

1. Is there a power node? In which activity?
  a. If yes: What about the future?
  b. If no: Answer questions 2 and 3
2. Can you create or acquire a power node?
3. Are there ways to maximize returns if you can't obtain a power node?
	1. Maximize the use of existing power nodes
	2. Create or acquire a power node
	3. Maximize returns from businesses without power nodes

of a company like this is Nestlé. While Nestlé has boasted of its 8,000 brands, they are not power node brands. Most of them do not have global recognition. Nestlé has no truly remarkable secret ingredients or proprietary formulas, no leverage over processes or distribution channels, no captive or loyal customers, and none of the other power nodes.

Since it does not have a power node strong enough to orchestrate its entire system (or even most of its system), Nestlé cannot control all of its activities by owning just one part; it must own a huge global infrastructure. Nestlé has expressed a wish to trim its number of brands, focus, and move into higher-growth categories, but for the moment has a large investment in a wholly owned, fully integrated business model.

Other examples of companies without power nodes are makers of plastic household bags brands like Ziploc, Glad, and Hefty. Their returns get hollowed out by power nodes above as well as below them in the value chain. They are in the same kind of tough spot as antifreeze producers without favorable supply deals. First, they are at the mercy of the manufacturers of their main ingredient—plastic—who, in turn, are at the receiving end of the cost of oil. Second, these brands are not powerful. The retail chains will drive tough bargains with them. The brands are not strong enough to generate leverage with large stores in discussions about shelf space or pricing. Their relative power node strength, or rather weakness, makes such companies vulnerable on several competitive levels.

If your company has no power node and you find yourself investigating the possibilities of allying with companies with stronger nodes, be sure to look several layers up and down—to the customers of your customers and the suppliers of their suppliers—as you consider potential relationships. Watch out for shifts in power and for changes in membership of business arrangements.

Power Node Action Plan

If you own a power node: congratulations! You are in an ideal position to generate extraordinary economic profits for your company and its shareholders, as well as to produce positive sums for yourself, your employees, and eventually for any partners in your distributed business arrangement. Companies and investors in this enviable position should review all options for maximizing the use of their power nodes.

If your company does not have a power node or is about to lose its power node, you need to take action. There are several possible strategies. One set of options involves extricating your company from the predicament by creating or acquiring a power node; another involves finding ways to make the most of a difficult situation by optimizing your share of the positive sums possible from arrangements with power node companies. Any of these strategies may be challenging to execute, but they can make the difference between a low-margin, struggling company and a company that earns sustained profits.

In chapter 13, I have provided illustrations of companies that have successfully created, or acquired power nodes (for a summary see table 13.2).

1. Maximize the Use of Existing Power Nodes

If you want to be the best, act like the best. These pages are rife with examples of companies that have made exemplary use of power nodes in every category. Success stories range from Apple to Zara, with many victories in between. Small companies can use power nodes to become very big, and big companies can use power nodes to increase their profits and achieve an even more commanding position.

In general, companies seeking to upgrade their existing power nodes will need to consider the following options:

- *Restructure to make optimal use of a power node within a distributed business arrangement.* Shift your company's ownership away from low-return activities. Be like Pepsi-Cola, which spun off its bottlers to focus on the brand power node and wound up earning double-digit returns on its beverage business.
- *Find the gold in existing products or processes.*
  - Be like Parker Hannifin, which raised prices and boosted its operating income by $200 million in about five years when it realized that many of its products possessed a special-ingredient power node.
  - Be like Cargill, which embarked on an array of initiatives to develop higher-margin specialty products related to its core grain business at the same time that it invested $1 billion in ethanol and biodiesel production.
  - Be like IBM, which makes billions by licensing the intellectual property in its patents.[1]
  - Be like Jeffrey Katzenberg, the former head of Disney's motion picture divisions, who recognized that his own creative special ingredient was worth more than Disney was willing to give him for it. Katzenberg quit to cofound DreamWorks, where he built a personal fortune by producing *Shrek* and a string of other top-grossing animated-movie hits.

2. Create or Acquire a Power Node

Fortunately there are many avenues to create or acquire a power node. Table 13.2 provides a summary of at least one notable example for each of the 12 power nodes. Each of these examples has been discussed in the pages of this book. For instance:

Create a Power Node
Be like De Beers, which lost its proprietary ingredient power node (raw diamonds) and reinvented itself as a company with a luxury brand power node (De Beers stores selling finished jewelry).[2] Or Hindustan Unilever, which organized a sales force of thousands of poor women into a new distribution power node.[3] Or Procter & Gamble (detergents in China, diaper manufacture in Asia), which reformulated existing products to develop secret ingredient and proprietary process power nodes. Or Unilever or Mars, which seized opportunities to extend their existing holdings and establish a dominant-position-in-a-layer power node (Unilever in ice cream, Mars in candy).

Acquire a Power Node
A company without a power node can sell its non–power node businesses while these businesses still command a good price and buy a new business *with* a power node. Be like Tata Tea, which bought a distribution power node in Tetley Tea and sold off its tea plantations. This is a bold strategy that may be very effective for those who take the leap. Be like Boise Cascade, which sold off its forests and paper-making operations, whose profits were fading, and purchased OfficeMax, which had a strong distribution power node in the form of its retail stores, or be like SBC, which bought AT&T for its business customers.[4]

3. Maximize Returns from Businesses without Power Nodes

If a company cannot create or acquire a power node, it still needs to take action to improve its returns. For example, it could:

Add value to the business by joining a group of players that can bestow positive sums.
Examples:

- It is better to be a Coke bottler than to be an independent no-name soda producer.
- If a company is an aviation component manufacturer, it will do better if it is included in a group that will have responsibility for a major aviation/weapons system.

Sell the non–power node business, especially if:

- There is no net positive sympathetic business arrangement to fit into.
- The business is temporarily overvalued due to changing industry fundamentals. Sell before other players catch up to your understanding of industry and power dynamics. (Examples include the initial public offering for Level 3 and the sale of AOL to Time Warner.)
- You can sell out at a high price to somebody who has a power node that can protect your powerless business. (Example: IBM's sale of a majority stake in its PC business to Lenovo, which as a Chinese government-affiliated company enjoys regulatory protection.)

Avoidable Mistakes about Power and Power Nodes

Even smart companies make mistakes about power nodes. If you can avoid these common errors, you will be well on your way to achieving profit power.

Do Not Give Power Nodes Away Needlessly—or Sell Them

Shell gave up on its exploration and production capability; Philips sold its share in the proprietary technology for manufacturing compact disks.

Do Not Use Nodes Carelessly

Power nodes represent your critical means to increase profits, decrease risk, lower your capital employed, and capture greater growth potential. If you use nodes poorly, you squander those opportunities.

Do Not Overlook the Nodes You Have

Parker Hannifin, a leader in motion and control technology, undertook an analysis that revealed that one-third of its product line had special-ingredient-type power nodes, and as a result implemented a new price structure that improved margins. This was a success story. However, until the incoming CEO addressed the incumbent strategy of not extracting such profits, this was a story of neglect—or worse, of outright failure to appreciate the ownership of power nodes.

Do Not Invest in "Phantom Nodes"

Phantoms are opportunities that appeal to you but have no relationship to the 12 power nodes. If it does not fit one of the 12 categories, an asset is unlikely to increase your profitability and returns. Moreover, not every asset that falls under a power node heading actually has profit power. You have to consider your asset's ability to succeed against the power nodes arrayed against it in horizontal and vertical competition. Do not waste shareholders' money by investing in anything that does not yield profit power.

Do Not Strengthen the Power Nodes of Your Competitors

Finally, do not invest in anything that benefits an entire industry. For example, IBM's investments in Linux cost the company several billion dollars. The emergence of the Linux community benefits many companies, but the returns are not accruing to IBM.

In the next chapter, we will raise your game by looking at the ways in which competition within and among distributed business arrangements can lead to better returns for power node–based leadership.

Chapter 16

Rule #2
21st-Century Business Model Evaluation and Action Plan Templates

As you will recall, the optimal 21st-century "firm" is a *focused* company that is connected to other firms via *power relationships,* which are ruled by power nodes, in a great variety of possible new business arrangements. The company with the power node(s) orchestrates the business model. Companies face a widening range of options about how to focus their own activities as well as how to relate to the activities of potential corporate partners. The 21st-Century Business Model Evaluation and 21st-Century Business Model Action Plan will help business leaders devise a company structure with maximum profit power.

The evaluation and action plan templates are shown in figure 16.1.

21st-Cenury Business Model Evaluation

Are you set up to make the most of your power node? Once a company has a power node, it must wield its power. If you have the strongest power node, you have the power to negotiate terms and grab the low-risk/high-return part of the business. The company with the strongest power node constantly presses for better terms. Are you ready to do this?

Figure 16.1

21st-century business model evaluation and action plan templates

21ST-CENTURY BUSINESS MODEL EVALUATION	21ST-CENTURY BUSINESS MODEL ACTION PLAN
Are you set up to use your power node?	Optimize business model structure and management to make the most of your power node.
1. Do you own (only) the right pieces?	1. Focus on ownership of the right pieces
2. Do you have an optimal business model?	2. Implement the optimal business model
3. Third bucket: are you orchestrating your power relationships well?	3. Third bucket: manage your power relationships

1. Do You Own (Only) the Right Pieces?

Let's assume that you have a power node. How best to exploit it? Is the correct structure to be stand-alone and focused on just the power node activity? Vertically integrated? Part of a distributed business arrangement? Do you want to be market-reliant, in a long-term relationship, or bound to formal contracts?

2. Do You Have an Optimal Business Model?

This is a key question, and to answer this you should use figure 16.2, figure 17.3, and table 7.1 to determine which power node you will use as the linchpin for the distributed business model. The parent's choice of activities and ownership in the distributed business arrangement must be based on understanding profit power. The parent focuses on and owns those activities that have profit powers and allocates away the activities that have low profit power, high risk, and high investment requirements. By focusing ownership on the power node activities/pieces, the parent can orchestrate the distributed business model, maximize profits and minimize risk.

The parent company should refer the Three Buckets Checklist (table 7.1) to determine the feasibility of a specific business structure and to decide on the optimal shape. As you remember, the three buckets categories were considerations regarding the cost of information (remember, the decline of information costs eliminates one of the prime motivators for vertical integration), performance (there are strong arguments that focused companies operate more efficiently and generate higher returns), and positive sums (will the pie grow bigger for everyone if a distributed business arrangement is created?).

Whatever the structure, the guiding principle is to focus on the power node and its potential for profit extraction. If you own a non–power node company and there is a power node anywhere near you, you should get hold of the power node, get out of your own non–power node businesses, or do both.

Figure 16.2

Determining the linchpin of the distributed business model

By focusing ownership on the power node activities/pieces, a company can orchestrate the distributed business model, maximize profits, and minimize risk. Consult the Three Buckets list (see table 7.1) to decide on the shape and ownership structure of your business model

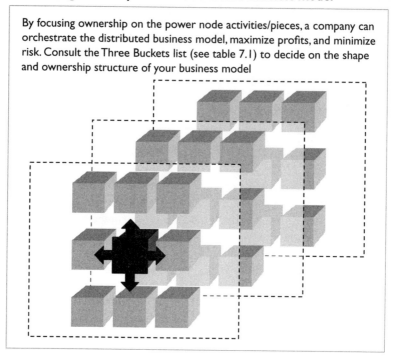

As a rule, do not integrate by keeping low-return businesses and adding a power node business. You should get rid of the low-return business. If you integrate upstream or downstream to offset the bargaining power of buyers or sellers, you will generally dilute your own potential for returns.[1] There are rare exceptions. Sometimes a vertical structure can be useful, either for the long term—as in the case of the oil companies discussed in chapter 8—or as a temporary means of accomplishing a larger end. Later in this chapter I will present an in-depth look at the example of Pepsi-Cola, which used vertical integration with bottlers as a transitional phase in its campaign to expand into global markets.

If you own the power node, the optimal distributed business arrangement should generate superior returns for you and also produce positive sums for all. Ask yourself the following questions. Does your distributed business arrangement:

- allow you to use your power node to maximize economic profits by extracting profits from others?

- allow you to create positive sums for yourself and your partner companies?
- allow you to optimize your risks by allocating many risks to other companies?
- allow you to optimize capital deployed over time (either financial or managerial)?
- have the optimal distributed arrangement partners?

3. Are You Orchestrating Your Power Relationships Well?: Taking Care of the Third Bucket

Here you focus on the third bucket or positive sum considerations in the Three Buckets Checklist. It is important to be sure that you give your partners reasons to belong to your distributed business arrangement. Managing power relationships in such arrangements will be an essential leadership skill for the 21st century. Check repeatedly whether your company maximizes profits across the distributed business arrangement, including adding value to the partners. Does your company:

- maintain the financial health of the business model members, including balancing risks and returns?
- create positive sums for the other members of the business arrangement?
- extract profits from other companies in the arrangement in a sustainable manner?

Business Model Action Plan

You should optimize business model structure and management to make the most of your power node.

1. Focus on Ownership of the Right Pieces

Instruct senior management to concentrate their efforts on managing, developing, and growing the high-return businesses. They need to leverage, protect, build, and create power nodes.

Take the company apart if necessary—before someone else does it for you. Focus on your power node and jettison the low-return, high-risk pieces. You should control these through an optimal business model.

2. Implement the Optimal Business Model

Choose and build the best specific business model to leverage your power nodes and to deal with considerations on the Three Buckets Checklist. You have a wide range of choices: vertical integration, federations with long-term relationships, implicit or explicit contracts that might maximize contract and relationship creativity (options, monitors, etc.), or even arm's-length markets.

Select optimal distributed business partners—in other words, try to take the "motley" out of the crew.

Structure the business model to maximize your own economic profits. For instance:

- Optimize (reduce) your own risk, and thereby reduce your weighted average cost of capital, by laying off risks to other companies in your distributed business arrangement.
- Reduce your capital employed by transferring capital-intensive activities to other members of your distributed business arrangement.
- Control the other businesses in your distributed business arrangement by means of your power node and associated power relationships.

3. Manage Your Power Relationships

Actively manage the business model. You need your distributed business arrangement members to be healthy because this is the source of the common pool of profits (of which you intend to extract the lion's share). For instance:

- Continuously balance profitability and spread risk across your distributed business arrangement. You want to extract as high a percentage of returns as possible while still maintaining the health of these businesses and retaining their good will.
- Provide positive incentives and benefits to members. This includes tending to risk management (planning for investment and technology cycles, etc.) and providing support/guarantees for members' financing. You can greatly enhance control through such minimal financial investments or support.

Example: Coca-Cola and Pepsi-Cola

As we have noted, Coca-Cola and Pepsi-Cola manage to extract very high returns relative to those of their bottlers. How specifically do these two companies manage to extract such returns?

Coca-Cola and Pepsi-Cola control a large system of which they own only a small part. It is important to note that the parts they do own—the Coca-Cola and Pepsi-Cola companies—are the parts that own the global brands, not the parts where most of the work is done and most of the capital expenditures are required. Because Pepsi-Cola and Coca-Cola have all the profit power in this value system, they are able to balance the economics and risk sharing so that they receive superior return on capital.

The scope of the relationship between the parent companies and the bottlers is clearly defined in contracts. For Coca-Cola and Pepsi-Cola, the returns are relatively risk-free. They don't have to own a truck, hire a deliveryman, or run a filling line.

For their part, the bottlers get the right to use the brands in a well-defined sales territory. Bottlers pay for concentrate, often on the basis of a percentage of their revenue; they pay a share of their revenue to be used in the global marketing budget; they pay a share of their revenue for marketing in their own markets. The bottlers are also responsible for the bulk of the capital expenditures in the system. In 2000, for example, Coca-Cola's capital expense per unit case was $0.04, compared to an average of $0.17 for its bottlers. At Pepsi-Cola the difference was even more dramatic: $0.05 for Pepsi-Cola versus $0.42, on average, for the bottlers.

The bottlers must set up bottling operations according to specs from Atlanta, Ga., or Purchase, N.Y. When it comes to brand advertising, they must use ads Coca-Cola and Pepsi-Cola make or approve. Coca-Cola and Pepsi-Cola direct the introduction of new packaging, the size and color of each can and bottle, and, of course, new products. Coca-Cola and Pepsi-Cola advise how many SKUs belong on each truck. Coca-Cola and Pepsi-Cola set standards for factory and warehouse cleanliness. They dictate how their products will look in the grocery aisle and the refrigerator case—right down to how many colors go on each shelf.

It is the bottlers who need to buy trucks in Warsaw, Poland; manage union labor in New Jersey; take responsibility for water purification in Shanghai, China; deal with bottle theft in St. Petersburg, Russia; and ferry crates and cans upstream in Bangkok, Thailand. This is what it means to be at the receiving end of a power node.

Example: Sprint Wireless

As of 2001–02, both AT&T Wireless and Sprint had a power node based on having rights to use part of the wireless spectrum. This is power node #3, *regulatory protection*.

Let us see how Sprint used this wireless spectrum power node to create and orchestrate its distributed business arrangement.

Table 16.1

Details of two distributed business arrangements in the beverage industry in 2005–06

Parent company	Coca-Cola Co. (KO)	PepsiCo, Inc. (PEP)
Parent's economic interest in bottlers	Coca-Cola has financial interests in approximately 50 unconsolidated bottling and distribution operations.	PepsiCo. has interests in approximately 40 franchised bottlers outside of the United States and Canada. It also has interests in franchised bottlers in the United States and Canada.
Parent's strategic rationale for distributed business arrangement	Focus parent's resources on brand management. Make use of local expertise. Leverage marketing budget. Increase capital availability and efficiency. Share risk.	Focus parent's resources on brand management. Make use of local expertise. Leverage marketing budget. Increase capital availability and efficiency. Share risk.
Profit sharing	Parent collects a share of bottles revenues via sales of concentrate. Affiliates contribute to global advertising budget.	Parent collects a share of bottler revenues via sales of concentrate. Affiliates contribute to global advertising budget.
Brand names	Parent company-owned brands.	Pepsi-Cola and other company-owned brands.
Production and distribution, financing	Production and distribution are handled by bottlers. Each bottler operates in a well-defined territory.	Production and distribution are handles by bottlers. Each bottler operates in a well-defined territory.
	Bottlers are responsible for: working capital; capital expenditures for production and distribution; plant and equipment.	Bottlers are responsible for: working capital; capital expenditures for production and distribution; plant and equipment.
	Bottlers raise financing based on their own balance sheets and cash flows.	Bottlers raise financing based on their own balance sheets and cash flows.
	Bottlers manage local regulations and labor relations.	Bottlers manage local regulations and labor relations.
	In 2006, parent-controlled (and consolidated bottling)	In 2006, after the restructuring of domestic and international

(Continued)

Table 16.1

(*Continued*)

Parent company	Coca-Cola Co. (KO)	PepsiCo, Inc. (PEP)
	and fountain operations produced and distributed approximately 18 percent of the worldwide unit case volume. Independently owned bottling operations produced and distributed approximately 23 percent of the company's worldwide unit case volume. Bottlers in which the company owns a noncontrolling ownership interest produced and distributed approximately 59 percent of the worldwide unit case volume.	bottling operations, Pepsi owned a minority stake in 3 U.S. bottlers that produced approximately 70 percent of U.S. volume. The remainder was produced by independent bottlers. Internationally, Pepsi relies predominately on minority-owned and independent bottlers, while also owning selected bottling businesses in certain countries.
Promotions, advertising, and marketing	Parent promotes consumer awareness and product appeal for its brands using integrated global marketing programs. Through its relationships with bottlers, the company implements these programs locally.	Parent develops the global marketing, promotion, and advertising programs that support the brands and brand images. Pepsi-Cola North America and Pepsi-Cola International and their bottlers jointly develop the national market, promotion, and advertising programs.
Technical support	Parent conducts product and packaging research, provides technical standards and manufacturing support, and approves equipment and packaging suppliers.	Parent conducts product and packaging research, provides technical standards and manufacturing support, and approves equipment and packaging suppliers.
Procurement	Global contract for key inputs and capital equipment.	Global contract for key inputs and capital equipment.

Sprint is a wireless telephone service provider in the United States. It could have decided to do all the work necessary to exploit that license and deliver service to all the customers. Instead, it licensed the rights to use the spectrum and its global brand in a number of its territories to so-called affiliates. At one point in 2001, Sprint had 13 affiliates, four of which were large, publicly traded companies. These affiliates covered about 19 percent of Sprint's potential customers.

In Sprint's case, the affiliates were responsible for the high-risk, low-return work. In exchange for access to the wireless spectrum, the affiliates had to follow Sprint's rules regarding capital expenditures—it was the affiliates that paid to erect transmission towers and build out the network. The affiliates also were required follow directives regarding technology migration, storefronts, pricing, and marketing plans.

The affiliates made the effort to win new customers, but Sprint maintained ownership of the customer relationships from then on. The affiliates tapped the public equity and debt markets by themselves and raised capital to expand the Sprint national system. Sprint had no equity in these affiliates and spent little or no capital in the affiliates' territories.

The affiliates paid Sprint 8 percent of their revenues, regardless of whether those affiliates had any profits. Affiliates can go bankrupt, as several of Sprint's did in the 2000s, with little effect on Sprint.

These wireless affiliates therefore were in a role very similar to that of the Pepsi-Cola and Coca-Cola bottlers.

This example shows how one can use a regulatory power node to control a large business model and extract the bulk of the returns without owning all of it. The specifics of the relationships between the wireless companies and their affiliates are summarized and compared in table 16.2.

As we have seen, the optimal business model is dynamic. Managing power relationships, for example, may mean adjusting the economics of the distributed business arrangement members in order to:

- *Keep all the players healthy.* In the late 1990s, for instance, Coca-Cola asked several of its international bottlers to increase production capacity or buy other bottlers, some of them partially owned by Coca-Cola. This stretched the bottlers' already thin returns and financial resources. The shareholders of Coca Cola Enterprises, for instance, the bottler that was spun off from Coca-Cola in 1986, complained. Coca-Cola responded by adjusting several elements in its bottler arrangements, such as charges for concentrate, to provide the bottlers with more capital.
- *Attract external sources of financing.* For instance, a power node company may want a distributed business arrangement member to demonstrate fast top-line growth when public equity markets are likely sources of financing. When debt financing is the likely source, the arrangement member may need to show steady cash flows.

Sometimes it is necessary to own quite a bit of the vertically integrated system even if you have a power node that would allow you to own only the highest-return part. For instance, the power node company may want or need to temporarily invest more of its own capital than will be optimal in the long term when:

- entering into a new market (e.g., in various stages of international expansion)
- leading a dramatic expansion in an existing market
- suitable partners are not available
- the external cost of capital for a would-be stand-alone "affiliate" is not appealing
- the parent needs to move fast to make the most of a window of opportunity or to establish a competitive advantage
- the 3-D competitive landscape has changed: note, e.g., Pepsi's reorganization of the ownership structure of its U.S. bottlers in 2009

In such cases, the parent or power node company might own a big part of the system—but only as long as necessary to achieve its objectives or until the businesses with the less powerful positions can stand on their own.

Once the conditions are right, parents or power node companies can implement the distributed business model. Operations of non–power node businesses can be transferred to third-party partners or affiliates, or, if financing is available through capital markets and other external sources, those non–power node businesses can be spun off.

For example, in the late 1980s, Pepsi-Cola made a conscious decision to expand internationally to capture the growth in emerging markets. The parent planned to first build and own many international operations outright, then spin off the new bottlers (laying off the investment and risk) at a later date. In the 1990s, Pepsi-Cola built largely company-owned operations in Thailand, India, Poland, Hungary, Czech Republic, China, and Russia. Pepsi-Cola bought and leased real estate, trained people, bought trucks, built plants, and bought soda manufacturers. Every country had a different story. Some of these operations, such as India, did well from the start; others, such as parts of Latin America and Eastern Europe, involved a struggle and needed to be revamped several times.

But by the late 1990s, most of the worldwide system was set up, and Pepsi-Cola could start the process of separating the bottlers from the parent. Pepsi-Cola's largest U.S. bottler, the Pepsi Bottling Group, was separated by means of an IPO in 1998. PepsiAmericas, which includes bottlers in Eastern Europe and in the United States, was reorganized in a reverse

Table 16.2

Comparisons of details of two distributed business arrangement in the wireless industry in 2001–02

	AT&T Wireless Services	Sprint PCS
Number of affiliates	5*	13**
Number of publicly traded affiliates	2	4
Total licensed POPs*	251 million	280+ million
Affiliated licensed POPs	60 million	75 million
Total covered POPs	217 million	227 million
Affiliated covered POPs	51 million	44 million
Strategic rationale	Affiliates alleviate parent's EPS dilution, provide incremental leverage and capital expenditures. Affiliates provide ubiquitous coverage.	Affiliates provide ubiquitous coverage and nationwide branding.
Spectrum contributed	Utilize balance sheet of affiliates to deploy and manage networks in lower-tier markets.	Utilize balance sheet of affiliates to deploy and manage networks in lower-tier markets.
Economic interest in affiliates	Parent AT&T Wireless contributed 20 MHz of spectrum in certain markets to its affiliates in exchange for substantial ownership interests (~20 percent). Approximately 20 percent equity ownership in each affiliate. Parent is not entitled to royalty fees or revenue sharing.	Sprint retains ownership of spectrum but has granted access to at least 10 MHz in each of its affiliate markets. Parent collects royalty revenue stream of 8 percent of local service revenue. No direct equity ownership; warrants in certain later-stage agreements.
Branding	Affiliates are allowed to create and market their own consumer brands, i.e., "SunCom, Member of the AT&T Wireless Network."	All products are marketed under the Sprint PCS brand; no private branding is permitted.
Pricing/product design	Affiliates are permitted to design their own product	Affiliates offer Sprint PCS products and pricing within

(Continued)

Table 16.2

(Continued)

	AT&T Wireless Services	Sprint PCS
	offerings and set their own prices.	their regions; Sprint must approve any deviation from national plans.
Network and capital expenditure requirements for affiliates	Minimum build-out requirements with specific timing targets. Requirements re compatibility with AT&T network standards and core services. AT&T can require new technology adoption by affiliates if AT&T has deployed the technology in a majority of its markets.	Minimum covered POP and market launch build-out targets with specific timing targets. Requirements re compatibility with Sprint network standards and core services (including technology upgrades). Sprint PCS has the right to supervise network construction and has unconditional access to the affiliates' PCS networks.
Customer care and billing	Affiliates are individually responsible for all customer care, billing, and provisioning.	Sprint PCS owns the customer relationship. Sprint PCS provides all customer care, billing, collections, provisioning, activation, call centers, etc., to its affiliates at rates per subscriber per month that reflect Sprint PCS's economies of scale.
Roaming agreements	Different agreements for each affiliate, generally 20 years at a fixed declining rate; not necessarily reciprocal in nature. AT&T allows each affiliate to be a party to its roaming agreement with other affiliates. Affiliates arrange their own roaming agreements for other service areas.	Sprint PCS retains complete discretion to set reciprocal roaming rates between itself and the affiliates, which generally share the same fixed rate; initially set at $0.20 per minute but reduced to $0.10 by 2002. Affiliates benefit from all of Sprint PCS's off-network and affiliate roaming agreements.
Distribution and marketing	No formal distribution arrangements.	Sprint PCS's national distribution agreements

(Continued)

	AT&T Wireless Services	Sprint PCS
Table 16.2		
(Continued)		
		with national retailers, such as Radio Shack, are shared with affiliates. Sprint national account teams provide additional subscribers, as does Sprint 1-800 telemarketing and online initiatives; affiliates benefit from Sprint PCS's national television and print ad campaigns.
Equipment procurement	AT&T is only committed to commercially reasonable efforts to assist affiliates in obtaining price discounts.	Affiliates purchase equipment under the same purchase contracts negotiated by Sprint PCS.

Source: Public filings.
*Affiliates list includes TeleCorp PCS, Triton PCS, Cincinnati Bell Wireless, Edge Wireless, and American Cellular (JV with Dobson Communications) but exclude minority investments in other wireless ventures.
**Includes all Sprint PCS affiliates. Pro forma for expected and pending acquisition activities. (Sprint originally affiliated 18 carriers.)
*** POP = Points of Presence

IPO transaction. Several Latin bottlers were reorganized or purchased by the publicly traded Gemex, Pepsi's Mexican bottler. Through such deals, Pepsi-Cola restructured itself so that by now it owns just a small percentage of its worldwide bottlers. Pepsi-Cola had to build its global system itself, but once it was in place, up and running, and financially independent, Pepsi-Cola no longer had to own all of it to control it. The company's leverage extends beyond financial resources to include human resources as well. Pepsi-Cola's global business is managed at the parent level with a minimum of staff.

Similarly, General Electric started GECIS, a back-office processor located in India, to access a low-cost, highly educated workforce. GE apparently did not actually want to be in the business of running back-office functions without a power node. It only wanted access to the functionality, but, in order to get this component of its global business model in place, had to create and nurture it. Once the GECIS business had been proven, GE was able to sell the majority of GECIS to two private companies while maintaining its access to security.

Avoidable Mistakes Regarding 21st-Century Business Arrangements and Their Application

When it comes to structuring a 21st-century firm, there are innumerable illustrations of avoidable mistakes. Companies often fail to focus on power node businesses and insist on holding on to businesses when their power has gone. Others fail to nurture their distributed power model.

Do Not Fail to Focus—and Therefore Own Too Much

Anheuser-Busch InBev NV and other large beer companies own their own bottlers. Over the past 10 years, these and the other top brewers have acquired well over 100 other beer brands. Now, a small number of major beer companies own the majority of the world's beer bottlers, trucks, and equipment. This extensive ownership forces them to plow their cash earnings back into capital infrastructure, lowering their returns. They ought to consider focusing on their power nodes—in brand and modus operandi, for example—and transform their excessive investments into a distributed business arrangement. In 2007, Coors and Molson had the right idea: the two companies took the bold step of merging their capital-intensive, low-return manufacturing operations in North America, but they retained separate ownership and management of their brands.

Do Not Fail to Develop Power Nodes

Vodafone, a leading mobile telecommunications company, owns majority and minority stakes in companies. For a long time, most of these companies have operated under their own brand names rather than under Vodafone's global brand. This greatly limited the strength of Vodafone's brand as a global power node. Therefore Vodafone could not rely on the power node of its global brand and its ownership rights to the wireless spectrum in many countries to distance itself from the ownership of physical operations.

If Vodafone had transitioned all these companies over to its own brand, it might have been able to move faster to adopt a high-return, low-resource-intensity global business model, akin to Sprint or AT&T Wireless and their affiliates.

Do Not Cling to Businesses When Their Power Node Has Evaporated

The prime illustrations of this phenomenon in recent years involve some of the leading telecommunications companies. A non-telecom example is IBM, which continued to produce PCs even when the power nodes at Microsoft and Intel were hollowing out its returns. Eventually, IBM sold the bulk of its PC business to Lenovo, which, as we have said, has a power node in the semiregulatory protections against foreign companies in the Chinese market.

Do Not Undermaintain Your Distributed Business Arrangement

If participants doubt that all parties to an arrangement are holding up their end of the bargain, the arrangements can fracture, with difficult consequences for all. This has happened at various times in the oil and copper industries, for example, where distributed business arrangements of several decades disintegrated as a result of opportunistic behavior. Remember also that seemingly minor parts of your distributed business arrangement can cause the power node company great trouble if they are not attended to. For example, as we mentioned in chapter 8, British Airways' global operations were halted for several days by problems related to its discounted food caterer at Heathrow Airport in 2005.

Chapter 17

Rule #3

3-D Competition Evaluation and Action Plan Templates

In the new 3-D competition, companies use their power nodes to battle over a pool of returns, risks, and assets. As we do with all four categories of strategic decision, we have evaluation and action plan tools. The 3-D Competitive Strength Evaluation establishes how well the company *is* performing in the 3-D battles, and also compares this to how well it *could* possibly perform. The 3-D Competition Action Plan will help the company to meet new goals. These templates are shown in figure 17.1.

The 3-D Competitive Strength Evaluation

How well will your company stand up against the greatly intensified competitive pressures in transparency? As you now know, companies in transparency will use their power nodes as weapons in their 3-D battles over the allocation of common pools of returns, risks, and assets. To assess any company's long-term profit potential, business leaders and investors must evaluate the relative strength of its power nodes in three critical competitive dimensions: vertical within a value chain, horizontal within a traditionally defined industry (market share), and horizontal across industry lines. In the 3-D Competitive Strength Evaluation portion of this chapter, I will offer a

Figure 17.1

3-D competition evaluation and action plan templates

3-D COMPETITIVE STRENGTH EVALUATION

1. Determine your RPS: 12 × 12 matrix
2. Assess 3-D performance: RPS vs. risk-adjusted ROIC
3. Determine gap: strength vs. performance

Dimension	RPS (>1, 1, <1)	ROIC
Vertical: up and down	_____	_____
Horizontal in industry	_____	_____
Horizontal across industries	_____	_____

3-D COMPETITION ACTION PLAN

1. Use power nodes to win in 3-D competition
2. Increase returns to match your RPS (12 × 12 matrix)
3. Manage your distributed business arrangement to maximize economic profits

Dimension	RPS (>1, 1, <1)
Vertical: up and down	_____
Horizontal in industry	_____
Horizontal across industries	_____

new method for judging the Relative Power Strength (RPS) of your power nodes versus your competition's power nodes. You can chart your company's current performance in 3-D battles—and compare that to your vision of how well it *could* perform. As you set new goals, the 3-D Competition Action Plan will help you to meet them.

1. Determine Your RPS: 12 × 12 Matrix

How strong are your power nodes relative to those of competitors? To assess this, a company needs to look in all applicable dimensions. The strength in each dimension is expressed in terms of 3-D Relative Power Node Strength (RPS).

You compute your company's RPS by gauging the strength of its power nodes versus the power nodes of your competitors (see figure 17.2). In transparency, we will see an endless series of matchups among potential power node battles. Does my company's special ingredient top your distribution network? Does my brand top your regulatory protection? Can my hub undo whatever advantage you built with your proprietary process? In any of these encounters, as we have seen, there is a continuum of possible outcomes. To keep things simple as we start off, we will categorize the results as win, draw, or lose. When we calculate RPS, a winning hand is RPS > 1 (my company's power node is stronger than yours), a likely draw is indicated by RPS = 1 (we are equal), and a losing position looks like RPS < 1 (my power is node weaker than yours).

Next we proceed to figure 17.3, the 12 × 12 Matrix of 3-D Competition and Relative Power Node Strength. To create your company's own grid, list all 12 power nodes horizontally across the top—these are all the power nodes that your company might potentially have access to. Do the same thing on the vertical axis—these are your competitor's power nodes.

Figure 17.2

Determining 3-D competitive position using indices of relative power node strength (RPS)

Dimension	RPS (>1, 1, <1)
Vertical: up and down	————
Horizontal in industry (*)	————
Horizontal across industries (*)	————

*The relative power indexes in the horizontal planes are measured as standard relative market share.

Complete the grid using the RPS ranking system that we outlined in our discussion of figure 17.2. If you are looking at a vertical competitor and your power node is equally as strong as your opponent's, the relative power node strength, or RPS, is recorded as 1. This is equivalent to a standoff in a profit tug-of-war. If your power node is stronger, its relative power node strength is greater than 1 (RPS > 1). If your power node is weaker, its relative power strength is less than 1 (RPS < 1). As you well know, the stronger power node has the potential to extract profits. You can do this for vertical competitors inside and outside your arrangement.

Use the same system for a horizontal competitor, whether that competitor is inside your industry or outside of it. If you have sustainable relative market share dominance, enter >1. If your standing in the marketplace is roughly equal over time to your nearest competitor, or to a serious group of competitors, then enter 1. If another firm has sustainable market share larger than 1 and you are nowhere near its size, enter <1.

The resulting chart will allow you to see how your company stacks up against its competitors—power node by power node, or cell by cell.

Even as you are filling in the squares, think outside the box. Review every possible area of power node competition, even if you assume there's no relevance. (For years, Parker Hannifin didn't realize it had a special-ingredient power node.) Think in terms of potential—of all the things your company could realistically do. If you are not sure about some of these answers, then tell or write someone else the story of your competition. Try to look at it as an outsider would; strive for a dispassionate and reasonably fair assessment of your prospects over a three- to five-year period. Who has the clear advantage in which power nodes?

You can fill out one sheet per competitor. When you compare the sheets, you will have a comprehensive view of the 3-D competitive universe in

Figure 17.3

12 × 12 matrix of 3-D competition and relative power node strength

Your Own Power Nodes

Power Nodes of Your 3-D Competitors	#1	#2	#3	#4	#5	#6	#7	#8	#9	#10	#11	#12
#1	◈	◈	◈	◈	◈	◈	◈	◈	◈	◈	◈	◈
#2		◈	◈	◈	◈	◈	◈	◈	◈	◈	◈	◈
#3			◈	◈	◈	◈	◈	◈	◈	◈	◈	◈
#4				◈	◈	◈	◈	◈	◈	◈	◈	◈
#5					◈	◈	◈	◈	◈	◈	◈	◈
#6						◈	◈	◈	◈	◈	◈	◈
#7							◈	◈	◈	◈	◈	◈
#8								◈	◈	◈	◈	◈
#9									◈	◈	◈	◈
#10										◈	◈	◈
#11											◈	◈
#12												◈

which you operate. Highlight the power node battlefronts. These documents record your company's potential. Now you need to look at its performance.

2. Assess 3-D Performance: Relative Power Node Strength (RPS) versus Risk-adjusted Returns (ROIC)

Now it's time to look at the hard evidence. Map out your own company's ROIC for each of its activities, and compare to competitors' ROICs in similar areas. *A company's competitive strength in terms of RPS ought to be reflected in its performance, that is, in its risk-adjusted returns.* Find the places where you have a potential power node advantage: the places where you scored >1. To what extent are you using this advantage to win in 3-D competition? To what extent is this power node's potential actually being realized in terms of achieving outstanding risk-adjusted returns? Do the same for every power node battle.

3. Determine the Gap: Strength versus Performance

By comparing strength with actual performance, you can assess where the company is not using its power node advantage, and what the returns might be if it did. You can also determine to what extent a power node disadvantage is damaging your returns and decide whether something needs to be done about this.

3-D Competition Action Plan

I. Use Power Nodes to Win in 3-D Competition

The 3-D Competitive Strength Evaluation, with its assessment of RPS versus risk-adjusted returns, may lead to a number of possible action plans. If you have power node advantages but are not realizing them in terms of profits, you will need to make plans to build and better deploy your power nodes in order to increase returns. Alternatively, if your RPS 12 × 12 matrix looks weak, which is to say that your power node strength is limited and you presumably have limited returns as well, then you will need to use the matrix to make a plan for improving your overall standing in terms of 3-D competition.

Whatever your situation, you will need to return to the fundamentals: strengthening your power node and using it to extract the maximum possible benefits from your distributed business arrangement. The action plan therefore has two steps:

2. Increase Returns to Match Your RPS: Use Nodes to Win in 3-D Competition

Table 13.1, entitled "Using Power Nodes in 3-D Competitive Battles," summarized many examples of power node battles that by now will be familiar from the text, labeling the leaders in every battle. When it comes to competition, power nodes are the key. Therefore, readers who want to devise a winning plan for improving their competitive position should return to chapter 15: "Rule #1: Power Node Evaluation and Action Plan Templates." Use the templates there to develop new strategies for making the most of existing power nodes or creating new ones, and thereby maximizing returns.

3. Manage Your Distributed Business Arrangement to Maximize Economic Profits

As you know, the companies with the mightiest power nodes are those that can extract the greatest share of profits from and transfer the greatest share of risks to their business model partners—and that can do it over the long term, because their power nodes are generating positive sums for all involved. If you are a company with a strong RPS and your risk-adjusted returns are proportionately low, it may mean that you are not extracting as much as you could or should from the vertical competitors in your value chain. Alternatively, if your RPS is low, but your risk-adjusted returns seem even weaker, you may be able to position yourself within another distributed business arrangement where the power relationships are more favorable to you. For this component of the action plan for improving competitive position, readers should return to the discussion in chapter 16 about implementing the superior business model. Use the templates there to develop new strategies for getting the most out of your business arrangements. Consider the best strategies for dealing with arrangement partners who act as friends (> 1, losers, weaker than you), enemies (< 1, winners, potentially stronger than you), or esteemed adversaries (1, draw, power nodes in symbiotic standoff).

Avoidable Mistakes Regarding 3-D Competition

Three-dimensional competition has already arrived in many industries—and if it is not yet in yours, it will come soon. No company or investor should rely any longer on 20th-century classifications of industries, spheres of competition, or rates of return.

Specifically:

- Do not find false comfort in your horizontal leadership within outdated and porous industry boundaries.
- Do not base your investment or business plans on industry profitability standards.
- Do not focus only on head-to-head competition over horizontal market share and lose sight of vertical fights.
- Do not assume your distributed business model is about friendly "co-opetition."
- Do not invest in anything if you don't control the power nodes necessary to hold on to the returns of your investment.
- Do not invest in anything that benefits the entire industry but brings no returns to you.

Finally: if someone else makes any of these mistakes, be sure to exploit them.

Chapter 18

Rule #4

Powerlaw Marketplace Evaluation and Action Plan Templates

Transparency will transform marketplaces, as we have discussed. The marketplaces most likely to display powerlaw dynamics will be those with many participants or many choices. Many of these will be markets for final products with many end-customers.

In some cases, hub dynamics will enable products to gain such broad horizontal market share that the horizontal position will become a useful weapon in vertical competition. New tactics will be required to create,

Figure 18.1

A network in the transition to transparency

MARKETPLACE EVALUATION	MARKETPLACE ACTION PLAN
1. Diagnosis of aggregates and marketplace	1. Prepare to win with speed
2. Are you using the right strategies?	2. Use hubs: three variations
3. Are you prepared to make the most of your power nodes in transparency?	3. Practice information aikido; use aikido assets

control, and compete with hubs and to respond to powerlaw distributions. Successful companies will need to develop an aikido approach to detect and respond to the movements of the marketplace.

The Marketplace Evaluation will help you to analyze your readiness to respond to powerlaw dynamics; the Marketplace Action Plan will outline strategies to create and control hub dynamics (see figure 18.1).

Marketplace Evaluation

1. Diagnosis: Which Generation of Aggregates and Marketplace Are You Facing?

- *Powerlaw*: a marketplace in transparency where the four conditions for powerlaw networks are satisfied; large economic groups or aggregates will function like powerlaw networks and therefore express powerlaw distributions.
- *Unruly* (in-between or transitional): a marketplace where we may find a spectrum of distributions.
- *Old world* (also called past, 20th-century, or hypothetical): a marketplace where normal distributions may be found.

2. Are You Using the Right Strategies?

Strategies in old-world marketplaces were based on building and maintaining a competitive *position*. Markets in transparency will require changing strategies based on rapid response to more fluid *dynamics* of power laws. Old tactics of increasing market share by means of low prices may no longer apply if a competitor product has become a winning hub. The companies that respond most quickly to the new realities of transparency will have an edge.

3. Are You Prepared to Make the Most of Your Power Nodes in Transparency?

You should evaluate your readiness to wield your power nodes in a transparent environment (evaluate your competitors' power nodes, too). Can your power nodes be enhanced to take advantage of powerlaw network dynamics? New-era power nodes include hubs and aikido assets. Hub dynamics can be encouraged and aikido assets can be developed to strengthen or complement older power nodes.

1. Prepare to Win with Speed

Remember, transparency is the prevailing condition in the age of perfect information—which is instantaneous information. If transparency hasn't reached your industry yet, upgrade your technical capabilities to be ahead when it comes. Investments in speed and connectivity will enable you to maximize performance as a focused company in a distributed business arrangement, and they will be essential to success in the marketplace.

As we saw in chapter 5, it pays to overlay a slow network with a faster one. E-mail beats snail mail, a product's reputation may build faster through online gossip than firsthand experience, and so forth. Make it easier and faster for customers to reach you. With such approaches, you will enhance your opportunities of creating a hub. If your product begins to spark preferential attachment, it will help to have an infrastructure (aikido assets) that allows you to respond to the market's movements in a rapid and flexible manner.

2. Use Hubs: Three Variations

There are several ways to benefit from hubs: either you are or create one (the surest route to profit power), you acquire one, or you control one without owning it. You can attempt to create a new hub from scratch, but you may also be able to enhance the hub potential of an existing power node. If you have no prospects of being a hub, there are ways to employ or manipulate other hubs to your advantage. There are two types of hubs, those based on power of attraction and those that are focal points of search; you can consider following strategies for either type.

Create a Hub

As we have mentioned, some older power nodes have hub potential. Two power nodes that may be converted into hubs by building on their power of attraction are brand (power node #1) and secret, special, or proprietary ingredients (power node #2). Two power nodes whose strength will be greatly enhanced if the underlying product or service becomes a hub are customer base with switching costs (power node #5) and increasing mutual utility (power node # 9).

Methods that may be used to produce conditions that may inspire preferential attachment and therefore create a hub may include:

- cultivate a brand community around products that can be associated with desirable lifestyles (Apple, Harley-Davidson)

- introduce new products or services at a significantly lower price (Vizio, Flip)
- enhance the "fitness" of your potential hub: recruit personnel and industries to enhance reputation and desirability, as governments (Dubai, Singapore), localities (Washington, D.C.), and institutions (universities, consulting firms) have done
- ride the coattails of a leading hub (Dr. Phil/Oprah; Stephen Colbert/Jon Stewart and *The Daily Show*)

Whichever approach is right for you, position yourself to be seen as links reach out for information. Remember the rules of preferential attachment: links go where they know other links have gone before. Therefore:

- Be first; get the most links early on
- Broadcast that you are ahead; for example, unleash word-of-mouth campaigns and let customers know that you (or your product) are the go-to point
- Facilitate visibility as the go-to point for search (brands and reputations can be helpful here)

Acquire a Hub

- Acquire a hub product or company
- Hire hub employees with large client lists (star investment bankers, hair stylists, etc.)—but try to prevent such hubs from building a power node that could potentially undermine your profitability

Control Hubs without Ownership

People start their searches by querying the hubs, so you should encourage links by "loading up" hubs with information that favors your product or service. Try to turn a hub into a billboard that serves your interests. Methods include:

- product placement (free or paid, grassroots or mass media: mentions on *Oprah*; use on highly rated TV shows; mentions on blogs, YouTube, and other online hot spots; sponsorship of parties by scenesters in a desired demographic; signing up famous cricket or golf or movie stars to be seen with your product)
- endorsements (South Beach label on Kraft products, advertisements featuring hub personalities)
- charm, encourage, or compensate hubs to become involved with your product line or cause (graffiti artists designing sneakers for Nike, celebrity board members for charity organizations, etc.)

3. Practice Information Aikido; Use Aikido Assets

The information aikido strategy is based on an awareness that people reach out for information; information doesn't reach out to them. The winning companies are those that can most quickly and accurately assess the directions in which the quests for information are flowing. A company needs assets that help it to provoke, listen to, and react to the choices of new-era aggregates. It must harness the dynamics or the energy of the aggregate network that it encounters. This is akin to the approach of aikido martial arts.

Aikido assets are assets that you need to own to take advantage of customers moving en masse. Instead of attempting to win hearts and minds, you use the momentum of the powerlaw network by:

- *Sowing seeds:* To end up with a winner, toss out many seeds and see what happens. The assets that I term "sow assets" are those that help you in provoking the network into showing its preferences to you. (Continually test or experiment with products, ideas, etc.; be willing to fail repeatedly—the magnitude of success will reward the effort.)
- *Conducting surveillance:* Surveillance assets are assets that let you be a superior observer of the network's wishes and votes. Be the best at listening for messages from the network. Look for emerging hubs. (Collect anecdotal information from shoppers; conduct up-to-the-second analysis sales data; test ideas and listen to feedback from Web sites, brand communities, etc.)
- *Practicing aikido:* Go with the flow, quickly (develop an agile manufacturing response to meet consumer demand ahead of competitors, alter marketing strategies to capitalize on emerging hubs, etc.)

Avoidable Mistakes in Powerlaw Marketplaces

- *Do not plan to reach out for customer votes, or try to control the flow of information.* Create or facilitate the conditions so that customers, choices, votes can easily come to you.
- *Focus investment in product, services, ideas, people that are beneficiaries of the energy of powerlaw dynamics.* Therefore, do not invest in remnants of the so-called long tail. This was discussed at length in chapter 10.
- *Do not continue to invest in a strategy or a product if powerlaw dynamics have turned against or away from your product.* If links are not coming

your way, or if they are showing preferential attachment for some other point, try another approach.

- *Do not allow the hubs within your own company to emerge as power nodes that may undermine your profitability.* Once hubs take on a following of their own, they will have leverage over the rest of the company.
- *Do not rely on outdated concepts for investment or forecasting, that is, those concepts that rely on an assumption of random distributions.* These concepts include: regression toward the mean, wisdom of crowds, random walk.

PART VII

Strategies for Investors

Chapter 19

The Four Rules Method
Added Value for Investors

Look, don't congratulate us when we buy a company, congratulate us when we sell it. Because any fool can overpay
and buy a company, as long as money will last to buy it.
————Henry Kravis[1]

Over the course of this book, we have guided companies and investors toward
extraordinary profitability in transparency. Our methods have focused, as
promised in chapter 1, on the increases in value that can be obtained by the
skillful use of profit power in the transparent economy.

How will transparency and a new understanding of profit power affect
the investor's pursuit of maximum realized returns?

Our Four Rules for Maximizing Profits method allows business leaders
to create evaluations and action plans that will yield significant increases in
value. This same method supplies investors with a fresh approach to value
investing and to the management of their portfolios of companies in transparency. Any investor who studies the Four Rules templates presented over
the previous chapters will have all the grounding necessary to analyze which
companies have the greatest inherent value in transparency. In other words, the
Four Rules and the templates are of help primarily to those investors among us
who are commonly referred to as value investors or fundamental investors and
to investors who are considering taking equity or equity-linked investments in
companies. In this chapter, we will add two additional templates to help investors evaluate the returns they may realize. These are the Steps for Investors
Templates to Assess Current Value (V1) and the Steps for Investors Templates
to Assess Potential Value (V2), which you will find in figures 19.1 and 19.2.

Figure 19.1

Steps for investors to assess current value (VI)

POWER NODES

1. Find the power node. Which power node does the prospect own?
2. Could it create or acquire a power node?
3. Are there ways to maximize value if it cannot obtain a power node?

21ST-CENTURY BUSINESS MODEL

Is your prospect set up to use its power node?

1. Does the prospect own (only) the right pieces?
2. Could you break out or free up the power node pieces?
3. Does it have an optimal distributed business model?
4. Is the team orchestrating the business model well?

3-D COMPETITIVE STRENGTH

1. Determine the RPS: 12 × 12 Matrix
2. What is actual ROIC?
3. Gap between actual vs. potential ROIC?

Dimension		RPS (>1, 1, <1)	ROIC
Vertical:	Up or down	___	___
Horizontal:	In industries	___	___
Horizontal:	Across industries	___	___

MARKETPLACE

In product markets:

1. Diagnosis of aggregates and marketplaces of its products.
2. Is prospect using the right strategies?
3. Does it have the necessary power nodes for powerlaw dynamics?

In financial markets:

1. Diagnosis of marketplaces of prospects' equity, debt, etc., instruments.

Figure 19.2

Steps for investors to assess potential value (V2)

POWER NODES

1. Can the prospect improve returns to power nodes?
2. Can the prospect create or acquire a power node?
3. If so, what is the impact for change in value?
4. If no power nodes, what is the outlook for returns?

3-D COMPETITIVE STRENGTH

1. Can you close the gap between actual and potential ROIC, based on RPS (12 × 12 matrix)?
2. What is impact on value?

Dimension	Actual ROIC	Actual RPS	Potential ROIC	Value Change
Vertical	——	——	——	——
Horizontal (in)	——	——	——	——
Horizontal (across)	——	——	——	——

21ST-CENTURY BUSINESS MODEL

1. Is the prospect set up to use its power node?
2. Can you focus ownership on (only) the power node pieces?
3. If you break up the business, who will buy the parts?
4. Can you create an optimal business model?
5. Could the power node company control the business arrangement and improve value?
6. Can the team manage the business model?
7. What is the impact for change in value?

POWERLAW MARKETPLACES

In product markets with powerlaw dynamics:
1. Prepare to win with speed
2. Use hubs: three variations
3. Practice information aikido
4. What is the impact for changes in values of implementing best strategies?

In financial markets with powerlaw dynamics:
1. Practice information aikido, etc.

As we have seen, the Four Rules for Maximizing Profits method is designed to produce a comprehensive picture of any company's prospects for returns and to decide on an action plan to increase returns. It can be used to assess or compare the performance of companies in any industry or in any dimension of competition, whether the businesses are fighting the vertical battles that pit power node against power node or competing horizontally within or across traditional industry boundaries.

Both investors and managers may use the Four Rules templates to make an accurate assessment of intrinsic value, but investors will be able to apply the Four Rules method in an even wider range of contexts than most corporate leaders.

Investing in Transparency

The declining cost of information and its two inevitable consequences have enormous implications for investors as well as companies, and many of the changes will be truly exciting. Let us briefly consider the salient features of the new business landscape as they pertain to investors. What should investors do differently in transparency, especially given what they now know about profit power?

Transparency Will Open a New Set of Investment Opportunities for Investors

As transparency allows companies greater flexibility regarding what businesses they want to focus on, how they organize themselves, and how they finance their activities, investors obviously will have a greatly increased range of options as well. They will be able as never before to construct portfolios of investment opportunities involving businesses that exactly match their desired profiles of cash flows, risk, and other investor-specific financial requirements.

Perfect information enables many new kinds of investment opportunities and vehicles, and destroys many previous opportunities and strategies that were based on scarce information. The rise in the numbers of focused companies is both an opportunity and a challenge. In transparency, investors will be able to buy any slice of the business they want—but which will bring the most profit as an investment? An understanding of profit power, and specifically of power nodes, is essential to recognizing which pieces have the greatest potential for returns.

As transparency expands the set of investment opportunities for investors, they will need to know the intrinsic value and intrinsic returns of all of the pieces. By "intrinsic" I do not mean to introduce a new term, but rather to distinguish between the value of a *company* and its returns, as discussed in the previous chapters, and the returns as they may accrue to an *investor* who buys into an ongoing concern. The addition of "intrinsic" merely denotes that these are valuations and returns *from the company's perspective.* By "intrinsic returns," therefore, I mean the same ROIC as defined in chapter 1, and by "intrinsic value" I mean the net present value of a company's cash flows, discounted by the appropriate risk-adjusted discount rate, also as defined in chapter 1. The returns from the perspective of an outside investor differ, because those returns are also a function of what was paid to get into the investment and what was received on the way out.

As companies that were once vertically integrated split up into a multitude of focused pieces, intrinsic returns among the pieces will vary greatly. To understand the relative potential for intrinsic economic profits among various businesses, investors will need to distinguish among power node and non–power node companies and obtain a clear sense of how the power relationships will play out in terms of the apportionment of returns. It is also important to consider the specific financial and logistical structures of the distributed business arrangement.

In transparency, investors will find new prospects for growing value and returns in previously unthinkable places. Thanks to increasingly perfect information, for example, it is possible to build a huge global company in a finely focused activity. This has obvious implications for any investor who contemplates financing the start-up or ongoing operations of a focused company. Obstacles associated with decreasing returns to scale are likely to be encountered at far greater company sizes—or may never come up at all.

Transparency Will Define a New Set of Valuation Challenges for Investors

In transparency, it will no longer be safe to rely on generalities about the performance of any given industry or niche. We can expect large differences in profitability among the new spate of focused companies, even those that pursue similar activities. Investors will do well to drop diversification plans and forecasts based on industry-average profitability and trends, or even horizontal-within-industry market share. The rise of focused companies and perfect information mean that, more than ever, potential investments will need to be carefully analyzed on a case-by-case basis. For this, the Four Rules for Maximizing Profits templates, including the Steps for Investors, will be extremely useful.

The valuation challenge is even more interesting if the power laws (that we can expect in large markets that meet certain conditions) kick in.

Companies or products or services that trigger hub dynamics have greatly enhanced potential to achieve dominance in terms of horizontal market share. Thanks to preferential attachment, they will also have a significant advantage in maintaining their lead in the market and in sustaining a higher pricing structure even in the face of quality and price competition from rivals.

Transparency Will Create New Norms for the Behavior of Markets and Achievable Returns

Classical theory states that the invisible hand will drive markets toward equilibria in which all profit opportunities will have been arbitraged away and in which price will serve as an accurate reflection of value. Therefore, you can't outsmart the market; there is no way that over the long term any individual investor can do a better job of understanding value than the market itself. In this view, you will do as well with a sufficiently large portfolio of randomly chosen stocks as by carefully picking individual holdings.

Such views are based on classical theories that state that since markets are perfect and reflect all available information, it is not possible to outperform the broad stock market. This is related to the theory about general equilibrium. As we saw in chapter 4, investment approaches based on this theory will no longer be reliable in transparency.

In transparency, the ideas that one cannot outperform the market and that the price in the market will always be equal to the intrinsic value of the company will be demonstrably false. Why is this so? As we now know, perfect information will not bring about perfect markets; the trend toward interdependent decision making prevents markets from achieving any classical economic ideal of general equilibrium. The notion that all extraordinary profits will eventually be competed away is no longer acceptable as a simplifying assumption; price variations will often not be normally distributed; and the market's price will often not reflect underlying or intrinsic value. These are some of the important aspects of the new powerlaw economics.

For investors, these new economic realities may be translated into the following rules of thumb for markets in general:

- The economics of perfect information do not follow the familiar mainstream economics rule book.
- Investors *can* outperform the market averages.
- Market prices need not be correct; that is, they may not equal the intrinsic value of investment prospects.
- Extraordinary profitability is achievable and sustainable.

- Risk management and forecasts based on normal distributions will be less useful, or even dangerous.

With regard to specific prospects, the lessons of this book are that:

- Power nodes are the leading indicators of intrinsic value and returns.
- Transparency will drastically alter the building blocks of extraordinary returns. It will change the outcomes to the four critical decisions any company needs to make, namely about what the company should focus on (the activities to engage in and where to focus ownership), the business model, competition with other companies, and the market places for their products. This we have discussed in chapters 6 through 10.
- The guidelines for maximizing intrinsic returns in transparency are our Four Rules, as we derived them in chapter 11.

Market Prices versus Intrinsic Values

As the conditions in large economic aggregates increasingly come to match the four conditions under which scale-free computer and social networks exhibit power laws (see chapter 5), we can expect that powerlaw distributions will gradually supplant random distributions as the basis for important economic models. In a world of powerlaw economics, market imperfections will be the rule, not the exception.

As a value investor, you can exploit market imperfections to your own benefit if you understand the divergence between market prices and intrinsic values. As such a fundamental investor, you would start with a firm understanding of the investment's intrinsic value, a solid sense of exactly what it is worth as an investment to you, knowledge about the market price of the prospect, and a sense of where pricing is headed.

Value investing is not the only strategy that may be given a boost by transparency. Powerlaw economics will also enhance the potential for other approaches to investing and trading. As we have seen, one of the chief causes of the persistent disequilibrium in transparency is interdependent decision making. Just like markets for fashionable clothing or books, markets for publicly traded securities can be subject to herd behavior. This is hardly surprising, given that trading systems are now so sophisticated that traders can "see" the positions and directions of trades at other firms. At the retail investor level, services like Covestor offer peer-to-peer sharing and immediate copying of investment decisions. When we speak of "market sentiment," we are often describing the trends produced by interdependent decision making.

In transparency, in short, most financial markets will increasingly be subject to dynamics that do not drive to equilibrium. Patterns in prices will display nonnormal (nonrandom) distributions, including powerlaw distributions. Indeed, studies have shown that certain price movements already reflect powerlaw distributions. Although non-value investing and trading are huge subjects—and are outside the scope of this book—we can see that transparency will bolster the efficacy of approaches to trading that are based on the realities of the economics of perfect information, including approaches that practice a version of what we have called information aikido—developing winning strategies by anticipating how the energy of choices will flow.

Fundamental investors can outsmart markets at large. For you, the route to success lies in correctly assessing the current as well as potential value of a company and then playing these valuations off against the available market prices. As you know, value is one thing, but price is often something else, especially in transparency.

In markets in transparency, as we have observed, price need not be "correct" relative to value, and these differentials may become more pronounced than ever. This is good news for fundamental investors, as long as they understand the correct approach to valuing companies in transparency. This, of course, is where our profit power analysis enters the picture.

The returns of investors are related to the intrinsic value of a company and to the increases in this value, but they are not the same. Indeed, fundamental investors will do best when the intrinsic value of an investment and its market price are not in sync. It doesn't matter whether an investment prospect is overpriced or underpriced relative to its intrinsic value. The gap is what counts. Depending on their view of the underlying value, investors can decide to buy or sell a prospect, for example, or to go long or go short on an investment or a security that is related to this investment.

The Investor's Perspective

Throughout, we have addressed our discussion equally to business leaders and investors. The concerns of such managers and shareholders are often thoroughly intertwined. In order to fulfill their responsibilities as stewards of economic value, business leaders need to take the perspective of investors when they make the strategic and financial decisions for their companies. Investors, for their part, often take on the role of business leader when they guide their portfolio companies to take steps to maximize intrinsic value.

Of course, there are also several critical distinctions between investors and business leaders, which are as follows.

The Investor's Focus Is on Realizing Returns

The focus of investors is not just on building intrinsic value but on realizing a return on their investment. Realized returns are related not just to the changes in intrinsic value over time—which we will refer to as a shift from current intrinsic value V1 to future intrinsic value V2—but are also determined, as Henry Kravis has reminded us, by the investors' going-in and getting-out prices. ("Current" in this context means "at the time the investor makes the investment," and "future" means the time when the investor exits). P1 and P2 may or may not be equal to V1 and V2. As readers will be well aware, investors create value for themselves (or their investment portfolio) when the relationship between the going-in price P1 and the getting-out price P2 (adjusted for interim net investments) yields a return in excess of their required risk-adjusted rate of return.

An Investor's Control over Creation of Intrinsic Value Is Indirect: It Depends on the Managers of the Portfolio Companies

The ability of investors to influence strategies at the companies they invest in varies widely. If they own the company or hold a large stake, investors have a lot of say. If they own a small stake, they have very little say. In either case, it is important for investors to assess a management team's ability to execute strategies that will boost value and returns. Questions about management capabilities and motivation are an important element of the Steps for Investors valuation templates.

If an investor decides to acquire an entire company in a going-private transaction, for example, or take a meaningful ownership position, the investor will have a measure of influence over what the company does next. Such investors will have to take a hard look at their own skills as well as the company's prospects for maximizing profit power. They will need to assess to what extent they will be successful as owners in implementing the Four Rules action plans laid out in the previous section.

The Four Rules templates of the previous chapters and the investors' templates of this chapter are your tools. They should be part of investors' checklists for management reviews and should form the basis for board-level reviews.

The Four Rules templates can also be of help in motivating management teams and can be the basis for building consensus around business plans. To formulate a consensus business plan that aligns the interests of management and investors, joint teams may use the detailed templates and lessons of chapters 14 through 18.

Investors who hold smaller stakes will have less direct influence, but they may nonetheless be able to exert a strong influence over the corporation's management. Fresh eyes often see things that insiders do not. Outside investors may be able to agitate for changes such as the implementation of the Four Rules even in cases where corporate leaders have faced internal resistance. As investors considering potential value (and using the Templates for Assessing Potential Value), they will want a thorough evaluation not only of current and potential management teams but also of the likelihood that leaders can and will implement change. The Four Rules templates can be the basis of multiyear operating plans and can facilitate benchmarking of progress.

Investors Have a Portfolio of Investments to Consider

Investors' estimates of a company's value as an investment aren't entirely based on how the company performs on its own. They must weigh other factors, including whether a potential investment is a good fit for a portfolio's risk profiles and whether it would create any positive sum benefits with other holdings.

As you may remember, distributed business arrangements are supposed to solve the positive sum issues related to business organization. These we summarized in Category III in our Three Buckets Checklist of trade-offs (see table 7.1). Creating or orchestrating a distributed business arrangement can get done especially well, and any problems can be solved more easily, if the companies involved have overlapping owners. The Four Rules and the Three Buckets Checklist will help the investors to diagnose the situation and maximize the sources of potential positive sums.

Investors who own a number of focused companies that participate in distributed business arrangements may be able to increase the intrinsic value for several of the companies involved by managing the positive sum returns that can be generated from those arrangements. In this situation, the management of portfolios of privately owned or controlled companies equates to stewardship of a distributed business arrangement.

Better yet, investors can work out positive sum benefits before they buy a company. When they bring into their portfolio a company that helps to complete or complement a distributed business arrangement, the private equity group can create value (by setting up the conditions for the positive sums to be realized) that nobody else can. All of these positive sum considerations should be figured into the calculations of potential value.

Steps for Investors

In figures 19.1 and 19.2, I have created templates that trace the path of the Steps for Investors. I will provide an overview of this process here. The tools for investors are exactly the same as they are for companies, but we have added these templates to reflect the investors' specific concerns regarding value and its relationship to market price. We will assess current value (which we label V1) using the Steps for Investors Templates to Assess Current Value. We will assess potential value (V2) using the Steps for Investors Templates to Assess Potential Value. The two sets of templates will be very useful in providing investors with insights into profit power in each of the four key areas of ownership, organization, competition, and markets.

Our overview of the assessment process begins with the concept of intrinsic value. Managers increase value by building companies that will deliver extraordinary risk-adjusted returns, also known as economic profits. As we discussed in chapter 1, intrinsic value, or V, is a function of the trio of cash earnings, capital investments over time, and associated risks. These get translated into valuation metrics using a variety of models and approaches, many of which are described very well in *Valuation: Measuring and Managing the Value of Companies*,[2] to arrive at a measure of intrinsic value.

The value added by our approach is to improve the quality of investors' assessments of this trio (cash flow, investments, and risks). Investors will benefit from the Steps for Investors Templates to Assess Current Value, or V1 (figure 19.1), which are consistent with the evaluation templates discussed over the previous four chapters.

Having arrived at an objective valuation of current value, V1, investors will also need to factor in their own specific concerns. A number of investor-specific considerations are involved in individual return calculations, including the time horizon of the investment, the investors' own risk management parameters, the other holdings in their portfolio, the opportunity cost of their capital, and the cost of financing.

To assess potential returns, investors will first compare the going-in price, P1, with the current value, V1, of the prospective investment. The difference between P1 and V1 (factoring in the investor considerations that we just mentioned) provides an initial view.

Next, investors will be interested in comparing the investment's current and expected future value, V2, with its going-in price and expected exit price. At the time they enter most investments, investors have only a limited understanding of the exit price. In order to get a handle on P2, the investors can try to forecast the future value or V2 of the enterprise. Investors interested in the company's potential value can benefit from the Steps for Investors Templates to Assess Potential Value or V2 (figure 19.2).

Investors will ask: What are the prospects for increasing profit in each of the four quadrants of the templates?

As mentioned, investors should not neglect to evaluate their own potential to play a part in shaping the company's fortunes and thereby enhancing V2.

As a final step in their process, investors develop an estimate of their potential returns. They do this by using V2 to inform their estimate of a feasible P2, the exit price. When considering exit strategies, investors should also ascertain what the range of valuations might be for *other* prospective buyers of the enterprise. Ultimately, the exit price will be determined by what others will give for it. This exit price will be determined by a market process: it might be set by a public market, an auction, a recapitalization, etc.

Ideally, after all the hard questions have been asked, and when all the calculations have been completed, investors should have assessments of V1 and V2, as well as of P1 and P2, that should result, given the investors' parameters (time, financing, costs, etc.), in an estimate of the returns that they might realize.

How to Use the Steps for Investors Templates to Assess Current and Potential Value

As you have seen, the Steps for Investors templates are consistent with the Four Rules for Maximizing Profits method. These investor templates help investors judge the difference between the current and potential value of a prospect and its market price. Investors can use the Steps for Investors valuation templates to identify investment opportunities whose value may not (yet) be apparent to other investors or the public markets—in other words, to find the bargains that will yield the maximum realized returns.

Let us now take a closer look at each of each of these templates in figure 19.1 for current value V1 and figure 19.2 for potential value V2.

Rule #1: Power Nodes Impact

Begin with determining the impact of power nodes on current value V1.

V1: Current Value Assessment for Power Nodes

Let's suppose that you as an investor have been offered a chance to buy a company or a piece of a larger company, or you are considering adding an instrument of a publicly traded company to your portfolio. Is this company or this piece of the company worth investing in? Is it well situated to prosper in transparency's 3-D competitive battles for returns? You need to take a hard look at the existence or lack of power nodes in valuing your prospect. This template is very similar to the Power Node Evaluation template. For a discussion of how to conduct a power node evaluation, refer to chapter 15: "Rule 1: Power Node Evaluation and Action Plan Templates."

Next, proceed to assessing the impact on potential value V2.

V2: Potential Value Assessment for Power Nodes

Once you have completed your current value assessment, you ask: Could this company be worth more one day than it is today because of its power node strategy? Can the prospect improve returns to power nodes? Can the prospect create or acquire a power node? If so, what is the impact for change in value? If there are no power nodes, what is the outlook for returns? For this, readers should look at the chapters that detail the many ways that companies have bought or created power nodes, including chapter 15, which contains a summary chart (table 15.1).

Understanding power nodes gives you the confidence to invest in new ventures, build new companies, or buy pieces out of other companies.

Understanding power nodes keeps you from making poor investments. When the market price has run up (or down) as a result of fads or momentum investing, for example, you as a fundamental investor will know that you can make returns by taking the opposite view. Companies like Global Crossing, Level 3, and Williams Communications had huge market prices in 2000–01 based on their investment in long-haul network capacity. But, as our stories about the telecom industry have shown, these companies were lacking power nodes. Power node watchers could see that their intrinsic value was very weak. After a while, the market prices of these companies started to reflect their intrinsic value, and few of them exist today in their original form.

Do not spend time hoping for value increases from performance enhancement at your prospect if it does not have the profit power to hold on to additional returns. This has been the case for the Pepsi and Coke bottlers, for instance. If they perform better, Pepsi-Cola and Coca-Cola find ways to extract the profits.

Investors should stay away from, or short, any business that appears to be neglecting a power node that must be functioning at peak levels if they are to be winners in their chosen focused activity. For example, beware of a company that relies on a power node of modus operandi—but messes up its corporate directory. Or a service company that is cultivating its reputation as a hub of talent and brains—and then the chair tells the recruitment team that he does not want to hire the best and the brightest.

All this does not mean that you cannot invest in a company without power nodes. It does mean that you need to scale down your valuation to reflect the realities of the lack of profit power of this prospect.

Rule #2: 21st-Century Business Model: Impact on current and future value

VI: Current Value Assessment for 21st-Century Business Model

This part of the template is again very similar to the 21st-Century Business Model Evaluation template. For a discussion of how to conduct a business model evaluation, refer to chapter 16: "Rule 2: 21st-Century Business Model Evaluation and Action Plan Templates."

V2: Potential Value Assessment for 21st-Century Business Model

A company can improve intrinsic returns by shifting to a better business model. If we return to the Three Buckets Checklist, we see that we can affect performance of the pieces by addressing Category I and II items, and we can affect the creation of positive sums by addressing Category III items.

If, for instance, a vertically integrated company is broken into its components, we may see that the value of the parts is greater than that of the integrated whole.

It may also be possible to reorganize a vertically integrated company into a distributed business arrangement controlled by a power node company. As discussed, the power node company can use its profit power to enhance its own returns as it shifts risks and investments to companies without power nodes. The weaker companies will have access to a greater pool of profits as a result of their relationship with the power node player. We can see that value is enhanced all around, but intrinsic returns in particular will spike for the power node player.

The benefits of a power node strategy in the context of a distributed business arrangement apply, as we have seen, to almost all industries: from consumer products to telecom, and from hotel management to high-tech manufacturing. We have also seen how not using the leverage of a distributed business arrangement can hold back returns. The returns at Vodafone in 2008 could have been predicted nearly a decade earlier by an investor considering the likely consequences of the company's limited ability to shift to a superior distributed business model. Should you encounter an investment proposal for a global growth strategy that envisions that the company should own every single aspect of the new empire, you may want to send it back to the drawing board. As you know, one can achieve global expansion and preserve high returns, and more often than not it will be helpful to leverage a power node to exercise control without ownership over a distributed business arrangement.

Rule #3: 3-D Competition: Impact on V1 and V2

V1: Current Value Assessment for 3-D Competitive Strength

This template is akin to the 3-D Competitive Strength Evaluation template. For a discussion of how to conduct a 3-D strength evaluation, refer to chapter 17: "Rule 3: 3-D Competitive Strength Evaluation and Action Plan Templates."

V2: Potential Value Assessment for 3-D Competitive Strength

In order to assess the potential upside to value, we start by determining the relative power node strength (RPS) of this enterprise. In other words, when looking vertically, horizontally, and horizontally across industry boundaries, how do its power nodes compare to those of the competition?

You should already have used a worksheet like the 12 × 12 RPS matrix (figure 17.2) to display the current state of competitive strength, as suggested in the template for V1. Next, we look at the ROIC that would be expected based on the strength of the power node and compare that to the company's actual ROIC. If the company were able to close the gap, what might be the result in terms of incremental returns or value?

An example of a company doing this right, as we have said, is Parker Hannifin. The company recognized that many of its industrial components had a special ingredient power node and recalibrated its pricing in ways that greatly increased its returns and value. Similarly, as the strength of Pixar's special ingredient power node rose in relationship to Disney's distribution power node, Pixar fought long and hard for its share of the returns, ultimately vastly increasing its value. Steve Jobs bought Pixar for $10 million in 1986; when he sold it to Disney in a $7.4 billion, all-stock transaction in 2006, he became Disney's largest shareholder, with approximately 7 percent of the stock.[3] This is an excellent example of maximizing realized returns! Does your prospect have this potential?

Rule #4: Powerlaw Marketplaces: Impact on V1 and V2

V1: Current Value Assessment for Marketplace

This template is very similar to the Marketplace Evaluation template. For a discussion of how to conduct a marketplace evaluation, refer to chapter 18: "Rule 4: Powerlaw Marketplace Evaluation and Action Plan Templates."

V2: Potential Value Assessment for Powerlaw Marketplaces

For discussions of power laws, hubs, 80–20 powerlaw distributions, and other facets of markets in transparency, go to chapters 5 and 10.

As you can see in the relevant template for this segment, you need to diagnose the aggregates and marketplaces of the company's products. Is your investment prospect using the right strategies? Does it have the necessary power nodes for the powerlaw dynamics that are present or might be expected to emerge?

Remember that if a company or product is the beneficiary of powerlaw dynamics, it will be hard for competitors to catch up. This should give you greater confidence in the durability of the cash flows of a leading hub and cause you to be skeptical of a new product (even if it is better and cheaper) that is proposing to compete with an established hub.

The End

In sum, as a reader of this book, you are trained to look at the impact of profit power and transparency on value. Investors increase their chances for returns if they understand the value or potential value of a company better than other investors or the market at large. The Four Rules for Maximizing Profits method and these Steps for Investors will help you to detect the profit power strengths and weaknesses in investment prospects that others won't see. This gives you the route to extraordinary returns.

PART VIII

Conclusion

Chapter 20

On Gaining Perspective

Arma virumque cano ["I sing of warfare and man at war"].
—Virgil, *Aeneid*[1]

Throughout this book, I have identified powerful trends that will shape our future.

The impact on the profit-making potential of business will be undeniable; the advantage for investors and executives in understanding these trends is immense. The trends of transparency themselves are inevitable. The only uncertainty is in us: how we interpret and respond to them.

Looking for underlying drivers to make sense of the present and to foretell the future is a time-tested trick. That is why I quoted Virgil's *Aeneid*—a 2,000-year-old story about underlying drivers and inevitable trends—early on. Like Virgil's Romans, we have found ourselves in tempestuous circumstances. And like them, we have asked: what is going on, and what is the optimal way to proceed? Humanity has often found itself in situations of rapid change before and has learned that, with hindsight, the underlying drivers and the changes they caused were very clear. I believe that it is possible to step back right now, in the midst of tumult, and discern the patterns that will later seem obvious.

Virgil is said to have written his story to persuade the Romans to maintain their perspective during turbulent times. If we, too, can keep our perspective, we will almost certainly see that the advantages of this new era will outweigh the discomforts of adjustment. We all have to admit that the trends of our age will not go away. Indeed, they are as inexorable in our time as the trajectory of the history of the foundation of Rome as recounted in the *Aeneid*.

We can prosper by using the energy of the underlying forces of change: by sailing, in effect, with the prevailing winds rather than trying to steer against them. That is the logic flow that we have followed in this book. We began by examining the underlying cause of change in our economic environment and continued to pursue this thread until we were able to formulate the right strategies to deliver profits in a tumultuous business world.

Like the *Aeneid*, this book has been written in terms of challenges and battles, strategies and weapons. At the heart of this book is our song about the competitive weapons of our times, the power nodes: what they are, how to acquire them, and how to use them wisely for the sake of winning extraordinary returns. The Four Rules to Maximize Profits in Transparency are your strategies. The templates to execute each of them with specific, practical, step-by-step instructions are your battle plans.

Another important and encouraging lesson of this book is that you have countless options to shape your business's outlook, and in particular its profitability. Now you have all the basics you require to make the most of transparency to build extraordinarily profitable companies, and to discern extraordinarily profitable investments. You need to get to work straight away to focus ownership on the most profitable business elements, to structure modern firms and build global enterprises, to win in three-dimensional competition against global rivals, and to take advantage of the dynamics in powerlaw marketplaces.

As a leader, one of your big challenges will be to rally support for reshaping your company. Many of the practices advocated in this book require determination and savvy to deliver success. If you are to thrive, your decisions will be made on the basis of tapping into the underlying changes and shaping the flows of profit power around you, applying and deploying your power node leverage effectively, and making it worth their while for others to join you. The steadfastness of two chairmen of PepsiCo, for instance, as they executed a decade-long plan to build the international drinks business and to take it all apart again later into a distributed business arrangement, is legendary. Getting support from those in your company who prefer the old ways is a huge challenge. Often, the sheer intensity of their discomfort is a clue that they are coming up against a reality that they have not yet accepted. But sticking with conventions that are not in step with transparency will not help. Denial is not a strategy. Accepting the new reality is the first step to success.

There are many stories in this book of companies that have found ways to reinvent themselves and use their profit power. But in the end, the main character of the book is you, the reader. There is no zero-sum limit to the lessons about transparency and profit power; every reader of this book could create or enhance an enterprise using these insights, and there still would be room for more. So the end of this book is a set of strategic questions for you, the business leaders and investors who will lead the way in transparency:

Where do you need to put your attention in order to utilize the potential for profit power in your own business?

What are the dynamics of your own business environment? As transparency swiftly approaches and the economics of perfect information start to prevail, where is the profit power within that environment?

What opportunities are there for you and your business to apply the Four Rules for Maximizing Profits? To seize those opportunities, what do you need to do differently?

And in the process, what might you and your business become?

Chapter 1

1. Lasswell and Kaplan, *Power and Society*, 291.
2. Child, *Discourse*, 114–15.
3. de Geus, *The Living Company*.
4. *Economic profits* equals "the spread between ROIC less the cost of capital multiplied by the amount of invested capital." Copeland, Koller, and Murrin, *Valuation*, 49. Alternatively, "Economic Profit = Invested Capital × (ROIC—WACC)." Copeland, Koller, and Murrin, *Valuation*, 143.

   ROIC is short for return on invested capital, which is equal to "after-tax operating profits divided by the capital invested in working capital, property, plant, and equipment" and other assets. Copeland, Koller, and Murrin, *Valuation*, 48.
5. Value is expected economic profits plus existing investments. Copeland, Koller, and Murrin, *Valuation*, 144.
6. Kiley, "Giving the Boss the Big Picture."
7. "Core competencies of the firm: A form of economy of scope that arises out of a firm's ability to carry out some types of activities as well. Typically, this refers to the firm's ability to design, make, sell, or distribute a certain kind of product." Milgrom and Roberts, *Economics, Organization, and Management*.
8. Hart, *Firms, Contracts, and Financial Structure*.
9. "When there's more fiber in, there's a whole lot less work to do." Belson, "At Traditional Phone Companies, Jobs May Not Last a Lifetime."
10. Child, *Discourse*, 114–15.

11. For references to several power types see Clegg, *Frameworks of Power*.
12. Bowles, *Microeconomics*.

Chapter 2

1. The English translation by Fitzgerald reads: "Happy the man who has learned the cause of things." Virgil, *Aeneid*, 404.
2. Turnbull, "How to Be a Demographic Realist."
3. See also Keeney and Raiffa, *Decisions with Multiple Objectives* and Raiffa, *Negotiation Analysis*.
4. Arrow, *Limits of Organization*.
5. Gates, "The New Road Ahead."
6. "The costs of information, that is, the inputs needed for the installation and operation of information channels" (Arrow, *Limits of Organization*, 39), which are the ways of "acquiring relevant information" (Arrow, *Limits of Organization*, 37).
7. Reuters, "Chronology: Reuters, from pigeons to multimedia merger."
8. McCullagh, Declan, "Ray Kurzweil deciphers a brave new world."

Chapter 3

1. Foust, "Taking Off Like 'a Rocket Ship.'"
2. McCue, "Tesco to Track Milk Deliveries by RFID."
3. "Learning to Live with Big Brother."
4. Duguid, "Feel Like You're Being Watched?"
5. "Learning to Live with Big Brother."
6. Bradsher, "China Finds American Allies for Security."
7. "Learning to Live with Big Brother."
8. Claburn, "U.K. Kids Get RFID Chips in School Uniforms."
9. Zamiska and O'Connell, "Altria Is in Talks."
10. "Originally, this was an insurance term referring to the tendency of people with insurance to reduce the care they take to avoid or reduce insured losses. Now, the term refers also to the form of *post-contractual opportunism* that arises when actions required or desired under the contract are not freely observable." Milgrom and Roberts, *Economics, Organization, and Management*, 601.
11. Smith and Linebaugh, "Morgan Stanley Plans Reduction in Research Jobs."
12. Richtel, "The Long-Distance Journey of a Fast-Food Order."
13. Ibid.
14. Terhune and McKay, "Coke Shelves Initiative of Ex-Chief."
15. Nestle Family Monitor, 2004 as quoted in *National Reading Campaign*.
16. McKinsey, 2003 as quoted in Ibid.
17. Covestor, "How It Works."
18. "The Web View."
19. Surowiecki, *The Wisdom of Crowds*.
20. Strogatz, *Sync*.
21. Ibid., 262.
22. *12 Angry Men*, directed by Sidney Lumet (Orion-Nova Productions, 1957).
23. Allison and Zelikow, *Essence of Decision*.
24. "Podtastic."
25. Frank, "Economic Scene."

26. Yuan, "Sichuan Quake Shows Changing China."

27. Brand, *The Media Lab*, 202.

28. *Whole Earth Review*, May 1985, 49.

Chapter 4

1. Nocera, "The Heresy That Made Them Rich."

2. Important exceptions to this rule are situations involving externalities and non-private goods.

3. Markets can only function perfectly, as defined by contemporary economic theory, when information is perfect and plentiful (an infinite amount of information is available for free) and decision making is not interdependent (interdependence is 0). So the condition required by mainstream economics is $[\infty, 0]$. When information is free and decision making is extremely interdependent, the situation is $[\infty, \infty]$.

4. See for instance Durlauf and Young (eds.), *Social Dynamics*, 133–54; Lambert, "The Manipulation of Perceptions"; Colander, Holt, and Rosser, *The Changing Face of Economics*; Fullbrook, *A Guide to What's Wrong with Economics*.

5. Colander, Holt, and Rosser, *The Changing Face of Economics*, 284. Economists and financial types are not the only ones having problems with following the processes by which individual behavior gets converted into aggregate behavior. The physical sciences have also found it very tricky to explain aggregate order on the basis of individual behaviors. They speak of "spontaneous order," which has a familiar ring to those who have been brought up with the "invisible hand."

6. Soros, *New Paradigm for Financial Markets*.

7. Lowenstein, *When Genius Failed*.

8. Jesdanun, "Study: Google Gets Bulk of World Search."

Chapter 5

1. Mandelbrot and Hudson, *The (Mis)Behavior of Markets*, 94–96.

2. Barabasi, *Linked*.

3. Strogatz, *Sync*.

4. Watts, *Six Degrees*.

5. Adamic and Huberman, "Zipf's Law and the Internet"; Guenther, Hogg, and Huberman, "Controls for Unstable Structures"; Huberman and Adamic, "Information Dynamics in the Networked World"; Huberman and Wu, "The Dynamics of Reputations"; Wu and Huberman, "Social Structure and Opinion Formation."

6. Barabasi, *Linked*.

7. Ibid.

8. Barabasi calls this a "scale-free" network. Barabasi, *Linked*, 70.

9. Ibid., 86–88.

10. "In practice, power-law distributions always display a characteristic cutoff because of the finite size of the system. The observed degree distribution, therefore, is only ever a straight line on a log-log plot, over some range." Watts, *Six Degrees*, 112.

11. "The essential limitation with the scale-free view of networks is that everything is assumed to come for free. Network ties in Barabasi and Albert's model are treated as costless, so you can have as many of them as you are able

to accumulate, without regard to the difficulty of making them or maintaining them....Information also is assumed to be free, so a newly arrived node can find and connect to any node in the world, and the only relevant factor is how many connections each existing node currently maintains." Ibid., 113.

12. Strogatz, *Sync*.

13. Colander, Holt, and Rosser, *The Changing Face of Economics*, 267–68.

14. Ibid., 267.

15. Ibid.

16. Huberman and Adamic, "Information Dynamics in the Networked World."

17. Barabasi, *Linked*, 72.

18. "Collaborate to Innovate."

19. "How 51 Gorillas Can Make You Seriously Rich."

20. Barabasi, *Linked*, 86–88, 102–03. Barabasi offers a helpful metaphor: Nodes are like states of energy. Links are like particles.

21. Gardner, *Changing Minds*.

22. Barabasi, *Linked*, 95.

23. Ibid.

24. Ibid., 95.

25. "Most people sense the greater risk and shun it. Perhaps no great statistical analysis was needed at all: This fact of mass psychology, alone, might have been sufficient evidence to suggest there is something amiss with the standard financial models." Mandelbrot and Hudson, *The (Mis)Behavior of Markets*.

26. Adamic and Huberman, "Zipf's Law and the Internet"; Guenther, Hogg, and Huberman, "Controls for Unstable Structures"; Huberman and Adamic, "Information Dynamics in the Networked World"; Huberman and Wu, "The Dynamics of Reputations"; Wu and Huberman, "Social Structure and Opinion Formation."

27. Barabasi, *Linked*, 88.

28. Ibid.

29. Watts, *Six Degrees*, 112.

30. Huberman and Wu, "The Dynamics of Reputations."

Chapter 6

1. Evans and Wurster, *Blown to Bits*; Malone, *The Future of Work*; Cairncross, *Company of the Future*.

Chapter 7

1. Kay, "No Need to Own the Road."

2. Wright, "Western Retailers Shift Their Supply Chain Tasks to China."

3. "Originally, this was an insurance term." See Milgrom and Roberts, *Economics, Organization, and Management*, 601.

4. Similarly, after Freescale, a semiconductor business, was spun off from Motorola in 2004, it was able to win new customers such as Samsung and Nokia. These companies would have been "reluctant to do business with a supplier owned by a rival." See Morrison, "Hidden Value Let Loose."

5. Milgrom and Roberts, *Economics, Organization, and Management*, 581.

6. Terhune, "Coke to Buy Danone's Stake in Bottled-Water Joint Venture."

7. Vranica, "Partyers Knock Back a Few…Aquafinas."

8. Senge, *Fifth Discipline.*

9. Zuckerman and McDonald, "Time to Slice the Mergers."

10. Roberts and Authers, "The Harder They Fall."

11. Newbery and Stiglitz, *Theory of Commodity Price Stabilization.*

12. Porter, *Competitive Advantage,* 25–26, 307.

13. See, for instance, Engardio, Arndt, and Foust, "The Future of Outsourcing": "In theory, it is becoming possible to buy, off the shelf, practically any function you need to run a company." See also Holmes, "Online Extra: Boeing's Global Strategy Takes Off": "For the first time, with the 787, Boeing is outsourcing more than 70% of the airframe and is giving all aircraft suppliers the responsibility for doing the detail engineering designs."

14. Engardio, "Business Prophet."

Chapter 8

1. Arrow, *The Limits of Organization,* 33.

2. The discussion of the achievement and stability of a power position is consistent with the discussion of the stability and achievement of authority by Kenneth Arrow, who points out that "the existence of sanctions is not a sufficient condition for obedience to authority" (*The Limits of Organization,* 71). Obedience requires that the obedient obtain something worthwhile: "the functional role of authority, its value in making the system work, plays a part in securing obedience" (72–73).

3. Nalebuff and Brandenburger, *Co-Opetition.*

4. This is a term used by Frances Cairncross in *The Company of the Future.*

5. Wheatley, "Contract Electronics Makers Feel Heat."

6. "Nortel Networks on Tuesday agreed to sell most of its global manufacturing operations to Flextronics International": Bartash, "Nortel to Sell Manufacturing Plants."

7. Lawton, Kane, and Dean , "U.S. Upstart Takes on TV Giants in Price War."

8. Gallagher, "Syntax-Brillian."

9. According to Arrow, "Organizations are a means of achieving the benefits of collective action in situations in which the price system fails" (*The Limits of Organization*). He points out that under conditions of uncertainty, the price system can fail if a) there is not "a combination of prices and insurance" against contingencies; b) there is "moral hazard," that is, cheating after a contract has been struck; c) there is "inequality of information between the two parties to the contract," which may lead to "adverse selection." Thanks to the trend toward perfect information, moral hazard and information inequalities will apply less and less. The lack of complete insurance for any and all contingencies for all possible states of the world is bound to continue for a while. This is one of the reasons for forming a distributed business arrangement.

10. Groysberg, Nanda, and Nohria, "The Risky Business of Hiring Stars," 92.

11. de Kuijper, "Unraveling of Market Regimes."

12. Ibid.

13. "ArcelorMittal Signs Record Iron Ore Deal with Vale."

14. Caves, *Creative Industries,* 17, 87.

15. Newbery and Stiglitz, *Theory of Commodity Price Stabilization.*

16. Caves, *Creative Industries*.

17. Simon, "Organizations and Markets," 27.

18. Williamson's List (Williamson, *Markets and Hierarchies*). Concerning hazardous markets, Williamson's approach goes beyond Coase's and Arrow's. Williamson says that in addition to the factors discussed by his two colleagues, firms must also figure out how to handle the riskiness of market volatility in multiperiod settings under uncertainty. Williamson say that if markets are too inhospitable (for a number of reasons), firms resort to solving this problem by vertically integrating.

19. Williamson's List (Williamson, *Markets and Hierarchies*).

20. Malone, *The Future of Work*.

Chapter 9

1. As you will appreciate, in principle there are multiple competitive planes, and we ought to speak of multidimensional battles. We are using 3-D because three is the greatest number of dimensions one can conveniently visualize.

2. Aeppel, "Seeking Perfect Prices, CEO Tears up the Rules."

3. Byron, "Tensions Roil Estée Lauder Dynasty."

4. Chazan, "Rich Guys on the Production Side."

5. Holson, "Pixar to Find Its Own Way as Disney Partnership Ends."

6. Schlender, "Pixar's Magic Man."

Chapter 10

1. Collyns, conversation with author, January 2005.

2. Watson and Kellner, "J.K. Rowling and the Billion-Dollar Empire."

3. "Hold the Front Page."

4. "Microsoft v Google."

5. DiCarlo, "Ye Oprah Book Club Returneth."

6. "The Final Chapter."

7. Wyatt, "Oprah's Book Club to Add Contemporary Writers."

8. Stadtmiller, "Brand Aid."

9. Gardner, *Buzz Marketing with Blogs for Dummies*.

10. Li and Bernoff, *Groundswell*.

11. Agins, "With Her Own Line."

12. Capell, "Unilever Lathers Up."

Chapter 12

1. Our broader definition is similar to the definition of *Kellogg on Branding*, which is "a set of associations linked to a name, mark, or symbol associated with a product or service—a brand is much like a reputation." Tybout and Calkins, *Kellogg on Branding*.

2. AskOxford, s.v. "brand."

3. "The key for brand builders is to give empowered consumers a great product and the tools to use it however they want." Brady, "Cult Brands," 66.

4. Rust, Zeithaml, and Lemon, "Customer-Centered Brand Management."

5. Moore, "Beyond Lovemarks: Emergence."

6. Atkin, *The Culting of Brands*.

7. "World Gold Deposits," American Museum of Natural History.

8. Abboud, "An Israeli Giant in Generic Drugs Faces New Rivals."

9. "The Rich List."

10. Ibid.

11. Rarick, "Dubai Makes Waterfront Plans."

12. Baker, "Professional Protectionists."

13. Freeman, "Barriers to Foreign Professionals Working in the United States."

14. Rivette and Kline, "Discovering New Value in Intellectual Property."

15. Milgrom and Roberts, *Economics, Organization, and Management*, 310.

16. Ibid., 567.

17. "Poor People, Rich Returns."

18. Roberts, "The Plant That Gave Itself New Life and Vigour."

19. Waters, "Innovation in Process."

20. Young, "MCI Offer Shows Price War Persists in Long Distance."

21. Authers and Silver, "Slim's Pickings."

22. AskOxford, s.v. "modus operandi."

23. Arquilla and Ronfeldt, *Networks and Netwars*, 333.

24. Abboud, "How Eli Lilly's Monster Deal Faced Extinction—but Survived."

25. Grant, "Switch to the Low-Income Customer."

26. Byrne, "Search for the Young and Gifted."

27. Hoyos and Catan, "Shell's 'Hands Off' Approach Pushes up Costs."

28. Ibid.

29. Hoyos, "Nationals' Champion."

30. Wilson, *Profit and Power*, 27–28.

31. Ibid., 29.

32. Ibid.

33. Warner, "Its Wish, Their Command."

34. Byrnes and Berner, "Branding: Five New Lessons."

35. "No. 1 China Bank Gets IPO Clearance."

36. Prystay, "With Loans, Poor South Asian Women Turn Entrepreneurial."

37. Mayani, "Tata Tea."

38. "Indian Tea Company in Deal for Tetley."

39. Ellison, "Retailers' Appetite for Top Sellers Has Food Firms Slimming Down."

40. Sorkin, "Mars to Buy Wrigley's for $23 Billion."

41. This pattern has been called many names, including "network effects" or "Metcalfe's Law." Readers of this book will appreciate that this is an injudicious use of the word "network." According to Metcalfe's Law, a company's value supposedly quadruples when the number of users doubles. Laseter, Turner, and Wilcox, "The Big, the Bad, and the Beautiful."

42. Alexa; available from http://www.alexa.com/data/details/traffic_details/pampers.com.

43. Mullaney and Coy, "This Gift Just Keeps on Giving."

44. Rohwedder and Johnson, "Pace-Setting Zara Seeks More Speed To Fight Its Rising Cheap-Chic Rivals."

45. Kauffeld, Sauer, and Bergson, "Partners at the Point of Sale."

46. Agins, "Who's the Coolest Kid At Fashion Week?"

47. Karl, "A Palate with Power."

48. McCoy, *The Emperor of Wine.*

49. Karl, "A Palate with Power."

50. Johnson, "Critic Blamed for 'Raspy' Wine."

51. "The Fashion Oscars."

52. Horyn, "Please Don't Come."

53. Federal Trade Commission, "Bayer Settles FTC Charges."

54. Saul, "Pfizer to End Lipitor Ads by Jarvik."

55. Nalley, "Big Changes at the High End."

56. Elmer-DeWitt, Philip, "How to grow the iPod as the MP3 player market shrinks."

57. Gibson, Brad. "First on TMO—iPod #1 with American Teens, Survey Shows."

58. Piper Jaffray & Company. "16th Semi-Annual Piper Jaffray 'Taking Stock With Teens' Study Indicates Bottom May Be Nearing for 'Discretionary Recession'."

59. Apple, "iTunes Store Tops Three Billion Songs."

60. Yang, "Between Silicon Valley and Silicon Alley."

61. "Exports Spur Sharp Growth for Singapore."

62. Beatty, "In Spa Industry's Makeover, Some Tough New Regimens."

63. "The Fashion Oscars."

64. Casey and Orwall, "Running Underground to Sharpen Nike's Edge, CEO Taps 'Influencers.'"

65. Trachtenberg, "Diet Book Found Novel Ways to Get to Top—and Stay."

Chapter 13

1. *Safire's Political Dictionary*, 692.

2. Lohr, "A Step Back for Microsoft."

3. Agins, "Diamond Store in the Rough."

4. Vranica, "Partyers Knock Back a Few...Aquafinas."

Chapter 15

1. Rivette and Kline, "Discovering New Value in Intellectual Property."

2. Agins, "Diamond Store in the Rough."

3. Prystay, "With Loans, Poor South Asian Women Turn Entrepreneurial."

4. Latour, "For SBC, Fading AT&T Offers a Rich Prize."

Chapter 16

1. Porter, *Competitive Advantage*, 25–26, 307.

Chapter 19

1. Thomas, "For TXU, One of the Street's Fabled Barbarians Is Back in the Hunt."

2. Copeland, Koller, and Murrin, *Valuation.*

3. La Monica, "Disney buys Pixar."

Chapter 20

1. Opening line of the *Aeneid*: Vergilus, *Opera*, 89. This line can be interpreted in many ways. The English translation chosen by Robert Fitzgerald,

for instance, is "I sing of warfare and a man at war": Virgil, *The Aeneid*, 3. In the context of this book it means: I will foretell the new nature of competition, and the new weapons and strategies needed to win.

Glossary

1. Note that this definition is consistent with that of Arrow: "The costs of information, that is, the inputs needed for the installation and operation of information channels," which are the ways of "acquiring relevant information." Arrow, *Limits of Organization*.
2. Copeland, Koller, and Murrin, *Valuation*, 49.
3. Ibid., 143.
4. Ibid., 48.
5. Ibid., 144.

Annotated Bibliography

1. Arrow, *The Limits of Organization*.
2. Barabasi, *Linked: The New Science of Networks*, 86–88.
3. "In practice, power-law distributions always display a characteristic cutoff because of the finite size of the system. The observed degree distribution, therefore, is only ever a straight line on a log-log plot, over some range." Watts, *Six Degrees: The Science of a Connected Age*, 112.
4. "The essential limitation with the scale-free view of networks is that everything is assumed to come for free. Network ties in Barabasi and Albert's model are treated as costless, so you can have as many of them as you are able to accumulate, without regard to the difficulty of making them or maintaining them.... Information also is assumed to be free, so a newly arrived node can find and connect to any node in the world, and the only relevant factor is how many connections each existing node currently maintains." Ibid., 113.
5. Strogatz, *Sync: The Emerging Science of Spontaneous Order*.
6. Barabasi, *Linked: The New Science of Networks*, 88.
7. Ibid.
8. Watts, *Six Degrees: The Science of a Connected Age*, 112.
9. Schelling, *Micromotives and Macrobehavior*.
10. de Kuijper, "Unraveling of Market Regimes."
11. Schelling, *Micromotives and Macrobehavior*.
12. de Kuijper, "Unraveling of Market Regimes."

12 Power Nodes

1. Brand
2. Secret, special, or proprietary ingredients
3. Regulatory protection
4. Focused financial resources
5. Customer base with switching costs
6. Proprietary processes or modus operandi
7. Distribution gateways
8. Dominant position in a layer
9. Increasing mutual utility
10. Aikido assets
11. Filters and brokers
12. Hubs

3-D Competitive Strength

The relative power strength (RPS) of a company's power nodes relative to competitors in three dimensions. You need to know whether your power node is as strong as the power node of your vertical opponent (relative power node strength = 1), which would be equivalent to a stand-off in the profit tug-of-war, or whether one of the two of you is stronger (relative power node strength > 1) so that the stronger one has the potential to extract profits.

3-Dimensional or 3-D Competition

Focused companies will face competition in at least three conceptual dimensions, namely:
- They will fight *vertical* battles for returns with rivals in the same value chain.
- They will face *horizontal* competition from other focused pieces that do the same thing as they do; these fights occur within narrowly defined borders of "old" industries.
- Companies will also face competition horizontally and globally *across* traditional industry boundaries.

Broker

A network point (a person, service, etc.) that is one of the *few* points to be connected to several isolated cliques (of people, products, etc.) and is therefore able to spot opportunities for interaction between members of different cliques. A broker can bring members of isolated cliques together for deals and exchange of information.

Cost of Information

Shorthand for a set of related costs, including the cost of computing, storing, recording, processing, analyzing, and displaying information in myriad forms; the cost of communicating, including the cost of connecting to any other economic actor and exchanging information; the cost of finding and passing on information; and the cost of coordinating, monitoring, and assessing financial, business, and economic activities.[1]

Distributed Business Arrangement (aka the 21st-Century Firm)	An entity composed of focused companies connected to other companies in an array of possible business structures that are controlled through a nexus of power relationships rather than by ownership. A distributed business arrangement may be global. (Here, the word *distributed* refers to arrangements among entities that are separate, autonomous, but linked).
Economic Profits	"The spread between ROIC and the cost of capital."[2] Alternatively, in absolute terms, Economic Profit = Invested Capital × (ROIC − WACC).[3]
Filter	A network point (a person, service, etc.) that is effectively the *only* connection between two cliques (of people, products, etc.). A filter is theoretically the only point through which information can be passed from one clique to another. A filter is often a person whose recommendation or influence can influence others easily.
Focused Company	One that concentrates on a very narrow set of outputs (goods or services); often these are "intermediary" outputs that will be sold to other companies instead of to final customers.
Hub	A point that has an extraordinary number of links; in a network operating according to power laws, hubs are the points with the predominant number of links.
Information	A useful input into decision making, especially, in this book, decision making about commercial transactions. A piece of information, or input, is useful if it causes a difference in a commercial decision.
Interdependent Decision Making	A description of a process whereby economic actors make decisions based on

a set of inputs that include the decisions of other economic actors, or make decisions based on a set of (decision) functions that have been shaped by the decisions of others.

Layer

A conceptual horizontal slice of the vertical value chain.

Perfect Information

The immediate availability of, and connection to, all existing information regarding anything and anybody, at extremely low cost.

Powerlaw Distribution

In general terms, an 80–20 distribution, or one in which a few events, products, players, or ideas account for most of the action. In a network, a powerlaw distribution of links is one in which the great majority of points have very few links but a small number of points (hubs) have a lot of links. Powerlaw distributions may be precisely described and predicted using mathematical formulas.
A simple example of a powerlaw distribution formula is as follows: The probability that a new link (a connection with a newly arrived point) will be established to a given point is proportional (or some other function with a positive first derivative) to the number of preexisting links this point already has. One instance of this can be expressed as a curve where the probability of k links at a point is proportional to *(1/k) to the power p*. If you take logs of both sides you would get: *log(probability of k links) = p.log(1/k)*, which is the same as *log(probability of k links)) = −plog (k)*. And if you plotted that, you would get a straight line with slope $−p^1$. p has often turned out to be 2 or 3.

Powerlaw Network	A multidimensional aggregate or structure consisting of points (buyers, sellers, companies, products, etc.) with links between them (family ties, tastes, votes, etc.) in a transparent environment of perfectly fast and free information with no constraints to connectivity. These links are distributed according to power laws. A powerlaw network has the properties of a scale-free network.
Power Node	A source of profit power—that is, a thing, position, skill, dynamic, or process that a company can reliably use to influence the financial outcomes for itself and for other commercial enterprises in either a positive or negative way. Power nodes provide companies with the ability to help or hinder the cash flows, risks, and investments—that is, the inputs to returns—of other players over an extended period of time.
Profit Power	The ability to hold on to the value from your own activities as well as to extract value from the activities of others with whom you interact in your commercial dealings, to increase the value available to the entire group, and to optimize the risks for yourself and allocate to others the risks that you do not want.
ROIC	ROIC is short for return on invested capital. ROIC is equal to: "after-tax operating profits divided by the capital invested in working capital, property, plant, and equipment."[4]
Rule #1	Focus on profit power and own business with power nodes.
Rule #2	Organize as a focused company that orchestrates power relationships and capitalizes on the positive sums of distributed business arrangements.
Rule #3	Use power nodes to win in 3-D competitions and gain extraordinary economic profits.

Rule #4   Follow strategies designed to succeed among the marketplace dynamics of the transparent economy (power laws and hubs).

Transparency   A state in which the cost of information (as we have defined it, including the cost of computing, processing, communicating, searching, coordinating, and monitoring) is approaching zero or, equivalently, in which cheap connectivity is so abundant and easy, one might consider it infinite.

Value   Value is expected economic profits (plus existing investments).[5]

Vertical Battles and Vertical Competition   Fights with companies that come before or after your own company in the sequence of products or services and that once might have been part of the same vertically integrated company. Competitors encounter "buyer" opponents in the markets of your product and "seller" opponents in the markets for your inputs.

Profit Power Economics owes a great debt to many teachers and authors who have informed my learning and thinking over the years. Here, I add a few notes to identify sources in the bibliography that I have found to be of particular relevance and to indicate what they taught me or how their approach compares to mine.

Competitive Advantage (M. Porter)

Profit Power Economics builds on Porter's famous five-forces framework for industry analysis and strategy development in *Competitive Advantage*.

This book's 3-D competitive approach takes on board the lessons of the five-forces framework but also advances it. First, by noting that in transparency, with the competitive environment consisting of focused companies, we can expect that vertical pressures will be the key determinants of competitive success. (Porter recognizes vertical competition, if only implicitly, in that he says that one must assess pressures from suppliers and buyers in order to evaluate a company's overall strength.) Second, by defining competitive success in terms of superior risk-adjusted returns rather than in terms of market share. And third, by focusing on the sources of profitability, the power nodes, as the determinants of such success.

My prescription for dealing with vertical competition differs from Porter's as well. Porter has suggested that a firm should integrate forward or backward if market power is present among its customers or suppliers. *Profit Power Economics'* prescriptions differ. Buying a power node business is fine (depending of course on what you have to pay for it), but you would drag down your average returns by holding on to ownership of your old low-return business. You should aim to shed ownership of your old business and switch to controlling it with the power node business.

Co-Opetition (B. Nalebuff)

Co-opetition was one of the first books to point out that the nature of competition is changing and that companies can cooperate to increase the common pie of profits. *Profit Power Economics* builds on these insights. *Profit Power Economics* also proposes that in transparency the fight for returns will be vicious, even if these returns have been generated collectively. We may see cooperative action in the generation of profits. We are not likely to see cooperation in the splitting up of the pie.

Creative Industries (R. Caves)

Profit Power Economics was greatly helped by the teaching and writing of economist Richard Caves about industry dynamics and company structures. Since the days of my Harvard dissertation ("Unraveling of Market Regimes"), Richard Caves has encouraged me to investigate alternative corporate structures in the middle ground between vertical integration and pure focus.

In his book *Creative Industries*, Caves describes the multifaceted contingencies spelled out in contracts between movie producers and Hollywood stars, painters and galleries, musicians and agents. If this could be accomplished in the past, under conditions of far more limited information, we can imagine that there will be few limits to structuring future commercial arrangements under conditions of transparency.

Good to Great and Built to Last (J. Collins)

These books are great motivators for corporate teams. Delivering excellence is certainly a prerequisite for earning high returns. In transparency, however, being best is not good enough to assure high returns. You need *profit power* to hold on to the profits that your company has generated by being excellent.

Hierarchies and Markets (Oliver Williamson), *Blown to Bits* (Philip Evans and Thomas Wurster), *The Future of Work* (Thomas Malone), *The Limits of Organization* (Kenneth Arrow), *The Company of the Future* (Frances Cairncross), *The Three Ways of Getting Things Done* (Gerard Fairtlough), "The Nature of the Firm" (Ronald Coase).

Profit Power Economics (especially chapters 7 and 8) has been informed by these articles and books on firms and organizational structure.

Profit Power Economics has incorporated the lessons of these works into its general framework for the organization of a firm. This comprehensive framework is presented in the form of my detailed, three-part Three Buckets Checklist (see Figure 7.1). For instance, Kenneth Arrow said, "Organizations are a means of achieving the benefits of collective action in situations in which the price system fails."[1] Arrow's "situations in which the price system fails" are included in my buckets, either in Bucket I or in Bucket III. This checklist will help corporate leaders and investors shape their companies. This checklist helps to decide what business model or corporate structure is appropriate for a company given the state of the cost of information and the state of its industry.

While the considerations of these authors have been included in *Profit Power Economics*, if we refer to this comprehensive list we can see that many of the outcomes that these authors discussed are in fact often special cases.

Many of the books by modern-day followers of Coase have focused almost exclusively on the implications of information-cost trade-offs per the Coase model—i.e., they are focused on my Bucket I considerations. They predict outcomes according to a single criterion, namely internal versus external coordination costs. On this narrow basis, they predict the emergence of loose bits, which henceforth deal with each other only in arm's length, market-based transactions. Several other authors mention another criterion, which is one of my five performance-related reasons (Bucket II) for creating focused companies: the motivational benefits of freeing the pieces. I believe it wiser to apply the checklist of three buckets of multiple trade-offs.

One of the other differences with *Profit Power Economics* is that these authors describe the alternative to vertical integration as "loose hierarchies" or "cooperating constellations," rather than considering a distributed business model with long-lasting relationships. They nod to the continuing vertically integrated entities without considering *why* there should or should not be such structures or what these structures are to achieve.

Decisions with Multiple Objectives: Preferences and Value (R. Keeney and H. Raiffa), *The Limits of Organization* (K. Arrow)

These books have informed my thinking about information. *Profit Power Economics'* concept of information is consistent with their work: as Howard Raiffa taught me in his decision analysis seminar at Harvard, if a new piece of information does not alter your decision, it has zero value. This definition is also consistent with that deployed by Arrow, when he said that "the costs of information" are "the inputs needed for the installation and operation of information channels," which are the ways of "acquiring relevant information." As noted, Arrow's book also influenced my work on organizational design.

Linked (A. Barabasi), *Six Degrees* (D. Watts), *Sync* (S. Strogatz), various articles by B. Huberman and coauthors

These three books and Huberman's articles collectively form the basis for much of the discussion about power laws and networks in *Profit Power Economics*. Each of these three books offers a part of the puzzle, and jointly they support the conclusions of *Profit Power Economics*.

Profit Power Economics pulls the pieces of the puzzle together. *Profit Power Economics* has translated the mathematical and statistical findings (of these and other authors) into economic terms and shows readers how they can apply them to solving general management and marketing problems in modern markets.

The valuable contributions to my work from these books are as follows:

The first two conditions about preferential attachment and growth can be found in Barabasi.[2] Watts made the point regarding the infinite size criterion[3] and points out the importance of zero search cost in hyper-speed networks.[4] Strogatz mentions the critical condition of zero search cost in an almost offhand manner.[5]

If the conditions are not all satisfied, we will not get powerlaw distributions. Barabsi pointed out that if there is preferential attachment, but no growth (i.e., a completely static model), we will not see the generation of power laws.[6] He also pointed out that if there is growth, but no preferential attachment, we end up with "an exponential degree distribution, which is similar to a bell curve in that it forbids the hubs" from forming.[7]

Huberman's simulations and empirical work helped me put the pieces together and gave validity to theoretical hypotheses.

Watts pointed out that if we are not dealing with a large group, we get truncated distributions instead of the long, fat tails of a power law distribution.[8]

The Long Tail: Why the Future of Business Is Selling Less of More (C. Anderson), "Should You Invest in the Long Tail?"(A. Elberse)

Profit Power Economics agrees with *The Long Tail* that the low cost of information and connectivity will lower distribution and marketing costs and will therefore facilitate a wide range of options for many consumer goods. However, *Profit Power Economics* takes issue with the hypothesis of *The Long Tail* that a wide range of options ex-ante will result in an equally broad range of actual consumer selections ex-post.

Recent empirical evidence is confirming the logic of *Profit Power Economics,* and is questioning the predictions of *The Long Tail.* Such evidence in support of *Profit Power Economics* is reported, for instance, by Elberse in her article in the *Harvard Business Review,* "Should You Invest in the Long Tail?"

Micromotives and Macrobehavior (T. Schelling).

Micromotives and Macrobehavior was the first book that inspired me, several decades ago, to explore the economic phenomenon of interdependent decision making.

This book also introduced me to tipping. Tipping can occur when we deal with a small number of players. Schelling's segregation puzzle is a famous example.[9] We also may see flip-flops in market structure when we have a limited number of players, as can be seen in the copper industry and in the oil industry.[10]

Micromotives helped me understand the dynamics of markets and industry structures, in particular, the connection between the two, as I have described in "Unraveling of Market Regimes." This understanding helped me to see the patterns in the copper industry and copper market in the 1950–80s. It also helped me to predict the developments in the oil industry in the mid-1980s and the subsequent emergence of futures, derivatives, etc., markets for oil.

This micro-motives and macro-behavior theme has been further developed in *Profit Power Economics,* where I look at micro-motives and macro-behavior in light of this modern and evolving economic landscape (especially in chapters 3, 4, and 5). As we head for free information and as the other conditions for hyperspeed networks apply, such as large and expanding numbers of participants, we transition from tipping phenomena to powerlaw network dynamics and multiple hubs.

The (Mis) Behavior of Markets (B. Mandelbrot), *Black Swan* (N. Taleb)

These books report that non-normal distributions can be observed in financial markets as well as in many natural phenomena, like rock formations. They point out the dangers of using normal distributions in modeling when actual distributions are not normal. This book very much agrees with this.

In addition, *Profit Power Economics* explicitly derives and provides the exact conditions for why, where, and when we can expect powerlaw distributions among behaviors and choices of groups.

The Origin of Wealth (E. Beinhocker)

Origin of Wealth offers an impressive survey of a number of research efforts pertaining to "complexity economics." Many of these explorations involve "complex adaptive systems" consisting of agents who process information and then adapt their behavior. The dynamics of systems in which "know everything" actors make interdependent decisions that are described in *Profit Power Economics* (as powerlaw networks) are a subset of the dynamics that can be found among this large family of complex adaptive systems. *Origin of Wealth* agrees with *Profit Power Economics* in finding that such complex adaptive systems generally do not achieve a general equilibrium. *Profit Power Economics* goes beyond this to define situations in which we can expect to see a very orderly, understandable, and predictable set of dynamics (i.e., in case of the four conditions that are likely to be met in mass markets in perfect information). For instance, our framework can predict Anita Elberse's empirical results.

The Tipping Point (M. Gladwell)

The Tipping Point was marvelous for popularizing many of the tipping matters that authors like Schelling had raised earlier.

When might we see tipping? In a world of cheap information, tipping will become rarer. When conditions for powerlaw dynamics are present, there will be no tipping. In many consumer markets in transparency, tipping will become a very special case. (See chapters 5 and 10.)

Tipping will be limited to situations in which one of the four conditions for powerlaw networks does not hold. We know which conditions are required for powerlaw networks. If any of those do not apply, we might have tipping. Tipping may occur, for instance, in exponential growth situations without preferential attachment, i.e., without interdependent decision making. Tipping can also occur if there is some kind of information asymmetry or decay. Finally, tipping can occur when we deal with a small number of players. Thomas Schelling's segregation puzzle is a famous example.[11] We also may see tipping in market structures when we have a limited number of players, as has been seen in the copper and oil industries.[12] In summary, as we head for free information and as the conditions for hyper-speed networks apply, tipping will become rarer.

The Wisdom of Crowds (J. Surowiecki)

The underlying assumptions of *The Wisdom of Crowds* are based on regression toward the mean, i.e., it assumes normal distributions. As should be clear to readers of *Profit Power Economics*, the assumption of a normal distribution is incorrect in most situations when information is cheap and abundant and interdependent decision making has entered the mix (see chapters 3, 4, and 5).

Valuation: Measuring and Managing the Value of Companies (T. Copeland, T. Koller, and J. Murrin)

This book is the basis for *Profit Power Economics'* approach to valuation and value maximization. The definitions in *Profit Power Economics* of profits, economic profits, extraordinary returns and profits, etc., are consistent with the definitions in *Valuation*.

Abboud, Leila. "How Eli Lilly's Monster Deal Faced Extinction—but Survived." *Wall Street Journal*, April 27, 2005.

———. "An Israeli Giant in Generic Drugs Faces New Rivals." *Wall Street Journal*, October 28, 2004.

Adamic, Lada A., and Bernardo A. Huberman. "Zipf's Law and the Internet." Palo Alto, Calif: HP Labs, 2002.

Aeppel, Timothy. "Seeking Perfect Prices, CEO Tears up the Rules." *Wall Street Journal*, March 27, 2007.

Agins, Teri. "Who's the Coolest Kid At Fashion Week?" *Wall Street Journal*, February 9, 2006.

———. "Diamond Store in the Rough." *Wall Street Journal*, May 20, 2005.

———. "With Her Own Line, Pop Star Rides Rise in Celebrity Fashion." *Wall Street Journal*, June 9, 2005.

Alexa. http://www.alexa.com/data/details/traffic_details/pampers.com (accessed February 18, 2009).

Allison, Graham T., and Philip Zelikow. *Essence of Decision: Explaining the Cuban Missile Crisis*. 2nd ed. New York: Longman, 1999.

Anderson, Chris. *The Long Tail: Why the Future of Business Is Selling Less of More*. New York: Hyperion, 2006.

Apple. "iTunes Store Tops Three Billion Songs." Press release, July 31, 2007.

"Arabia's Field of Dreams." *The Economist*, May 29, 2004, 61–62.

"ArcelorMittal Signs Record Iron Ore Deal with Vale." Reuters, April 29, 2008.

Arquilla, John, and David Ronfeldt, eds. *Networks and Netwars: The Future of Terror, Crime, and Militancy*. Santa Monica, Calif.: Rand, 2001.

Arrow, Kenneth J. *The Limits of Organization.* New York: W. W. Norton, 1974.

AskOxford. S.v. "brand," http://www.askoxford.com/concise_oed/ brand?view=uk (accessed February 23, 2006).

———. S.v. "modus operandi," http://www.askoxford.com/concise_oed/ modusoperandi?view=uk (accessed December 13, 2008).

Atkin, Douglas. *The Culting of Brands: When Customers Become True Believers.* New York: Portfolio, 2004.

Authers, John, and Sara Silver. "Slim's Pickings: Latin America's Richest Man Eyes up His Next Undervalued Target." *Financial Times,* April 25, 2005.

Baker, Dean. "Professional Protectionists: The Gains from Free Trade in Highly Paid Professional Services." Center for Economic and Policy Research, 2003, http://www.cepr.net/documents/publications/ protectionists.PDF.

Barabasi, Albert-Laszlo. *Linked: The New Science of Networks.* Cambridge, Mass.: Perseus, 2002.

Bartash, Jeffry. "Nortel to Sell Manufacturing Plants." CBSMartWatch. com, June 29, 2004, http://www.marketwatch.com/News/Story/Story. aspx?guid={4B552844-78EF-40D3-B085-AA9AA3771734}&siteid=mktw (accessed February 18, 2009).

Beatty, Sally. "In Spa Industry's Makeover, Some Tough New Regimens." *Wall Street Journal,* January 19, 2005.

Beinhocker, Eric D. *The Origin of Wealth.* Boston: Harvard Business School Press, 2006.

Belson, Ken. "At Traditional Phone Companies, Jobs May Not Last a Lifetime." *New York Times,* December 5, 2005.

Bowles, Samuel. *Microeconomics: Behavior, Institutions, and Evolution.* Princeton, N.J.: Princeton University Press, 2004.

Bradsher, Keith. "China Finds American Allies for Security." *New York Times,* December 28, 2007.

Brady, Diane. "Cult Brands." *BusinessWeek,* August 2, 2004, 64–71.

Brand, Stewart. *The Media Lab: Investing the Future at M.I.T.* New York: Viking Press, 1987.

Byrne, John. "The Search for the Young and Gifted." *BusinessWeek,* October 4, 1999, 110.

Byrnes, Nanette, and Robert Berner. "Branding: Five New Lessons." *BusinessWeek,* February 14, 2005, 26–28.

Byron, Ellen. "Tensions Roil Estée Lauder Dynasty." *Wall Street Journal,* February 27, 2008.

Cairncross, Frances. *The Company of the Future: Meeting the Management Challenges of the Communications Revolution.* Boston, Mass.: Harvard Business School Press, 2002.

Capell, Kerry. "Unilever Lathers Up." *BusinessWeek,* February 15, 2008.

Casey, Nicholas and Bruce Orwall. "To Sharpen Nike's Edge, CEO Taps 'Influencers.'" *Wall Street Journal,* October 24, 2007.

Caves, Richard E. *Creative Industries: Contracts between Art and Commerce.* Cambridge, Mass.: Harvard University Press, 2000.

Chadha, Radha, and Paul Husband. *The Cult of the Luxury Brand: Inside Asia's Love Affair With Luxury.* London: Nicholas Brealey International, 2006.

Chazan, Guy. "Rich Guys on the Production Side." *Wall Street Journal*, April 16, 2008.

Child, Josiah. *A Discourse of the Nature, Use, and Advantages of Trade: Proposing Some Considerations for the Promotion and Advancement Thereof by a Registry of Lands, Preventing the Exportation of Coyn, Lowering the Interest of Money, Inviting Foreign Families into England*. London: Randal Taylor, 1694.

Claburn, Thomas. "U.K. Kids Get RFID Chips in School Uniforms." *InformationWeek*, October 25, 2007, http://www.informationweek.com/news/mobility/RFID/showArticle.jhtml?articleID=202601660.

Clegg, Stewart. *Frameworks of Power*. London: Sage, 1989.

Coase, Ronald. "The Nature of the Firm." *Economica*, November 1937, 16(4): 386–405.

Colander, David C., Richard P. F. Holt, and John Barkley Rosser. *The Changing Face of Economics: Conversations with Cutting Edge Economists*. Ann Arbor: University of Michigan Press, 2004.

"Collaborate to Innovate." Workshop held at the World Economic Forum Annual Meeting 2007, Davos, Switzerland.

Collyns, Napier. Conversation, January 2005.

Copeland, Thomas E., Tim Koller, and Jack Murrin. *Valuation: Measuring and Managing the Value of Companies*. 3rd ed. New York: Wiley, 2000.

Covestor. "How It Works." From Covestor Web site, Covestor.com (accessed February 19, 2009).

de Geus, Arie. *The Living Company: Habitats for Survival in a Turbulent Business Environment*. Boston Mass.: Harvard Business School Press, 1997.

de Kuijper, Mia. "Unraveling of Market Regimes: In Theory and in Application to Copper, Aluminum, and Oil." PhD diss., Harvard University, 1983.

DiCarlo, Lisa. "Ye Oprah Book Club Returneth." Forbes.com, February 27, 2003, http://www.forbes.com/2003/02/27/cx_ld_0227bookclub.html

Duguid, Sarah. "Feel Like You're Being Watched?" *Financial Times*, January 28, 2006.

Durlauf, Steven N., and H. Peyton Young, eds. *Social Dynamics*. Cambridge, Mass.: MIT Press, 2001.

Elberse, Anita. "Should You Invest in the Long Tail?" *Harvard Business Review*, July-August 2008, 88–96.

Ellison, Sarah. "Retailers' Appetite for Top Sellers Has Food Firms Slimming Down." *Wall Street Journal*, Nov 28, 2004.

Elmer-DeWitt, Philip. "How to grow the iPod as the MP3 player market shrinks." Apple 2.0, January 29, 2008, http://apple20.blogs.fortune.cnn.com/2008/01/29/beyond-the-incredible-shrinking-ipod-market/ (accessed February 18, 2009).

Engardio, Pete. "Business Prophet: How Strategy Guru C.K. Prahalad Is Changing the Way CEOs Think." *BusinessWeek*, January 23, 2006.

Engardio, Pete, Michael Arndt, and Dean Foust. "The Future of Outsourcing." *BusinessWeek Online*, January 30, 2006, http://www.businessweek.com/magazine/content/06_05/b3969401.htm.

Evans, Philip, and Thomas S. Wurster. *Blown to Bits: How the New Economics of Information Transforms Strategy*. Boston, Mass.: Harvard Business School Press, 1999.

"Exports Spur Sharp Growth for Singapore." *New York Times*, July 13, 2004.

Fairtlough, Gerard. *The Three Ways of Getting Things Done: Hierarchy, Heterarchy and Responsible Autonomy in Organizations.* Axminster, U.K.: Triarchy Press, 2005.

"The Fashion Oscars." *Wall Street Journal,* March 3, 2006.

Federal Trade Commission, "Bayer Settles FTC Charges," news release, January 11, 2000.

"The Final Chapter." *Economist.com,* April 11, 2002, http://www.economist.com/books/displaystory.cfm?story_id=1077398.

Foust, Dean. "Taking Off Like 'a Rocket Ship.'" *BusinessWeek,* April 3, 2006, 76.

Frank, Robert H. "Economic Scene: The Intense Competition for Top Students Is Threatening Financial Aid Based on Need." *New York Times,* April 14, 2005.

Freeman, Eric. "Barriers to Foreign Professionals Working in the United States." Center for Economic and Policy Research, 2003, http://www.cepr.net/documents/publications/professional_supplement.htm.

Fullbrook, Edward. *A Guide to What's Wrong with Economics.* London: Anthem, 2004.

Gallagher, Mark. "Syntax-Brillian: 'It's the Overhead, Stupid.'" *Seeking Alpha,* February 20, 2007, http://seekingalpha.com/article/27430-syntax-brillian-it-s-the-overhead-stupid.

Gardner, Howard. *Changing Minds: The Art and Science of Changing Our Own and Other People's Minds.* Boston, Mass.: Harvard Business School Press, 2004.

Gardner, Susannah. *Buzz Marketing with Blogs for Dummies*: Hoboken, N.J.: Wiley, 2005.

Gates, Bill. "The New Road Ahead: What's Next for the Knowledge Economy?" *Newsweek,* Special Edition on Technology, December 2005. http://www.microsoft.com/presspass/ofnote/12-05Newsweek.mspx (accessed February 18, 2009).

Gibson, Brad. "First on TMO – iPod #1 with American Teens, Survey Shows." Mac Observer, April 6, 2005, www.macobserver.com/article/2005/04/06.4.shtml (accessed February 19, 2009).

Grant, Jeremy. "Switch to the Low-Income Customer." *Financial Times,* November 15, 2005.

Groysberg, Boris, Ashish Nanda, and Nitin Nohria. "The Risky Business of Hiring Stars." *Harvard Business Review,* May 2004, 92–100.

Guenther, Oliver, Tad Hogg, and Bernardo A. Huberman. "Controls for Unstable Structures." Palo Alto, Calif: Xerox Palo Alto Research Center, 1997, http://www.ece.ubc.ca/~guenther/ControlsForUnstableStructures.pdf.

Hart, Oliver D. *Firms, Contracts, and Financial Structure.* Oxford; New York: Oxford University Press, 1995.

"Hold the Front Page: How to Replace the Editor with a ß Computer." *The Economist.* March 6, 2008, 90.

Holmes, Stanley. "Online Extra: Boeing's Global Strategy Takes Off." *BusinessWeek Online,* January 30, 2006.

Holson, Laura. "Pixar to Find Its Own Way as Disney Partnership Ends." *New York Times,* January 31, 2004.

Horyn, Cathy. "Please Don't Come." *New York Times,* February 18, 2008.

"How 51 Gorillas Can Make You Seriously Rich." *The Economist*, August 21, 2004, 77.

Hoyos, Carola. "Nationals' Champion: How the Energy-Rich Rely on Schlumberger." *Financial Times*, July 29, 2008.

Hoyos, Carola, and Thomas Catan. "Shell's 'Hands Off' Approach Pushes up Costs." *Financial Times*, November 7, 2005.

Huberman, Bernardo A., and Lada A. Adamic. "Information Dynamics in the Networked World." Palo Alto, Calif: HP Labs, 2004, http://www.hpl.hp.com/research/idl/papers/infodynamics/infodynamics.pdf.

Huberman, Bernardo A., and Fang Wu. "The Dynamics of Reputations." Palo Alto, Calif.: HP Labs, 2004, http://www.hpl.hp.com/research/idl/papers/reputations/reputation.pdf.

"Indian Tea Company in Deal for Tetley." *New York Times*, February 28, 2000.

Jesdanun, Anick. "Study: Google Gets Bulk of World Search." Associated Press, October 9, 2007.

Johnson, Richard. "Critic Blamed for 'Raspy' Wine." *New York Post*, February 13, 2008.

Karl, Jonathan. "A Palate with Power." *Wall Street Journal*, July 14, 2005.

Kauffeld, Rich, Johan Sauer, and Sara Bergson. "Partners at the Point of Sale." *strategy + business*, Autumn 2007.

Kay, John. "No Need to Own the Road: Buy the Tollbooth." *Financial Times*, March 18, 2008.

Keeney, Ralph L., and Howard Raiffa. *Decisions with Multiple Objectives: Preferences and Value Tradeoffs*. New York: John Wiley & Sons, 1976.

Kiley, David. "Giving the Boss the Big Picture." *BusinessWeek*, February 13, 2006.

Knowledgerush. S.v. "Bell Curve," http://www.knowledgerush.com/kr/encyclopedia/Bell_Curve/

Kurzweil, Ray. *The Singularity Is Near: When Humans Transcend Biology*. New York: Viking, 2005.

Laboy, Carlos. In company reports, ed. Bear Stearns Equity Research, 2000.

Lambert, Craig. "The Manipulation of Perceptions." *Harvard Magazine*, March–April 2006.

La Monica, Paul R. "Disney Buys Pixar." CNNMoney.com, January 25, 2006, http://money.cnn.com/2006/01/24/news/companies/disney_pixar_deal/index.htm.

Laseter, Tim, Martha Turner, and Ron Wilcox. "The Big, the Bad, and the Beautiful." *strategy+business*, Winter 2003.

Lasswell, Harold Dwight, and Abraham Kaplan. *Power and Society: a Framework for Political Inquiry*. New Haven: Yale University Press, 1950.

Latour, Almar. "For SBC, Fading AT&T Offers a Rich Prize: Business Customers." *Wall Street Journal*, January 28, 2005.

Lawton, Christopher, Yukari Iwatani Kane, and Jason Dean. "U.S. Upstart Takes on TV Giants in Price War." *Wall Street Journal*, April 15, 2008.

"Learning to Live with Big Brother." *The Economist*, September 29, 2007, 62–63.

Li, Charlene, and Josh Bernoff. *Groundswell: Winning in a World Transformed by Social Technologies*. Boston, Mass.: Harvard Business School Press, 2008.

Lohr, Steve. "A Step Back for Microsoft." *New York Times*, May 5, 2008.

Lowenstein, Roger. *When Genius Failed: The Rise and Fall of Long-Term Capital Management*. London: Fourth Estate, 2001.

Malkiel, Burton Gordon. *A Random Walk down Wall Street*. New York: W.W. Norton, 1999.

Malone, Thomas W. *The Future of Work: How the New Order of Business Will Shape Your Organization, Your Management Style, and Your Life*. Boston, Mass.: Harvard Business School Press, 2004.

Mandelbrot, Benoit B., and Richard L. Hudson. *The (Mis)Behavior of Markets: A Fractal View of Risk, Ruin, and Reward*. New York: Basic Books, 2004.

Mayani, Rajesh. "Tata Tea." Morgan Stanley Dean Witter equity research report, January 12, 2001.

McCoy, Elin. *The Emperor of Wine: The Rise of Robert M. Parker, Jr. and the Reign of American Taste*. New York: Ecco, 2005.

McCue, Andy. "Tesco to Track Milk Deliveries by RFID." CNET News.com, June 1 2006, http://news.cnet.com/Tesco-to-track-milk-deliveries-by-RFID/2100-1033_3-6079022.html.

McCullagh, Declan, "Ray Kurzweil deciphers a brave new world," CNET News, September 29, 2005.

"Microsoft v Google." *The Economist*. February 7, 2008, http://www.economist.com/business/displaystory.cfm?story_id=10650607 (accessed February 19, 2009).

Milgrom, Paul, and John Roberts. *Economics, Organization, and Management*. Englewood Cliffs, N.J.: Prentice-Hall, 1992.

Moore, Johnnie. "Beyond Lovemarks: Emergence." Johnnie Moore's Weblog, August 7, 2004, http://www.johnniemoore.com/blog/archives/000416.php.

Morrison, Mark. "Hidden Value Let Loose." *BusinessWeek*, November 14, 2005, 116.

Mullaney, Timothy J., and Peter Coy. "This Gift Just Keeps on Giving." *BusinessWeek*, August 25, 2003, 72–73.

Nalebuff, Barry, and Adam Brandenburger. *Co-Opetition*. London: HarperCollinsBusiness, 1996.

Nalley, Richard. "Big Changes at the High End." *Wall Street Journal*, August 16, 2007.

National Reading Campaign. 2006. www.literacytrust.org.uk (accessed March 21, 2006).

Newbery, David M. G., and Joseph E. Stiglitz. *The Theory of Commodity Price Stabilization: A Study in the Economics of Risk*. Oxford: Oxford University Press, 1981.

"No. 1 China Bank Gets IPO Clearance." *International Herald Tribune*, July 19, 2006.

Nocera, Joseph. "The Heresy That Made Them Rich." *New York Times*, October 29, 2005.

Piper Jaffray & Company. "16th Semi-Annual Piper Jaffray 'Taking Stock With Teens' Study Indicates Bottom May Be Nearing for 'Discretionary Recession'." News release, October 9, 2008.

"Podtastic." *The Economist*, January 12, 2006.

Porter, Michael E. *Competitive Advantage: Creating and Sustaining Superior Performance*. Rev. ed. New York: Free Press, 1998.

"Poor People, Rich Returns." *The Economist*, May 15, 2008, 93.

Prystay, Cris. "With Loans, Poor South Asian Women Turn Entrepreneurial." *Wall Street Journal*, May 25, 2005.

Raiffa, Howard. *Negotiation Analysis*. Cambridge, Mass.: Belknap Press, 2002.

Rarick, Gina. "Dubai Makes Waterfront Plans." *International Herald Tribune*, May 31, 2006.

Reuters, "Chronology: Reuters, from pigeons to multimedia merger," May 15, 2007, http://www.reuters.com/article/ousivMolt/idUSL1541685720070515 (accessed February 18, 2009).

"The Rich List." *The Sunday Times*, April 3, 2005.

Richtel, Matt. "The Long-Distance Journey of a Fast-Food Order." *New York Times*, April 11, 2006.

Rivette, Kevin G., and David Kline. "Discovering New Value in Intellectual Property." *Harvard Business Review*, January–February 2000, 55–56.

Roberts, Dan. "The Plant That Gave Itself New Life and Vigour." *Financial Times*, September 14, 2005.

Roberts, Dan, and John Authers. "The Harder They Fall: Conglomerates Are Stricken by a Shift in Investor Preference." *Financial Times*, October 28, 2005.

Rohwedder, Cecilie, and Keith Johnson. "Pace-Setting Zara Seeks More Speed To Fight Its Rising Cheap-Chic Rivals." *Wall Street Journal*, February 20, 2008.

Rust, Roland T., Valarie A. Zeithaml, Katherine N. Lemon. "Customer-Centered Brand Management." *Harvard Business Review*, September 1, 2004.

Safire's Political Dictionary, Oxford: Oxford University Press, 2008.

Saul, Stephanie. "Pfizer to End Lipitor Ads by Jarvik." *New York Times*, February 26, 2008.

Schlender, Brent. "Pixar's Magic Man." *Fortune*, May 17, 2006, http://money.cnn.com/2006/05/15/magazines/fortune/pixar_futureof_fortune_052906/index.htm (accessed on February 17, 2009).

Senge, Peter M. *The Fifth Discipline: The Art and Practice of the Learning Organization*. New York: Doubleday, 2006.

Simon, Herbert. "Organizations and Markets." *Journal of Economic Perspectives* 5 (1991): 25–44.

Smith, Randall, and Kate Linebaugh. "Morgan Stanley Plans Reduction in Research Jobs." *Wall Street Journal*, March 22, 2006.

Sorkin, Andrew Ross. "Mars to Buy Wrigley's for $23 Billion." *New York Times*, April 28, 2008.

Soros, George. *The New Paradigm for Financial Markets: The Credit Crisis of 2008 and What It Means*. New York: PublicAffairs, 2008.

Stadtmiller, Mandy. "Brand Aid: Sponsorship Isn't Just for Celebs Anymore." *New York Post*, March 13, 2008.

Strogatz, Steven H. *Sync: The Emerging Science of Spontaneous Order*. New York: Hyperion, 2003.

Surowiecki, James. *The Wisdom of Crowds: Why the Many Are Smarter Than the Few and How Collective Wisdom Shapes Business, Economies, Societies, and Nations*. New York: Doubleday, 2004.

Terhune, Chad. "Coke to Buy Danone's Stake in Bottled-Water Joint Venture." *Wall Street Journal*, April 25, 2005.

Terhune, Chad, and Betsy McKay. "Coke Shelves Initiative of Ex-Chief: Goal of Rekindling Growth to Eclipse Efforts to Alter Profit Sharing with Bottler." *Wall Street Journal*, September 28, 2004.

Thomas, Landon, Jr. "For TXU, One of the Street's Fabled Barbarians Is Back in the Hunt." *New York Times*, February 26, 2007.

Trachtenberg, Jeffrey. "Diet Book Found Novel Ways to Get to Top—and Stay." *Wall Street Journal*, June 30, 2004.

Turnbull, Lord Andrew. "How to Be a Demographic Realist." *strategy + business*, November 8, 2007, http://www.strategy-business.com/resiliencereport/resilience/rr00052.

Tybout, Alice M., and Tim Calkins, eds. *Kellogg on Branding: The Marketing Faculty of the Kellogg School of Management*. Hoboken, N.J.: Wiley, 2005.

Vergilius Maro, P. *Opera: Bucolica, Georgica, Aeneis*. Translated by Dr. G. J. D. Aalders. Haarlem: H. D. Tjeenk Willink & Zoon, 1961.

Virgil. *The Aeneid*. Translated by Robert Fitzgerald. New York: Random House, 1983, 1990.

Vranica, Suzanne. "Partyers Knock Back a Few…Aquafinas." *Wall Street Journal*, July 13, 2004.

Warner, Melanie. "Coke Bottlers Challenge Wal-Mart Deliveries." *New York Times*, March 3, 2006.

———. "Its Wish, Their Command." *New York Times*, March 3, 2006.

Waters, Richard. "Innovation in Process: Plugging Together Business Software May Soon Be Painless." *Financial Times*, May 4, 2005.

Watson, Julie, and Tomas Kellner. "J.K. Rowling and the Billion-Dollar Empire." *Forbes*, February 26, 2004, http://www.forbes.com/2004/02/26/cx_jw_0226rowlingbill04.html (accessed February 18, 2009).

Watts, Duncan J. *Six Degrees: The Science of a Connected Age*. New York: Norton, 2003.

"The Web View." *Financial Times*, February 20, 2006.

"World Gold Deposits." American Museum of Natural History, http:amnh.org/exhibitions/gold/incomparable/world.php (accessed February 18, 2009).

Weideger, Paula. "'I Ask the Art Where It Wants to Be.'" *Financial Times*, May 26, 2007.

Wheatley, Jonathan. "Contract Electronics Makers Feel Heat." *Financial Times*, March 2, 2005.

Whole Earth Review, May 1985, 49.

Williamson, Oliver E. *Markets and Hierarchies, Analysis and Antitrust Implications: A Study in the Economics of Internal Organization*. New York: Free Press, 1975.

Wilson, Charles. *Profit and Power: A Study of England and the Dutch Wars*. The Hague: M. Nijhoff, 1978.

Wright, Robert. "Western Retailers Shift Their Supply Chain Tasks to China." *Financial Times*, March 27, 2007.

Wu, Fang, and Bernardo A. Huberman. "Social Structure and Opinion Formation." Palo Alto, Calif.: HP Labs, 2004, http://www.hpl.hp.com/research/idl/papers/opinions/opinions.pdf.

Wyatt, Edward. "Oprah's Book Club to Add Contemporary Writers." *New York Times*, September 23, 2005.

Yang, Catherine. "Between Silicon Valley and Silicon Alley." *BusinessWeek*, August 30, 1999, 168.

Young, Shawn. "MCI Offer Shows Price War Persists in Long Distance." *Wall Street Journal*, May 14, 2004.

Yuan, Li. "Sichuan Quake Shows Changing China." *Wall Street Journal*, May 14, 2008.

Zamiska, Nicholas, and Vanessa O'Connell. "Altria Is in Talks to Make Marlboros in China." *Wall Street Journal*, April 21, 2005.

Zuckerman, Gregory, and Ian McDonald. "Time to Slice the Mergers." *Wall Street Journal*, January 10, 2006.

Page numbers in bold indicate figures or tables. Power node number is indicated in bold braces like {1}.

FiatAvio, 95
fiefdoms, 194
filters and brokers. *See* power nodes, filters and brokers {11}
Financial Times, 97, 101, 161, 163
First Boston, 41, 154–55, 180
First Data Corporation, 98, 166
fitness, 78
five forces framework, 124
flexibility, 100–101, 108
flexible pricing, 54
Flextronics, 111
Flip, 138, 237
flip your perspective, 132
focal-point-of-search hubs, 176–77
focused companies. *See also* 21st-Century Business Model
    business models, **109**
    collective action, 107
    cost of information, 91, 98
    definition, 6, 92
    distributed business model, 32–33, **109**, 118
    extraordinary profits, 184–85
    flexibility, 100–101
    Four Rules, 147, 200, **201**, 247–48
    investors, 88, 91–93, 101
    marketplace action plan, 236
    monitoring costs, 96–97
    outsourcing model, 103–4, 269n13
    perfect information, 32, 88, 92–95, 107
    performance considerations, 95, 98–102
    positive sums, 107
    power nodes, 6–7, 32–33, 194
    power nodes and, 21
    power relationships, 119
    risks, 99, 101
    search costs, 96
    Three Buckets Checklist, **93**
    three dimensional business models, **110**, 111
    transparent economy, 4, 89, 92, **94**
    value chain, 32, 95
focused financial resources. *See* power nodes, focused financial resources {4}
Food and Drug Administration, 155

food industry, 162–63, 167, 169–70, 209
Forbes, 136
Ford. *See* car industry
Four Rules for Maximizing Profits in Transparency, 6–9, 147, 184, 190, 199–204, 200, **201**–3, 204, 243, **244–45**, 246–48, 251–52, 258, 262
franchises, 32
Fredriksen, John, 129
Freeman, Eric, 157
Freescale, 94
Friedland, Danielle, 181
Frito-Lay, 140, 162–63, 168–69
Fullbrook, Edward, 267n4 (ch. 4)
future information, 40
The Future of Work, 120
futures market, 38

game theory, 20, 29–30, 130
Gate Gourmet catering service, 114
gatekeepers, 82
Gauthereau, Guillaume, 173
GE, 161, 224
GECIS, 224
Gecis (Genpact), 95
Gemex, 224
general equilibrium, 61
General Mills, 164–65
General Motors. *See* car industry
Gillette, 51, 152
Gladwell, Malcolm, 285
GlaxoSmithKline, 179
global economy, 3, 32–33, 49–50, 58, 66
gold, 154
Goldman Sachs, 179, 180
Good to Great, 282
Google, 8, 51, 56, 66–67, 70, 132–36, 172, 176–77, 179–80
gossip networks, 84
government selling prices (GSPs), 115
Grameen Bank, 159–60
Groundswell, 138
group decision making, 131
groupthink, 56
growth and change, 73
Gulf & Western, 92

hackers, 59
Harley-Davidson, 153, 178, 181, 236

perfect information. *See also* cost
    of information; transparent
    economy
  aggregates, **69**
  asymmetrical information, 51–52
  competition, 33, 49–50
  consequences of, 46–54
  consumers, 33
  contracts, options and conditional
    deals, 53–54, 118
  coordination of activities, 50
  definition, 46
  distributed business model, 106
  80–20 principle, 141
  extraordinary profits, 87
  focused companies, 32, 88, 92–95, 107
  global economy, 3, 49–50
  hubs dynamics {**12**}, 132–33
  independence of decision making,
    248
  inefficiencies, 54, 59
  inequality of information, 269n9
    (ch. 8)
  interdependent decision making,
    9–10, 45, 57, 59–60, **69**, 87,
    89–90, 145
  intermediaries, 49
  investors, 246
  law of large numbers, 56
  market failures and, 60–65
  monitoring costs, 50–51, 88
  moral hazard, 266n10
  and perfect markets, 1–2
  power nodes, 33
  power relationships, 7
  powerlaw distributions, 69, 76
  powerlaw networks, 73
  preferential attachment, 139
  pricing, 61–63
  profitability, 103
  and profits, 2
  regression toward the mean, 56
  search costs, 47–49
  star drivers, 42
  transaction costs, 52–53
  value chain, 106
  vertical integration, 49, 87–88
  wage and price competition, 49–50
  wisdom of the crowds, 56

perfect markets, 1, 267n2, 267n3
performance considerations, 95,
    98–102, 103, 105
permits, 157
Pfizer, 155, 174
phantom nodes, 210–11
pharmaceutical companies, 162,
    173–74
pharmaceutical industry, 155
Philip Morris, 152–53, 157
Philippines, 139
Phillips, 113, 210
phone companies, 26–28, 157–58. *See
    also* AT&T
Piper Jaffray & Co., 178
Pixar, 129–30, 257–58
Poland, 221
popularity contests, 131
Porter, Michael, 103, 124
positive sums
  collective action, 106
  computer industry, 130
  cost of information, 107
  distributed business model, 107,
    109, 112–18, 146, 214–15,
    232, 252
  focused companies, 107
  focused financial resources, 160
  non-power node companies, 118
  Oprah Winfrey, 136–37
  power nodes, 102–3, 209–10
  Power Nodes Evaluation and
    Action Plan, 206–8
  profit power, 30, 106–7
  Three Buckets Checklist, 103, 105,
    215, 252, 256
potential value, 243, **245**, 251, 253–58
power, 29
power laws. *See* transparent economy
power nodes
  main discussion
    {**1**}, 151–53
    {**2**}, 153–56
    {**3**}, 157–58
    {**4**}, 158–60
    {**5**}, 160–62
    {**6**}, 162–64
    {**7**}, 164–65
    {**8**}, 166–67